The

DEAF HOUSE

The
DEAF HOUSE

JOANNE WEBER

thistledown press

Thistledown Press Ltd.
118 - 20th Street West
Saskatoon, Saskatchewan, S7M 0W6
www.thistledownpress.com

Library and Archives Canada Cataloguing in Publication

Weber, Joanne, 1959–, author
The deaf house / Joanne Weber.

Issued in print and electronic formats.

ISBN 978-1-927068-48-9 (pbk.). ISBN 978-1-927068-49-6
(html). ISBN 978-1-927068-79-3 (pdf)

1. Weber, Joanne, 1959-. 2. Deaf–Canada–Biography.
3. Poets, Canadian (English)–21st century–Biography.

I. Title.
PS8645.E235Z53 2013   C811'.6   C2013-903951-1
C2013-903952-X

Cover painting, *Butterfly Pudding* by Susan Dupor
Cover and book design by Jackie Forrie
Printed and bound in Canada

"All one people" by Joseph Naytowhow and Cheryl L'Hirondelle, Miyoutakwan Music, 2000. Used by permission

Canada Council
for the Arts

Conseil des Arts
du Canada

SASKATCHEWAN
ARTS BOARD

Canadian   Patrimoine
Heritage   canadien

Thistledown Press gratefully acknowledges the financial assistance of the Canada Council for the Arts, the Saskatchewan Arts Board, and the Government of Canada through the Canada Book Fund for its publishing program.

Note

The use of the capital "D" as in "Deaf" represents identification with the Deaf community, use of American Sign Language (ASL), and the participation in Deaf culture as a way of life, whereas use of the lower case "d" as in "deaf" indicates a diagnosis of hearing loss by the medical profession and a primary desire to belong only to the hearing world. Such deaf individuals may identify themselves as "hearing impaired" and primarily rely on technology (hearing aids, cochlear implants, assistive listening devices) in order to hear and speak. Many of these individuals do sign but have adopted a sign code invented by hearing people (Signed English or a variation of a manually coded English). Even though they may sign, they do not identify with the Deaf community nor participate in Deaf community events. Instead, they may see themselves as disabled and as belonging to the hearing world only whereas the Deaf do not perceive themselves as disabled but as belonging to a linguistic minority. Sign languages are now recognized as bona fide languages and are accepted as additional languages of study at the PhD level in many universities throughout the world.

The use of upper and lower case "d/D" is strategically used throughout this work. Likewise, the word "hearing" is capitalized in order to stress the Deaf perception of Hearing people as belonging to their own linguistic groups characterized by spoken languages.

For Murray,
Anna and Paula

BOOK ONE

One

"WHERE IS THE BABY?"

My mother stands blinking in the hall light, her nightgown tumbling forward as she bends down to hold me.

She says: "What baby? There is no baby."

The baby is crying. It won't stop.

I insist: "You have to find the baby. I can hear the baby crying. Listen."

I run to her with my hearing aid. She fits it into my ear. Strangely, I can't hear the baby anymore. I think: *Oh yes, he is still crying, but not so loud.*

My mother shakes her head. Her hair is all awry and because she isn't wearing her glasses, her eyes are piercing. My father shifts underneath the blankets on the bed behind her.

She says: "There is no baby, Joanne. Go back to bed."

"Yes, there is. I can't sleep. The baby won't stop crying. It sounds like it's right in my bedroom with me."

My mother sighs: "Let's go and look." She takes my hand.

We turn on the light, and my bed reveals crushed blankets, and a pillow cratered by my head.

I say: "It's under the bed." I think: *Yes, it must be.* I drop to my knees, feeling the rough carpet beneath my hands. I see a sock and a doll that slid down the other side of the bed. I think: *Maybe she was crying.* I slide my hand under the bed and pull her out.

My mother says: "Joanne, you have ringing in the ears. That baby sound is in your head."

I say: "But I can't sleep. Make it go away."

She explains: "I can't. There is nothing that will make it go away."

"Why not?"

My mother sighs. She leads me to the kitchen and sits me down at the dining room table. She draws a picture of an ear and puts a spiral at the end of a long tunnel. She draws little lines along the seashell (like the one I see in my favourite seashore book). She says: "It is called the 'coke-lee-a'. There are the hairs, see? We all have them along these circles. Yours are damaged." She erases some of the lines. There are now shortened or broken hairs. She looks at me carefully. She draws a line by the cochlear spiral and upwards into a mass of curls. She says: "This line is your nerve going into your brain." She points to the curly mass. "The nerve is damaged. Those noises are coming from that damaged nerve that goes into your brain."

I ask: "So the baby isn't real?"

She shakes her head: "No, it isn't."

"But how do I make it stop crying?"

"You can't."

I can't. The enormity of this sinks into me. I am eight years old. I can't stop the noises in my head. I suddenly realize: *I've always had these noises. They're not always baby cries, but a vacuum cleaner going full tilt over a carpet, high pitched hissing noises as if an angry snake was nearby, the clanging of church bells, which I thought I heard when I woke up to go to the bathroom a few nights ago.*

My mother bends down again toward me. She suggests: "Keep your hearing aid on, Joanne. See if you can go back to sleep with your hearing aid on."

In the morning, I stir sleepily, with the hearing aid cord wrapped around my neck, and the hard bulge of the ear mold in my cheek. The little white box is in its harness on my chest.

My mother comes into the room and shakes me. She says: "Your hearing aid is whistling, the mold is not in your ear. Shut it off."

I grope for the switch and turn over. My mother pulls the blankets up around me. She knows I've had a hard night, but now I'm fully awake. I'm not hearing the baby anymore, but a fire truck is going down the street. I'm sure of it.

Wilkie, Saskatchewan

A strange woman is sitting in the living room with my mother. I've just come home from school. My mother's tea set is out on the coffee table. Usually it's covered with books and papers, but now the old brown teapot stands on a tray beside fine china cups emblazoned with the Saskatchewan prairie lily. And my mother has dug up napkins from somewhere. The woman is rather burly and mannish. She wears a black dress with pearls and matching pumps. Her face is broad and her dark hair is simply combed back.

My mother's face reddens as she says: "This is Miss Lorraine O'Connor. From Regina."

Miss O'Connor smiles and takes my hand. She says: "This must be Joanne." She nods at my mother, with a flush of pleasure. "Joanne, how would you like to come to Regina to talk to a group of parents about your life?"

My mother begins: "We'd put you on a bus."

Miss O'Connor finishes: "And I'd pick you up when you get off. Then you can stay at my place. Oh Joanne, they'd love to hear from you about what you are able to do."

Sitting in the humming but stationary bus beside the only gas station in our town, waving through the window to my parents, my suitcase stowed in the cavity of the bus, the driver in his grey suit and cap is strolling down the aisle, counting as he taps the tops of seats, I wave again, hardly able to see my parents' faces in the dark morning. Then the bus lurches down the quiet streets of the sleeping town away to the highway and the pink flush of morning spreading over fields locked in ice and snow, my nose pressing against the glass, the telephone wires between poles form noises inside my head, *swe-eoop, swee-oop*, not being afraid, travelling to Regina, a city I've never visited, and a woman I've only met once, or what I'm supposed to do there, thinking of the book I'm reading, *A Stranger at Green Knowe*, how I really don't understand it although I feel compelled to finish it because it's about a mysterious house set in a leafy, green thicket choked with vines, and there's a gorilla in the house, hiding from humans, and the secret of the house goes back centuries, enters the present, and then darts back, although I can't make head nor tail of Ping, a small boy who skips through the novel's centuries, but I want to know why the gorilla is hiding in the attic in Green Knowe.

Yesterday, at school, I held up that book to a boy sitting across from me, the one with the freckles across his nose, who wore striped T-shirts every day.

I said: "This book has no pictures." I held it up in front of him, thinking that he, this boy I liked so much, would marvel that words had the power to form pictures in the mind. Instead, he stared at me and said, "You ah stoopeh," and then turned to chatter with the other boys along the aisle.

It's already evening when Miss O'Connor meets me at the bus depot, standing tall with her cane at her side, watching the men quickly unload my suitcase from the bus. Soon I'm looking out of the windows of her small car, as she drives through Wascana Park. Her voice drifts over me and I smell peppermint on her breath. I've no idea what she's saying, but I politely nod my head.

That evening, I stand in a drafty church basement somewhere in Regina, with my boots squeaking in melting puddles of snow, a necklace of indigo windows circling the ceiling, the parents I've come to meet sitting on hard straight-backed chairs stenciled with the name of the church, St. Peter's Parish, all leaning forward to catch my slightly muffled words, except for a man at the back, who sprawls in his chair, his head thrown back as he looks up at the brown mould staining the ceiling. I eye him. Mostly, I just see his stomach.

I say: "I'm just like the other kids. I'm eleven years old and in grade six. My favourite subjects are English and Social Studies."

A woman raises her hand. Her hair is straggling out from a loose bun. She asks: "Your spee perect. Are you reaee pro unn deee eaf?"

I say: " . . . " Something has slid into my brain, and caused it to stop. I hang suspended in a cage atop of a ferris wheel while the operator has thrown the switch to let someone else out on the ground.

Miss O'Connor steps up and leans on her cane: "Joanne's progress is very remarkable. She is profoundly deaf, yet as you can see, she is able to develop speech and reading skills comparable with her peers, or even higher. She is an excellent example of what can be done if one is willing to do the hard work and make all the necessary sacrifices."

The room erupts in a buzz of voices. Finally the woman tucks a strand of hair behind her ear and pats her bun. I wish I could do that, tuck my hair behind my ear, leaving my hearing aid fully exposed. I've watched the nonchalant gestures of the girls in class, the sudden flips of locks, and the mild shakes of their heads in order to straighten the hair around their shoulders, but I feel the thick swath of bangs pushing down on my eyebrows as I check the narrow twisted cord from the ear mold that plugs my left ear. My right ear lies flat and snug against my head and the cord wraps around my neck and snakes down the middle of my chest to the small white box that nestles in a body harness underneath my clothes.

The woman with the bun turns to me again and asks: "What yuh readee leveh lie?"

I push my ear mold impatiently. The sweat in my outer ear is causing the mold to slip.

I hear: "How are you able to heah what go on in the claaaroom?" The woman with the bun. I still can't understand the question, but I have a faint idea of what she might mean, only I'm not sure if she wants to know how much I can hear or how much I can do without hearing. Suddenly, the question feels like a trap, waiting for me, an innocent snare lying casually atop of the grass.

I say: "Well, I don't need any help."

It's the end. I clutch the lottery ticket given to me as a "thank you" for the presentation while the women shrug into their coats and huddle near the stairs leading up to the outside doors, with their heads outstretched like ravens looking for food, turning toward each other to monitor looks of surprise or dismay, the men have left to warm the cars, the exhaust is already curling up against the indigo windows. Miss O'Connor weaves her way through the now disheveled rows of chairs toward me and speaks carefully: "Joanne, how would you like to meet their deaf children? We've been invited to a party for you at one of their homes."

The house has been scrubbed for the occasion. The smell of ammonia tinges the air. The house is noisy with the laughter of adults, the shrieks of small children running about the forest of their legs, and the television blaring, deaf children bouncing boisterously and shouting vociferously on the living room couch, a boy chasing a girl around the heavy coffee table, oblivious to the spilled Kool Aid dripping onto the floor. None of them look at me. They're intent on jumping on the couch. A girl flees down the hallway toward a bedroom.

I am introduced to them, one by one. Their names crash over me until I finally hear one: *Caroline.* I hear her name because I've read it before. I sat down one afternoon with my father's saxophone music, the song that had words under the notes. I slid my finger over the words and sang: *Can't you hear me calling for you, Caroline?*

The others wander off after the short introductions, but Caroline stays on the couch. Her wide skirt spans over her drawn up feet.

I ask her: "How old are you, Caroline?"

A series of croaks, gawks, and yelps spill from her mouth. Her face is strained as she tries to form the words. I can lipread her enough to see that she can make the right movements with her lips and tongue to form the words, but the sound coming from her mouth is nasal, high pitched, strained, and raw.

Her mother turns to me. She says: "Caroline is eight. We're so happy to know that she will become like you one day."

I nod slowly, unsure of what to say to this creature before me. She hardly seems human, though she is anxious about her dress, smoothing it over her legs. A woman stands beside me, stroking her poodle at the same time. She must be the owner of the house.

Afterwards, Miss O'Connor drives slowly back through the park toward her apartment in Hillsdale. The street lamps light the serpentine road sweeping past the Legislative Building, stark and brooding in the dark. The river is pocked with broken ice, and the low moon casts eerie shadows over the high snow banks.

The next morning, still in the dark, Miss O'Connor takes me to the bus station, again my luggage is stored in the cavernous reaches of the bus, I better go to the bathroom at the end of the bus before it moves, I can't stand to sit on a toilet that jiggles under my thighs, and when I finish washing my hands I notice my eyes, hyper-focused, even at seven-thirty in the morning, the light over the small steel sink barely outlining my face, and the sun hasn't even risen outside yet. I mouth my name *Joanne Weber* and see how my mouth movements are exaggerated, unlike those of the children in my class then, over the quiet hum of the bus, I speak, listening carefully, my voice hollow, as if I am speaking from behind a door.

Green Knowe is a familiar weight in my lap. I lean my head against the glass as the bus hums its way through sleeping Regina. A snow plow moves slowly south on Albert Street. Half asleep, behind a door, I hear voices in the other rooms of Green Knowe, talking about the gorilla who must hide in the attic, the gorilla's name is Caroline, and the voices are making plans, no, have already made plans, for all the years I've been alive, because time is different in that book, nothing is straightforward from birth to death, and I've never known these architects of Green Knowe before, they're not my parents, can't be my parents, but they're stronger, more powerful than my dogged mother who coaxed me into wearing headphones on my ears when I was two, more resourceful than my father who made wooden puzzles out of scrap wood, puzzle pieces of barnyard animals, *oink, oink, bow wow, meow, meow, neigh, neigh, hush, hush,* the voices babble to me in dull cadences, lulling me until I wake in the screech of another sundog day, mesmerized by the *swe-oop, swe-oop* of the telephone wires.

Two

"Mom, I'd rather live in a different family."

My daughter, Paula. Nine years old. Tears are streaming down her face. She places her hand lightly on my throat. My throat constricts. I shouldn't let Paula do this to me, yet I think somehow I deserve it. The queerness of the gesture is a reminder of something I can't quite grasp.

Then I see it. As a baby, she began to put her hand on my throat while I breastfed her, with her eyes gazing steadily into mine and her petite body nestled into my arms.

Now I scoop her up and we snuggle down between the covers on her bed.

I ask: "What do you mean?"

Anna comes in then, my oldest daughter, and sits on the bed, already in her pyjamas, ready for our nightly episode of the *The Lion, the Witch, and the Wardrobe*. She holds it in her hand.

"Something isn't right, Mom," Paula says. "I want to live with other people."

I say: "Have I hurt you? Have I done something wrong to you?"

My mind races frantically, yes, I yelled at her the other day to get out of bed, to move more quickly, to look for her coat, and boots, on the double quick, otherwise I'd be late for work.

"No," Paula says. She shakes her head from side to side. "It's just that we don't have a dad and you're . . . "

She pauses. But I'm too busy to notice the pause just then as I only hear about every third word she is saying and I must knit the meaning together at breakneck speed.

I do, into: "Lots of kids don't have their fathers with them." Thinking: *The pause, what was the pause about?*

I take her hand. She must be grieving. This must be difficult for her.

Paula looks at me steadily as I entwine my fingers with hers. Her eyes suddenly too deep, she is too young to live with so much inside her. I ask: "What are you thinking, you with your half-wise thoughts?" Paula says: "Mom, it's time to make peace with Dad. You two can work it out."

Anna is listening intently.

I ask Anna: "Do you ever think about your dad, Anna? Do you ever want to see him?"

Anna shrugs. Then she shakes her head. She says: "It's okay, Mom. I'm happy here. I don't need a dad."

I say: "Well then, we need to just do the best we can without him." I add: "He has not contacted us for nine years."

Paula says: "But it's time, Mom." She insists: "You can do it." She looks steadily into my eyes.

"It's time to brush your teeth," I say.

Our elbows bump each other as we shift for space in the tiny cramped bathroom. Each of us has our own way of fighting for possession of it. Discarded clothing and towels mark out the floor. I've made an effort at decorative domestication. I've dumped all the soap gifts into dusty wicker baskets half tilted on the torn linoleum.

The girls creep into my bed with me, lifting their legs onto my feet in order to warm them. I reach for *The Lion, the Witch, and the Wardrobe*.

Anna asks: "Did you lock the door?"

I feign forgetfulness and dash downstairs to bolt the locks and set my purse right beside the door so that a thief will find exactly what he is looking for and be satisfied, and, no, I do not want to explain to my daughters how a thief might not be satisfied. Then I slide my cold feet atop of Anna and Paula's.

Paula giggles. She says: "Ouch, your feet burn."

Paula's voice runs silently beneath my careful articulation of the words in the book I am reading: "*We don't have a dad and you're . . .*" Oh. She meant to say, "*and you're deaf.*" I read, snap off our bedside lamp, and wait for the restless forest of legs to quieten, thinking: everything was too sudden, too soon, ten years ago, our rushed affair, the birth of two daughters fifteen months apart, the unspoken question in each other's eyes, *what are we doing*, as I struggled through the pregnancies, hospitalized to keep the babies from coming too soon, Murray mired in a struggle to extricate himself from his marriage and to parent his two young sons, everything beyond repair — our wrongdoing in rushing into sex, the pregnancies, and our neglect of the business of our lives, actions that harmed Murray's two sons and their mother, and hurt my parents deeply. When things were beyond repair, I did what I always do: move somewhere else, after all, I had moved every two to three months, even every semester for most of my nine years of university, a running family joke. My parents counted: forty-seven times. My father kept a small trailer in his backyard, in case, and my mother always had a store of mops, brooms, and garbage bags for the cleaning before and after each move.

I thought: *There's nothing strange about it.* My reasons for moving are always compelling. The place is too small, too large, too expensive, too poorly kept up, and roommates come and go.

Move out. Pack, clean, move, clean, unpack. I played house with my daughters, marvelling at the spaces that once held towels, sheets, and blankets, exclaiming over the closets, the depths of shelves, the spaces that held a myriad of possibilities, the excitement always mounting in me on moving day even while our clothing and toys sat in black plastic bags like manatees beached on the living room floor, moving every year with the girls, my father aging with every move, my mother tight lipped, cleaning and sweeping while I set up the beds in the new rooms in what were never real homes but temporary places, and finally when Paula was five years old, I was standing in the kitchen of our townhouse in Saskatoon and announcing that we were going to move to North Battleford, and tears streamed down Paula's face.

She begged: "Mom, think of what we have, the good things we have."

I explained: "I have a good paying job waiting for me there, so we have to go, no question about it." Anna said nothing. She played quietly in the corner of the room, listening carefully.

The day we moved, into a small wartime house in North Battleford. Paula found a cross-shaped twig on the sidewalk, clutched it, and said: "This is a good sign, Mom. This is our home."

Anna waved from the living room window.

I took a deep breath and silently considered the house, I answered them: "We will call it Ladymint, because we are now ladies living in a house with white siding and green trim." And I assured myself: *It's a friendly house.*

Inside, detergents, bleach, and rags, bread and cheese poked out of plastic shopping bags, the old maple flooring had several splinters, so I wouldn't allow the girls to take off their shoes, I tried not to notice how the rooms were chopped up, designated for certain purposes, as if Ladymint already knew what was best for me, I tried to push the resentment out of my mind, and unpacked.

I argued with myself: *I like things open ended. I don't like people or even houses making decisions for me. That way anything is possible and I can always leave if I don't like it.*

I argued with myself a lot that day. I realized what the house would do to me: *It will make me look into rooms to find Anna and Paula: a frustrating search. Especially if they're in the basement or upstairs.*

Furthermore, the house said: *A bedroom upstairs must remain a bedroom. The living room must be a living room, where else to put the living room furniture? Anyways, it is the only room big enough for the large couch.*

I argued back: *All I need is one room. Size doesn't matter.* I stared down the stairs to the basement at the lurid carpet: green, orange, and brown, my eyes already hurting from too much visual noise, like static on a radio station.

I said: *You are not a Deaf house. You are not going to make living with deafness any easier for me.*

I watched my parents and my friends, who were carrying boxes and bags from the truck, sweating profusely on this October day, trusting that I had made good decisions, that I would finally settle down for many years, and I promised them silently: *I will never move again and I will make peace with this house that is not for me.*

I pause, holding *The Lion, the Witch, and the Wardrobe* in my hands, Anna and Paula leaning heavily on my shoulders. We're lying in my bed, pushed up against the window, my feather duvet is drawn up closely about our necks to protect ourselves from the winter night that always seems to seep through the window next to the bed. I hear a wild, shrieking noise. I smile to myself: *I know what that noise is and where it's coming from. I am tired. And I had too much coffee today. And I scarfed down that bag of chips after work. Too much salt.* The shrieking goes on and I realize: *It's rather interesting, how my brain has the capacity to generate that variation in internal noise inside my ears.*

Anna says: "Mom, that's weird." I think: *She means Aslan.*

I explain: "Well, it's a paradox. Aslan isn't safe, but he is good. Life is full of paradoxes like that. You know, two things that are opposite but somehow they work together."

Anna says: "No, Mom, the noise. That howling noise. Do you hear it? It's so spooky."

I listen again. I ask her: "Where is it coming from?"

She says: "I think it's near the window."

The window is a square of Prussian blue. *I had heard this before, and ran into my parents' bedroom screaming about a ghost rattling and howling in my room. I wanted my mother to tell me that it was all inside my head and I could go back to sleep. Instead she led me to the window and placed my hand on the cold glass.*

"Your hearing aid is on, isn't it?"

"Yeah, but I still hear noises inside my head, even with my hearing aid on."

"Well, what you are hearing is real. When there is a strong wind, it rattles the panes, especially if the window is old."

Anna throws her arm across my neck, "I wish that noise would go away. It's so creepy."

I turn on the night-lamp, "Shhh, it's just a strong wind. Turn your hearing aids off." I take out my own hearing aid and put it on the bedside table.

The girls giggle at my old joke, and burrow down under the heavy duvet. Paula puts her hand on my throat, and Anna lays her head on my right shoulder. For a few moments, I feel the vibrations through their bodies. They're talking to each other, jockeying for a position as to where they can put their hands, arms, and legs over my body. Soon I'm enclosed in the pen of their heavy and warm limbs as they sleep and I listen to the howling and shrieking in the house.

~

I was not often home. I worked long hours as a coordinator for literacy and university at North West Regional College, leaving Anna and Paula with my sister in her home three blocks up the same street, and often with my parents in Wilkie, forty minutes' drive away. I became the deaf-girl wonder, who travelled throughout the northwest and as far north as Makwa and Waterhen to learn how to foster literacy within aboriginal communities, and actually thought my hearing had improved, although my most recent audiograms all showed the same degree of hearing loss: profound deafness. But how could I explain my ability to attend meetings, to galvanize organizations into supporting the new programs, and my work with First Nations people who are so difficult to lipread?

I told myself: *You talk on the phone as smoothly as anyone.* Until I realized it was familiar territory, that my contacts and I were talking about the same thing over and over again: that what I didn't know, I looked up in articles, books, or reports, and what I didn't hear, I cobbled together from reasonable guesses, and my degrees in arts, education, library science, and deaf education had me well prepared, as I received plaques, awards, kudos, cards, compliments, and a nod from my supervisor *and the college president and was soon telling myself: It doesn't matter anymore that you don't understand what is being said at meetings and workshops. You are being applauded again and again for the work you are able to do.*

Between reports, programs, meetings, proposals, and more reports, I sprinkled crushed bay leaves by the baseboards to deter the ants from invading my cupboards; one morning Anna helped me chase a bat out of our front closet; late one evening, I was ankle deep in water, when the sewer backed up because the old trees had wrapped their roots around my pipes.

I murmured to myself: *Choking me.*

The house was not well insulated. During the hot days of summer, I packed picnic lunches and carried large coolers to Cochin, a half hour drive away, and only returned to Ladymint late at night, stepping past the tall evergreen trees and rattling my key in the sticky lock, as the house reached its arms toward us, mysterious and dark, then shuddered as I climbed the stairs, cradling sleeping Paula in my arms, urging Anna to follow me up the stairs, clutching her blanket. But Ladymint with its white wooden shutters on the kitchen window and creaking floors continued to demand things from me: *The broken garage door!* My father put in a new garage door. *The back steps!* My father built new ones. *The linoleum floor in the kitchen!* My father patched it. In a moment of appeasement, I brought all my remaining boxes from his garage in Wilkie. The look of relief on my parents' faces was palpable.

The furnace! It was late one spring evening. I stood in the cold basement, thinking, *I could move again.* But Joseph Naytowhow, a visiting storyteller working on a literacy project with me, trudged down the stairs to the basement and banged the furnace back to life. He lifted out a round plate from the furnace. Something I'd never seen before. He shrugged, and said: "It might last you the night, I don't know." He stepped away into the night.

I stood at the screen door, envious of his vagabond ways, of how he was able to live in hotel rooms and with other people nearly every night of the year as he wandered Canada telling stories, and now I wanted his freedom — to move from community to community, to meet new people, to forge new relationships, and to shake the dust off my feet at the hint of trouble: no more fighting for recognition, for success, for admiration or approval, or even for people's rights, and said, to myself, rather bitterly: *Not even my own rights.*

Joseph's drum beat through my dreams that night: *We are all one people. We are all one nation.* His kind eyes peered at me through a crowd of faces until I woke twisted in sheets and blankets, and weighted down by the limbs of my daughters, who had flung themselves over me, with my mind repeating over again: *No more fighting. No more fighting for anything anymore.*

☙

My parents became more sure I was going to stay in Ladymint. After all, it'd been two years already. I began to imagine planting flowers in the dirt bed outside the front window, began to save up for a deck wrapping around the entire house, sewed new pillow cushions for the couch, and planning new tiles for the kitchen and the bathroom. And then . . .

PAULA: *(Insistently)* "I don't want to live here anymore."

ABSENT MOTHER: " . . . " Paula began to run out of Ladymint after our arguments and roamed the streets near our house until I was frantic and found her at home again, curled up in the rocking chair, choking out between sobs: "I miss you, Mommy. You're never here anymore."

Anna became more absent, too. She wanted to go to hockey games with her friends. She insisted she didn't have any homework. I was uneasy. I talked to her teachers.

INCESSANTLY PRAISING TEACHERS: "I wish everyone in my class were like Anna."

ARGUING ABSENT MOTHER: "Anna is a gifted child, and you must find something stimulating for her."

Nothing changed. Anna never seemed to have homework and she was too quiet.

꩜

I hated the chopped up rooms in Ladymint: the badly worn front steps, the scrubby front yard, the tight staircase, and the worse thing was that I couldn't see into the rooms, every noise was a phantom noise, I always wondered if they were real or imagined, because I could never see where the sounds were coming from, and I was spooked by the house's incessant hums, buzzes, and howls during storms.

A June evening. A group of friends and I listened to Joseph tell a story to my daughters about the Mosquito Man, then he took out his drum, and began to beat a slow rhythm, and instantly we rose, held hands, and moved sinuously in an improvised round dance, and as I wove my way through the dance, I began to see what others saw in me: *A woman, smart, kind, funny, hard-working, single parent, with slightly defective speech but certainly nothing to worry about because she hears so well.* But why wasn't I celebrating my Deaf culture too? Why was I participating in a First Nations dance while being silent about my own language and culture? I watched Joseph settle my children for another story, and looked at my hands, arguing with myself: *You haven't signed to anyone in five years. But we've set down roots in North Battleford. And I no longer have difficulty living in Ladymint.* And more insistently: *God forbid, another move.* And that was when everything began to change.

∽❧

Fall, and then winter. Paula, Anna and I are still reading together at night. The tall evergreen tree leans toward our window to listen. It's a late February night. We reach the very last page of *The Last Battle* in the Narnia series. We are all quiet, until Paula says: "We have come to the end."

The forest of our legs falls heavy and I begin to move over Anna in order to back out of the bed, when Paula reaches for my throat, and says: "Mommy?"

"Yes, Paula. I'm still here." I settle myself between my daughters again.

A few moments later, Paula is asleep. I finally lift myself over Anna's still body, and move further away until I can feel the blanket covering only my shoulder and part of my hip. The rest of my back is cold and exposed. I slide my legs onto the floor until I come to a kneeling position. I ought to say a prayer. Instead, I smooth the blanket beside Anna's shoulders, pushing the pillows into the warm space where I was lying.

I enter my own bed. It's an old rickety double bed, but I don't care. I can't hear it creak, sigh, or moan. I go into a dream, sad and heavy with the weight of Murray's arms over my shoulders as I cover Paula's bony hips with my own generous flesh and rest my hand on Anna's back as she nestles against her sister. I'm naked in Murray's arms, my back to him. We're under a single white sheet, which, at intervals, Murray sends billowing over the four of us, a protective gesture. As the sheet settles, we lie fully awake, not moving, not speaking, aware of our breathing in tiny shallow hills. Words keeps forming in my throat and I want to speak, to define the small silences, but Murray tightens his arms around me, as if to bolt me into his body, and I soften and sleep.

In the morning, I stand in my tiny white kitchen, staring at the marbled Arborite counter. The florescent light is flickering overhead. The dishwasher is humming. Outside, the day is already grey, the colour of dirty water.

Water, dirty water, is in Ladymint, pushing me out, telling me to go. The water will take me where I need to go. Go with the water.

I struggle to push these thoughts away, and open the door to the new ice that has crusted over the melted snow on the front steps. As I start my car, leaving my children to prepare themselves for school, I tell myself: *They will be all right.*

A few blocks down the road in the humming car, however, I know that the water will not leave me. Later, I call Murray, the first time in nine years. I crisply suggest we meet in Davidson to discuss a reunion with Anna and Paula.

He is sitting in the far corner, almost a decade older, heavier, his face more lined, and his hair grey, and I have Unbidden Thoughts: *He is my beloved, and I am his.* These words spring open a cache of love that has remained between us after all these years. I try to remember my mother's cautionary words, *Joanne you are too impulsive,* but the rhythm of water carries me closer to him, pushing me along with a shoebox under my arm.

He weeps when he sees the photographs. *The girls at four and five, six and seven, eight and nine, ten and eleven.* The rhyme lobs itself into my head and churns me as if I am on a merry-go-round.

After coffee, I finally sign to him, the first time in nine years. "Can we start again?"

That evening, I drive in silence. There is a hum inside my head. It says, accusingly: *You've been stupid, impulsive, and careless. What do you know of this man whom you haven't seen in nine years? How can you possibly make a decision to reunite with him in a split second in that restaurant?*

I arrive home in silence, convinced that water has invaded my home and it is time to get out. I tell myself: *This is all I know.* I think: *It is enough for me.*

＊

My father's face sags just before we leave for Regina. He says: "You really don't have a place to live."

I say: "Yes, we do, Dad. It's just not ready yet. It's not Murray's fault that the tenants trashed the house."

He insists: "You don't have a home." And turns away. His eyes are pained. They seem to say: *This man is still not able to give you what you need after nine years. How can you be so naïve?*

I try to settle myself with: *I can always leave if I don't like it.* And I say: "We'll be in our home soon. Soon as we get the carpets cleaned. I'm sure there are no lice left in the house." I add: "And we'll redo the bathrooms."

My father nods, his eyes on the ground, his mouth drawn downward with worry, about to give up his role as surrogate father to Anna and Paula whom he's cradled in his arms since their birth.

＊

In Regina, I lug a backpack while the girls carry their suitcases into the hotel lobby where Murray is waiting for us, his arms opened wide. The girls nod stiffly as he rushes toward us, grabbing our bags. He fusses after the girls, as they're hungry, tired, and nervous. He phones room service for a late night pizza.

Ladymint appears before me the way I left her that morning, sullen, quiet in the early October morning, surrounded by brown patches of grass and dying juniper bushes. Her gaping mouth, the living room window now uncovered, accuses. I dispel her by promising myself an early morning swim before the girls get up for school. But I can't help thinking, already: *I am homeless.* I curl myself around a pillow, my back to Murray in the hotel room, casting an eye on the girls sleeping in the double bed next to ours. Already, the strangeness of what I've done prohibits me from turning to him, sliding into his arms. I think: *Not yet.*

The light under the hotel room door lures me with its: *You can leave anytime if you ever should have to.*

I think: *Not yet.*

Three

THERE ARE FOOTPRINTS ON THE CEILING in Murray's house in Regina. I am lying on the couch, trying to decipher the size and style of the shoes. I give up at the colour of the soles. The ceiling is smudged with greyness anyway. I try wiping off the footprints with a damp cloth, but some of it stays, and I slump on the couch. *Have I been too impulsive in reconciling with Murray and moving to Regina?*

The couch was a serious disappointment for both of us. In his hasty passion, Murray once pushed my bra down behind the cushions. Afterwards, we stood before the mirror. Murray had his hand on my shoulder, with a backward glance at the couch. Soon, our bodies became a ship of dreams sailing to nowhere, only because of my perverse need to run away from people whom I love.

In the relief of lying against Murray's side nine years later, I realize: *I wanted his body so badly that I have followed him in my dreams and in my waking intuitions. During all the years of my wandering, I must have always known I was going to come back to him someday, to the home I always had with him.*

I lie in bed now, holding a copy of *Jane Eyre*. The cover features the back of a young woman's head. I can see the freckles on her upper back, the lace straps of a chemise, and the untidy curls pinned up. I've always thought of Jane as an unattractive and prim governess, not as someone who'd be caught in her undergarments, but the publisher clearly wants to increase Jane's sex appeal, although her appeal lies in her sharp wit, intelligence, and wisdom, certainly nineteenth century virtues.

The school librarian handed me a well-worn *Jane Eyre* when I was fifteen and wandering about alone in the library at noon hour. She said: "It's about an English governess who falls in love with her master."

As I turned the pages, I began to hear the slamming of the windows, the strange scream from the upper floor, and the sudden scuffling of footsteps. I had some idea from the *Stranger at Green Knowe* that houses were haunted, their walls contained mysteries, and their windows opened onto the pasts of their inhabitants, but I'd *seen* sound in *Jane Eyre*, and now I *heard* more sounds in the classroom: the sudden roar of a teacher chastising a student, a thud made by the dropping of a book on a desk. The school became alive with sound, as I began to watch students walk, pick up books, scribble furiously in notebooks, and throw pencils carelessly on the ribbed wooden floor beneath my feet, and soon, McLurg High School became more my home than the one I lived in, where I could not understand the chatter of my sisters and brother, nor the muted conversations between my parents. My own house became alive at night only because of the strange sounds Jane heard in the dark: the hair-raising wails, and the sudden slam of a door. In the day, I began to dream of rooms I would inhabit in the school. The first thing I would do is to tear down the walls. I'd have to see everywhere at once. No more chasing people from room to room, trying to follow the trail of their sounds. I'd be able to *see* sound emanating from a physical place: from an open mouth, from the dropping of a book, from a suddenly upset cup.

The only difficulty that I could see with the gutted school is that I would have no furniture of my own. I planned to tear out lockers from the girls' changing room to make way for an oak vanity table and a large mirror. The shower, built to accommodate six girls at a time, would become a gigantic claw foot bathtub. My bedroom would be in the English room — my favourite subject. I'd sleep under posters of Shakespeare and grammar exhorting *subject verb object*. The old school would be mine, because nobody else lived there, not even the ghosts of former students, and I thought: *I could hear everything in this house, because I could see everything. If I stood before it in any light, at any time of the day, I might see Jane Eyre moving from window to window with a candlestick. I would even see Grace Poole slam a window shut in the midst of an eerie scream.*

Now, I lie awake with *Jane Eyre* spread open on my chest. All that pours through my mind is how quiet Murray's house is, even with the spirits of former tenants lurking in every tight little corner, hiding in rooms large and small. I can't hear anything. There is no sound in this house that I can see.

From the kitchen doorway the next morning, I study my two bedraggled daughters, still in their T-shirts and pyjama pants, and Murray, wrapped in his velour bathrobe, chatting at the breakfast table. Waiting. I can see their mouths move, the low hum of words sliding back and forth, an easy chatter, its intimacy, fluidity in contrast to my contrived system of nods and assurances. I snatch a tea towel. I am going to do something about this inequality right now. I am going to right it, balance it, and restore it somehow. I sign to Murray: "I won't be using my voice with you or the girls anymore."

Murray signs back: "That's not fair. The girls don't know sign very well."

My hands fly: "They're too dependent on my voice in communicating with me. They need to be forced to use sign language."

Murray's sign back: "You should've taught them when they were little."

I sign, in answer: "My hand . . . I couldn't . . . you know, the carpal tunnel."

And his: "Well, it's not fair that you spring it on them like this, right now."

And mine: "Well, it's not fair to me to have to live like this."

And his: "Well, you say it takes ten years to become fluent — only if we sign all day and nothing else. Besides, that carpal tunnel in your wrist isn't any better, is it?"

The girls are watching. I can see from the stricken looks on their faces that they understand some of it.

Finally, Murray signs: "Joanne, the pancakes are burning."

I slam the frying pan upon an unheated burner and turn toward them again. I sign: "They won't sign. They don't have to."

Murray signs back gently: "Of course they'll talk to you. It's easier for them."

I sign back, less gently: "But it is even easier for them to talk to you than to me."

And Murray, steadily: "Joanne, you're exaggerating."

And me: "It's about functioning in a group, a family, not in pairs or couples, a family."

Murray has already turned toward Anna to hear what she has just said. Paula is looking down at her plate. I think: *It is too late. The intimacy has already sprung its shoots around Murray and our daughters. Its vines are enclosing them in a bower which I cannot enter. The whispers, easy talk, intimate mumbling, sudden bursts of laughter, the jostling and embraces between father and daughters, have made me a spectator.*

I try to remind myself: *I can detach and not care about anything that goes on around me. I can become absorbed by the steady wash of images, nonsensical fragments of conversation, a theatre of the absurd, an aimless, empty, feckless, hollow, inconsequential, insignificant, insubstantial, nonsensical, black hole. Absurdity is a benign force offering to absorb my bones, to settle me into a warm and dark sleep.* If only I liked the theatre of the absurd.

I whisk the plate of pancakes to the dining room table. I can feel their eyes on me as I walk briskly into the kitchen and stand before the window. *Why, there are stains on the kitchen cupboard.* I reach for the dishcloth crumpled in the sink.

"No, not that one. A clean one." Murray. In the doorway.

Inflamed by Murray's correct guess at my intent, I slap the dishrag on the kitchen counter.

He says: "Joanne, sit down. Talk to me."

I shake my head and rush to the sink. *If I scrub the kitchen right now, this very instant, it will become my domain.* I begin to snatch the dishes piled in the drying rack, sending up a great clatter.

Murray says, loudly: "Joanne. Sit down. Look at me."

I sit on the kitchen chair, hands folded in my lap, while Murray scoots his chair over. Finally, his open knees squeeze my legs.

He asks: "What's wrong?"

I shake my head. If I speak again, I'll turn into an animal. I'll lean forward in this cramped, hot kitchen, and sink my teeth into Murray's throat. I'll threaten to leave him, flail my arms about, or let loose an endless stream of profanities, while he sits immovably, his arms folded.

He tries to take me into his arms. He says, soothingly: "Now, I don't want you to do that again."

In tears, I look up at him through the strands of my hair, now limp with sweat, and nod, vigorously. I have become a contrite little fox with dainty, limp paws. I see myself walk up the stairs to lie alone on our great bed, my tail twitching from under the quilt. I throw my arms around Murray and say: "I love you. I will do better next time," and then, "I'm very, very deaf. I know that my speech is nearly perfect and that I'm an excellent lip reader in one-on-one situations, but I need sign language in our home."

Murray touches my arm. "Why don't you wear your FM system more often?"

I shake him off. "I still need to lipread. The FM doesn't allow me to hear the way you guys can hear."

"Well, it would help."

I stand firm. "Can't you see I'm losing Anna and Paula? I can't have a relationship with them if you are going to be around. I need equal access to them."

"I've never discouraged Anna and Paula from talking to you."

"It's the group dynamics, Murray. God, you don't get it."

I turn away and go upstairs, leaving them to eat the cold and sodden pancakes. *Jane Eyre* lies on the night table, its spine already cracked. The novel is Jane's long journey to find a home where she can lay her head. Where she can live forever and never have to move again. Thornfield Hall. I glance at the winter rain skittering down the panes of our bedroom window and snuggle down to read, thinking: *I did this to myself.*

Four

A WEEK LATER, I HEAR: "I feel like you're not my mother anymore." Anna. We're sitting on her bed. Only because she beckons me to come in. My heart thudding. She actually wants to talk. To me. She's still here. She's still my daughter. The one I had in North Battleford.

So I say: "Why do you say that?" Cautious. Calm.

Anna, not so calm: "Well, Dad has taken over everything. He tells us what to eat, what clothes to wear, what to do. I want to be able to pick out my own clothes." My daughter. She adds, firmly: "He's too involved."

I touch her on the shoulder. "He's so happy to have you girls with him again. There are things he can give you that I haven't been able to."

I try to sound convinced. Secretly, though, I'm pleased.

My daughter says: "You should be more confident."

Hmmm.

Murray does dominate all the conversations. I'm drowning in his wet, cold words, too much talk, talk, talk, he can hardly contain his excitement about parenting the girls, while I sit, holding my memories, my life with my daughters, a deadness expanding in me. I can't say anything to his ideas, or his perceptions, I'm mute, as he goes on, and on.

I say: "..."

He says: "Paula is so open with her feelings, last night she was telling me about her math, how she finds it so difficult, she needs to develop confidence in herself, but Anna has dominated her all these years. We have to work on teaching Anna her boundaries."

I think: *Boundaries?* I listen. I can only say: "..."

All these new discoveries Murray is making are new to me too. How is it that I never knew these things about them before? My babies? Whom I've been with since birth? I breastfed them, bathed them, and sang to them. I sewed their clothes, cooked their meals, and took them to parks, swimming pools, museums, libraries, playgrounds. Jazz festivals by the Bessborough Hotel in Saskatoon. I read to them. Every night. And our games in bed. And Anna begging me to tell her again and again the story of how she was born, how my water broke, and her father, Murray, calmly ironed his pants before we went to the hospital, and I was still in my sodden dress, sliding on to the car seat atop a plastic bag.

I was strong. I was competent, resourceful, and hardworking. I owned a consulting business. I had contracts with school boards. I gave workshops to Deaf aboriginal women. I was the miracle worker. I churned out proposal after proposal. I took my children to all the Deaf socials. Anna and Paula romped with the Hearing children of Deaf parents. And I saw Anna read for the first time. Five years old. She came to me. I was sick at home. I was lying on the bed. She sat beside me. She asked me to write a word. I did, weakly. "Cat." She sounded it out. I was curious. I rolled over onto my queasy stomach and printed out: "See the cat." She sounded it out.

"No way," I said. "Try this." I wrote: *Uncle Joe has a pig.* She got, "Joe has a pig."

"Do you know what this means?"

She nodded. We did a dance on the bed.

I want to accuse Murray: *I have memories of them you'll never have.* I want to taunt him with memories. Paula at age two in the library, with a pageboy bob, opening the mockingbird book, and singing in a sweet clear soprano as she turns the pages, "Hush little baby, don't say a word. Mama's gonna buy you a mockingbird," because I sang it to her every night before sleep. Anna stopping reading to listen. The library staff stopping, and the other patrons, to listen. All this talk about boundaries. *Pfft,* I want to say to Murray. *What do you really know about the girls?*

I know: *Deep inside he is right. I carried Paula everywhere, like a fragile china doll. Anna stood on sturdy legs. I began to consult her more and more about decisions affecting us, as if she were a grown adult. The discrepancy was unfair. I weaned Anna at six months and Paula at two and a half years.*

My mother: "But they are so well adjusted."

My friends: "You are such a wonderful mother."

Their daycare worker one day: "Are you married?"

I say: "The girls have no contact with their father."

Curious daycare worker gasps: "But you look married. The girls are so grounded, not like most children from single parent families."

But according to Murray, they aren't grounded enough. A confusion is growing in me. I am sinking into a muddy pool of water. The house suddenly seems rank.

I complain to Murray: "There's mould on the basement bathroom ceiling."

Murray points out: "It's brown mould. You can wipe it off with a Javex solution."

I want to reply: "But I shouldn't have to wipe it off. There's something wrong somewhere. *Too much water.*" I want to say more about this water, but this is what I complain about instead: "I don't have a connection with the girls anymore. You've taken them away from me," and slam the door fiercely behind me and climb the stairs to the living room, where I sense the spirits of Murray's former tenants, dulled by ghostly television sets and computer games, giving me a glance sideways. I feel like I'm walking underwater. Murray, Anna, and Paula are muddy blobs, walking away from me. I slump on the brown velvet couch in confusion. *No one is listening to me in this house.*

The next day, Paula comes back from school for lunch, and announces: "Mom, they're really bad."

"Who?"

"The kids. Holy Family in North Battleford was a much better school. Here the kids don't do anything. And the teachers yell all the time."

I offer: "Well, it is a tough neighborhood."

But my confusion from the previous evening is deepening to panic: *They're not safe. I've delivered them into the hands of a controlling father and a neighborhood full of drug addicts, juvenile delinquents, and thieves.*

I say: " . . . "

In better moments at the supper table, I lean forward with pleasure into the conversations, when Murray talks about things I already know, like literature, stories, tidbits of history, footholds I can grip when navigating the conversation between the four of us before the incessant babbling brook of personal anecdotes, plans, problem solving starts up, leaving me to sit in a quiet pool, unable to derive any sense of the topic.

This moment. Listening to Murray tell Paula and Anna the story of Demeter and Persephone, for Paula's benefit, who complained about having to study Greek myths.

"It's about a mother who lost her daughter to Hades, the god of the underworld . . . "

Deaf Girl-Wonder treads water and says: "Those myths are very important . . . "

Paula, hearing everything, both said and unsaid, says: "Yeah, yeah." She sighs and turns away.

The Controlling Father Lover Companion and Family Everything glances at me, his eyebrows raised high, and swims on into: "Persephone starves in her grief and finally eats those pomegranate seeds underground when she is with Hades. Then her mother, Demeter, and Hades strike a deal. Persephone is to live with her mother above ground amongst the flowers, grasses, and trees, but underground with Hades, her husband, in winter."

Paula, who doesn't catch the significance of this little double-edged story, says: "Dad, this is not important. Who cares . . . "

But Deaf Girl-Wonder catches onto the topic and interrupts with: "I saw a picture of Persephone, white and cold, lying on a flat stone tomb, her warm breath rising against the raw and frozen earth walls of her home in Hades."

What I hear, however, is: *Continued chatter that pushes Demeter and her Persephone down the river of conversation.* I want to swim after that precious cargo that has been sent carelessly floating down the rapid waters. I want to shout: *I am Demeter! I've lost my girls to Hades, the god of the underworld, who says I can only have them part of the time.*

What I say instead is: " . . . "

I sit and glower at Murray, angry that he doesn't understand the power of stories, that he doesn't swim with me to rescue the story from oblivion.

We move into another house in south Regina, far away from that brassy yellow kitchen in the north end. My new kitchen has original metal Youngstown cabinets, no dishwasher, and a badly scratched and pocked enamel sink, but there is hope in the flowers outside, and there is water nearby, though certainly not in the house, I note, but in man-made Wascana Lake, where we walk in the evenings, brushing past dogs, people, and bikes, water too dirty to swim in, sidewalks dotted with goose poop, dried and frozen in November, where three months later, after supper, we are walking along on a path of grey snow, from which I keep veering every few paces so I can see Murray's hands and face, because how else am I going to have a conversation? I have to *see* what I hear.

I sign-complain: "The girls are still not talking to me much. They still spend too much time with you. And no one has any time for me."

Murray signs back: "It's important that Anna and Paula have their father."

With gloved hands, I sign: "It isn't healthy for the girls to have an invisible mother." I shiver as a cloud passes overhead and makes Murray's face seem even greyer.

Walking along, Murray signs: "Joanne, be honest, you are not invisible."

My woolen fingers sign: "Maybe that's how I am supposed to be."

Murray bends his head down toward me and reaches out to hug me: "Joanne, you're not invisible. You are important to us."

I think: *If I can't participate in any conversations, I can't feel that I am of significance to others.* I say: " . . . " My body says: *I am something.*

I follow Murray's gaze toward a small island standing sentinel, its shores dark with frost, in the middle of the Wascana Lake. A lone goose hisses nearby as it waddles past us. I push my striped scarf closer to my face to ward off the roar of the wind rushing in my hearing aid, and I think: *No. I am just nothing.*

A broad back with white-tipped needles scoots into a bush dark and wet with snow. A porcupine? Wild oats scratch my legs as I bend down to the ground, smelling the damp and cold earth, the dead leaves, the decay of insects, and the rich loam beneath. Murray standing, motionless, looking out over the lake, up at the last geese of the season flying overhead, as I look downward, caught by the layer of red and yellow leaves frosted with snow, and then something red catches the corner of my eye, a poor creature barely camouflaged by snow and autumn leaves: a fox, peering out from the bottom of the bush.

A call from somewhere within me, a high pitched whistle, a sound I am unable to ignore, reverberating in my ears, not the first time that tinnitus has intruded into the noise of everyday, now, but it's so insistent now that it unleashes Fear, and Fear screams: *Something calamitous is about to happen!* I stop suddenly on the footpath.

Murray. Bending down towards me. "Joanne, what's wrong?"

I am struggling in my mind for something to say because I'm too filled with nothingness, except for a vague fear. And other people's thoughts or stories. I think: *Stories.*

I begin. "Have you ever heard of fox wives?"

The answer, faint: "Hmm."

Excitedly now: "I saw a picture of a fox wife. She's wearing a navy blue kimono and her baby is lying on a cushion at her feet. She doesn't even look at her son."

Again that: "Hmm." The look in Murray's eyes is vacant.

In full flight: "There are two weird things about this picture. She has a tail that comes out from the edge of her skirt. She also has a cloth stuffed in her mouth, the ends of which she holds in her hand."

Murray asks: "Why the cloth?"

Taking the time to explain: "It's a cloth used for blotting ink. Apparently, this fox wife was a writer. The *kitsune*, that's the Japanese word for foxes, were intellectuals."

Which earns an: "Ah."

Which I fill out with: "Some kind of a vampire. A fox wife. She married a twelfth century nobleman and bore him a child. He was besotted with her."

Which earns this: "The fox wife bites him and turns to other men for their blood?"

Which I dispel with: "No, that's a European vampire. She just disappears, leaving him with the baby."

Murray, drawing me out: "But what do *kitsune* want, if they don't want blood?"

Drawn out now, I say: "Words. They want to fill themselves with words. Knowledge. They drain people because they are so needy for ideas, knowledge, and words. A *kitsune's* human lover or child will waste away because the *kitsune* is so demanding."

A sudden chill descends upon us. I think: *It must be the sudden gust of the north wind.* I say: "There's more. I looked up the story. The baby son became very sick, to the point of dying. The father was distraught, to the point where he forgot to sow his rice fields. The tax collectors then demanded taxes from a field of weeds."

"I don't see the point of this."

"One morning, the husband wandered to his field, now really worried that his son was going to die. Then he noticed that his field had been planted and rice was flourishing. When he looked more closely, he discovered that the arrowroot weeds were growing upside down, with their roots exposed."

Murray nods politely and his steps become quicker.

I hope to keep up with him on the snow-tracked path, until I have a clear enough view to say: "Wait, there's more. The husband ran back home to tell his wife, and discovered her sleeping in bed, with her fox tail switching out from the covers."

"Joanne, this is very interesting, but I really don't see the point of this story."

"But there's *more* to it. The wife took the dying baby into her arms and she and her husband walked back out to the field again. Then with tears in her eyes, the fox wife handed the child over to her husband, waved her hand at the sky, and the sky grew dark and heavy, and in the lengthening shadows she disappeared."

Murray is silent as we finish our brisk walk back home. He stamps the snow off his feet before he enters the house.

Me, at his large long back: "Don't you see the point of the story? The child only recovers when the fox wife leaves the husband."

Murray shrugs. His eyes are narrow and cautious. "It's just a story, Joanne. We have our own lives to live. How about some coffee now?"

Not to be put off, I say: "But there's something vampirish about deafness. We live off Hearing people, off their good will, because we can't hear well enough to participate in anything, everything is so complicated all the time, you'd have to interpret everything for me if I were to be involved. I just live off you. And maybe, Anna and Paula would be better off..."

The Hearing man says: "You're living in the Hearing world now. You aren't in the Deaf community."

His profoundly deaf fox wife says: "But..."

Wearing his husband mask now, the Hearing man says: "Remember Myklebust, that psychiatrist who did research on deaf children during the fifties? He said something like, 'Deaf people experience the world in a lesser way... are egocentric, paranoid...'"

MY MOTHER: "*Deaf people can be so self-centred. Be sure you don't ever get like that.*"

I sit in glum silence. Murray is reading the paper that he has sprawled over the scratched dining room table. I think: *Murray is too calm, he must not care. I can hardly bring myself to look at him. I know my eyes are smudged with fatigue and my face is pasty white. Surely I am a loathsome creature. To be pitied.*

PITIABLE CREATURE: "Murray, this isn't working."

MURRAY: "We made a commitment, we're in this together."

He pours me a cup of coffee as we sit at the kitchen table. He extracts a section of the newspaper from the pile on table.

PITIABLE CREATURE: (*Insists*): "But I'm lonelier now than ever. You spend all your time with the girls and we don't do anything together."

Murray pauses from his paper, and muses aloud: "It's the myth of North Battleford, isn't it? You and the girls, in that house, surrounded by your family, how things were so much better then, you weren't even around Deaf people there, either; somehow you managed to convince yourself that you were Hearing."

PROUD (BUT STILL PITIABLE) CREATURE: "Well, it's true, life was better then. I'm losing the girls now, they don't talk to me anymore, and they always talk to you."

Murray's signs are heavy and slow, his large fingers barely able to fully make the hand shapes, these hand shapes: "Look, Joanne, I'm so fortunate to have you, Anna, and Paula back with me again. You need to have some confidence that we can do this."

Silence.

Silence. That evening, Murray slides behind me in our bed. He holds me tight. I turn toward him, my nightgown a thin cotton shift twisted in ropes underneath me, exasperated, I pull it off, and Murray begins to tap on my body with his large fingers, a Morse code on my skin: I am surprised I know what it means. A panic rises in me, my ears roar with tinnitus, while the tapping becomes insistent, it increases in intensity, this is a language I cannot pretend not to hear or understand. I bury my nose in the hairs on Murray's chest while I explore the crevices and folds of his body with trembling fingers. I find a mole, a knotted muscle, and fine hairs, adjusting the cartography of his body in my head.

Later I wake in the middle of the night. I look over the twisted sheets, the thrown pillows and the humped blankets. Doubt assails me. *Is it worth having a Hearing husband, to go through the anxiety of not knowing what he will say in the dark, in the car, in the rain, in the middle of the night with the lamp turned off, in the middle of an accident, or a stirring moment? Or worse, having to endure long hours of boredom at family and social gatherings?*

I answer myself: *Books are more satisfying. I'd rather read words that remain bolted to a page instead of flying off in fragments from a person's mouth.*

What I don't want to see: the clumsiness in Murray's fingers, the unusual strain on his wrists as he chokes out the hand shapes. Doing all that for me.

Early light is creeping around the edges of the bedroom curtains. No. It is only the moon sliding through the slats of the window blinds. I kick the covers and Murray stirs slightly. I'm hungry and I rise, snatching *Jane Eyre* from the bedside table.

Jane Eyre bedecks herself in a white lace veil, a blushing bride ready for church, unaware that Rochester already has a mad wife in the attic. The wedding ceremony is interrupted by the one living relative of the mad wife. Humiliated, Jane flees across the moors, lugging an abominably heavy suitcase, and collapsing in a yard by a farmer's pigpen. She eats the pig slop, and is found huddled against the door of a manor house. She has returned to her beginnings: an orphan, penniless, without family or friends; she has reached too high. Despite her intelligence and uncommon good sense, she doesn't know her place. I think: *I too, have returned to the Hearing world, and I too don't know my place, living with a Hearing man, having Hearing children.*

Doubt says: *Maybe you should just starve yourself to death.*

The moon shines through the kitchen window as I stand waiting for the kettle to come to a full boil, the steam pasting itself against the glass pane; over the top of the mist, the sky is lit by the city's lights. When my tea is ready, I sit at the table and pick up *Jane Eyre*. I am playing Bible roulette with this book, but I must find out what to do. I stab a finger on a page, and I read: "All says I am wicked, and perhaps I might be so: what thoughts had I been but just conceiving of starving myself to death?"

I slam the book shut.

I make a sandwich.

I pick at it.

I think: *There's a mad wife somewhere in this house.* It's a lurid thought, a melodramatic device from Gothic novels, but it has settled in me like a fishhook. Soon the shadows in the kitchen crowd around me and the moonlight becomes a veil ready for Jane's wedding ceremony the next day, then I shake my head, and say, to myself, *I should not identify this closely with a Bronte heroine. It's unhealthy.*

I slip back into bed, wondering whether I can warm my cold feet on Murray's. I tuck myself in backwards between his head and his knees. But the mad wife has come along with me. She says, between us: *Why must I always rear up like a skittish horse when hearing people invite me into conversation and then their mumbling unplugs me without warning? Why can't I attach to them when they want so much for me to belong to them?* Murray stirs in his sleep, his body is like an iron pot-bellied stove. There are flames all around me now, licking at the edges of my tightly shut eyes.

I think: *Fox wives like to burn houses.*

JOANNE FOX WIFE: (*Cackles maniacally*) " . . . !"

Five

On an early July morning, Murray comes to me with a newspaper in his hand and points to an advertisement.

Teacher of the deaf position . . . Regina Public School system . . .

I counter: "No way."

It's been fifteen years since I last worked as a teacher of the Deaf. Since the closure of the R.J.D. Williams Provincial School for the Deaf in 1991, school boards have been responsible for educating deaf and hard-of-hearing, relying on special education teachers to address their needs and rarely hiring teachers of the deaf, using educational assistants with mostly no more than one or two years of postsecondary education and little formal training in deaf education or even sign language. Only the public and separate school boards in Regina and Saskatoon hire teachers of the deaf. Those positions have long been filled. I can't believe that this opportunity has come at last, after so many years of taking on jobs that didn't have much to do with deaf education, but now I'm not so sure I want this job, even though the opportunity will likely not appear again for another decade.

I buy myself time. "But they're going to want me to do the mainstreaming thing."

"Well, you were mainstreamed for all of your education."

I stall some more: "Yeah, well, it's a pretty word. Everyone wants the deaf to be part of one great happy family, but no one is willing to do the work of integrating them."

"Apply anyway. It's so much better than the job you have now."

I say: " . . . "

He's right. I'm miserable with my instructional design job at SIAST, endlessly cutting and pasting content from instructors' notes into web pages. A secretarial job.

And: Murray knows what I do best.

And how did he know? I met Murray for the first time in 1987. R.J.D. Williams School. He had been working there for five years. I reported to him as a practicum student, fresh from the College of Education at the University of Saskatchewan. On a dark February morning, we were in his science laboratory, with two Deaf boys, who were studying magnetism. At first our conversation included the boys.

The dark-haired one, curious, signed with his slender fingers, his eyebrows dark and heavy in thought: "Does your family sign?"

My fingers stuttered: "Actually no. We've all gotten along without it."

He turned away, already restless with my fumbling signed English. He dismissed me with a thin tight mouth and bounced *hh* off his fingers: "Oh, you're hard-of-hearing."

He and his lab partner began to play with the magnets on top of the laboratory table.

Murray signed to them: "Go ahead, here's the hammer, now smash them."

Their eyebrows shot up. They signed: "Are you sure you want us to do this?"

I interjected too, with my stumbling fingers: "You sure about that?"

Murray nodded slowly, his face expressionless.

Behind his back, I watched the two Deaf boys hold hammers hesitantly over the magnets.

I signed (and spoke): "Actually, I'm profoundly deaf."

Murray nodded and held up his index finger. He turned to encourage his Deaf students to break the magnets. Then he asked: "How did you learn when you were in school?"

I spoke (and then remembered to add sign, the Deaf boys had a right to see the conversations in the room): "Well, not like those boys."

I jumped slightly when the magnet snapped in two and the pieces reverberated against the walls in the science laboratory.

Murray turned to the boys and signed to them: "Now read these science sheets and complete them using those magnet pieces."

While he passed out the papers, I mulled over his question. The question no one has ever bothered to ask me. I thought: *He actually wants to know how I was able to write stories, poems, essays, research papers, and balance chemistry equations.* I fidgeted with my internship observation papers, and finally lay them down.

I began to sign with him, dropping my voice, even though he was Hearing and my speech was nearly perfect: "Well, basically, I'm self taught. The teacher was pretty much useless, talking endlessly at the front of the classroom. I didn't pay much attention."

His fingers carved out: "Why not?"

My fingers danced out: "I couldn't hear the teacher. I could hear his voice, but everything was so muffled. I'm not sure I learned everything I was supposed to learn."

His fingers: "Well, you did, didn't you? Otherwise, you wouldn't have made it through university, to here, would you?"

I paused. I thought about this some more. I signed: "You mean it's possible to learn without a teacher?"

He answered with: "I don't see why not. That way of learning is just as legitimate as anything else."

Murray's classroom was a science laboratory, with lab tables, sinks, and microscopes. The windows looked out onto the basketball court at the back of the school. A stack of educational journals rested on his desk. I pointed at them. I ask: "You read those?"

Murray nodded, busy with the boys again.

I sidled over to the desk. Language development, cognition, psychology of deafness, studies contesting the use of Signed English over American Sign Language. The steps inherent in the scientific method, outlined on the blackboard: hypothesis, test design, variables, methodology, experiment, observation, data, conclusion.

I thought: *He has confidence in me*, that I managed to learn with teachers who were there but not there. Maybe it was just their pity that pushed me along to higher grades, maybe I'm a fraud. I looked at Murray again. *He has confidence in me.*

I felt: *I don't.*

Nearly fifteen years later, at seven thirty in the morning, I let myself into the only carpeted room at a high school in Regina.

Will my new job unlock the mystery why I ran away from every home I've lived in and away from the people I love? Will it bring back to me the way I grew up and became integrated into the school and the Hearing world at large, will it spit up clues, hints, and memories and explain this incessant urge to flee? *Would it have been better for me if I'd joined the Deaf community and attended the School for the Deaf from the age of three? Would I have been any happier, more able to stay at home?*

This morning while our car idled in front of the school, Murray told me: "It can't have worked any other way. It's your parents, your tenacity, and your intelligence that's made you who you are. It's time you stopped complaining about the path you've taken." He kissed me. He tried to hold me, but I pushed him away as I slid across the front seat and out of our car. An inexplicable grief welled up within me as I watched him drive off to his own school a few blocks down the road.

The room is one third the size of a regular classroom, the Deaf and Hard-of-Hearing Resource room, once part of a large staff room and now facing the glass-walled administrative offices across a large wide hallway. A typical special education closet, smelling of sweat, dust and mould. The carpet not vacuumed in some time. Crammed with furniture. Five teacher desks. Two round tables. A small desk bearing a coffee machine and snacks. Two file cabinets. In 425 square feet. Painted cement brick walls. Three blackboards. Two bulletin boards. Full-sized. A computer workstation wedged between two of the interpreters' desks. Shelves. Class notes, in binders. Spines labelled with the names of classes and teachers. I take a deep breath.

Seven students. I flip through their cumulative files on my desk. Four are hard-of-hearing students. A quick check. Many of their hearing losses are the result of genetic disorders. Or maybe fetal alcohol syndrome. I nod grimly. I think: *That means they might have other problems. Not like the generation I grew up in, where the rubella epidemic produced many bright and able deaf children.* The two deaf students who use sign language rely on a staff of three interpreters who rotate between translating and taking notes for the other hard-of-hearing students. The sixth student has a hearing loss in one ear only. I do a mental tally in my head: *Five are oral. Only two use sign language.* I fill my coffee cup and nod brief smiles to the few teachers in the staff room. I say to myself: *I am not unfriendly. I just have no energy for pretending to laugh and smile at small talk. I used to be able to do that when I was younger, but I'm over forty. The years have left their mark of impatience.*

In the classroom, I find the students sitting around a table. One of them stares at the computer monitor.

Why aren't they chatting with each other? They'll have to spend four years in the same room at certain times throughout the day. Surely they have something in common. A bolt from the blue answers: They can't understand each other. Their speech is too poor. Not all of them can sign.

I pause by the girl on the computer. I sign and speak: "Your name?"

"M-e-l-i-s-s-a." She finger spells her name instead of using her voice. She shrugs. Her eyes are vacant. She unfolds her long legs under the desk.

I feel a tap on my back and turn around. The interpreter. A petite woman with a shock of blond hair, sprayed and moussed. She turns her back so that Melissa doesn't see her signs.

"Don't get her started on another stupid story about her cousins on the reserve." Her signs are light and swift, disappearing a nanosecond after they arc through the air.

I sign: "Reserve?"

"Yeah, Melissa comes from there. There's a note in her file about her going on and on about her family. By the way, I'm Lisa."

I sign: "Maybe it's all she's got."

I shake Lisa's hand and glance over my shoulder at the three hard-of-hearing students waiting at their table. They still aren't talking to each other. They are engrossed in painting their binders with whiteout fluid.

One is Casey. Her bright pink T-shirt dips barely above her breasts. Her father is Métis. It's in her file. She has his high cheekbones. Dark brown hair laps around her eyes. Her long narrow fingers tap her binder, which is painted with logos, tattoo designs, and the initials of her boyfriends.

"Do you know sign language?" I sign, using a pidgin mixture of American Sign Language, spoken and Signed English. "I am Ms. Weber, and my sign name is JW." I show them how to make the handshape *j* circle over my left hand and land with a *w* on the back of my hand. I realize: *I have three names: Joanne, Ms. Weber, and JW. And it's been so long since I've been known as JW.*

Casey's pea-green eyes shift to the right, past my shoulder as she says, in answer: "Boo, aeh, eh wha nnoo hea."

Lisa nods and smiles to acknowledge what Casey has just said. Me: *Puzzled look.*

Another girl nods in my direction. "She's my sister." Her black eyes flash as she speaks through carefully formed lips, concentrating on where to put her tongue in her mouth.

Her voice is authoritative: "Casey means that she doesn't know any sign and she doesn't want to learn."

Casey nods, a wide smile growing across her face, and vocalizes: "Tee ee Andrea. Andy."

I realize: They are twins. Identical. Except that this one is wearing black, the U shape of her shirt plunging between her breasts.

Their jeans are ultra-tight. Andy's arm is etched with old scratches. She catches me looking and quickly pulls down her sleeve. I nod and look at the other students. Their faces are immobile and uncomprehending.

I ask a deaf boy: "And what about you? Do you sign?"

His face is sullen. He shakes his dreadlocks over his eyes. He says: "I doan nee et, my spee ee fine."

An older woman, her hair dyed to a soft brown, who must've been in her early sixties, interrupts, exactly like this: "Yes, you don't need to sign as you do speak very well."

I see gnarled hands and think: *Signing hurts.*

She returns her gaze to the boy. So do I. His face is flushed with her praise.

I nod and turn to another student. Nolan. A tall aboriginal student built like a football player. I sign speak: "Did you just understand what he just said?"

He shakes his head.

At first, I say: " . . . " Then I say: " . . . "

I'm at a loss. I stand before the three students as the two additional staff arrive and huddle in the corner, conversing in soft tones. I can't make out anything they are saying.

I walk up to them. I sign, sans voice: "Uh, good morning. Can anyone give me a schedule, so I can decide who is responsible for which class?"

Lisa's eyes narrow at my signing.

I made a mistake. I tapped my left shoulder with slightly cupped hands indicating "responsibility" instead of crossing my fingers into the *r* handshape. She knows that I am an ASL signer, which is contraband in her eyes. She is a Signed English signer. She uses an Anglicized version of sign language. She signs like she is speaking Chinese in English word order, with an English accent, and using the English alphabet instead of characters. We Deaf don't sign like that. Sign language is not English. *Oh brother.*

Lisa signs in this Signed English to the deaf students in my classroom. Although I took a Signed English course a long time ago, I can't remember which signs are alphabetized. The older interpreter steps into the space between Lisa and me.

She says: "I'm Catherine."

Grateful, I shake her twisted fingers.

I turn to Lisa, "Is it just me, or is Casey's speech really that bad?"

"Her speech is terrible, but we're used to it."

"The other two students are not much good either. You'll have to interpret for them."

"They don't want to use sign language."

Catherine says: "Their parents want them to be oral."

I say: "It's not them. It's for me. I need to be able to understand them."

Catherine explains: "But I have to go and take notes in the class for them. I can't be here at the same time."

I sigh. I turn to my chair. The only window in the room is locked. With a narrow wooden stick. It is covered by curtains. Heavy with dust. They don't fit. A foot-wide strip of glass is exposed.

I feel another tap on my shoulder. Melissa. She is standing before me. Her large brown eyes are nearly black with anxiety. Her books are lying on the table.

Melissa and Ms. Weber sign together:

MELISSA: "I don't want to go to class."

JW: "You have to. Your interpreter's waiting for you."

MELISSA: "I don't understand my interpreter."

JW: "When did you start working with the interpreter?"

MELISSA: "Just today. I talked with her for five minutes."

JW: "You mean you signed with her. It's scary for all grade nines. You can come back and tell me about it in an hour."

MELISSA: "All the interpreters think they're wonderful."

JW: "Give her a chance. I promise you I'll think about this."

MELISSA: "But everyone thinks I'm a freak. They all stare at me."

JW: "It's the first day of Grade Nine. Everyone is scared shitless."
End of our signing.

I sit in my chair wondering if I should have signed "shit."

Five minutes later, Lisa stomps into the room. She throws her clipboard on her desk. *Ms. Weber and Lisa talk, loudly. It ends in a lecture.*

LISA: "Melissa's in a bad mood. Did she complain to you about my signing?"

MS. WEBER: "Why aren't you in the auditorium interpreting for her?"

LISA: "There's nothing going on. Just kids in the auditorium, milling around. The principal hasn't arrived yet."

MS. WEBER: "Maybe you'd better get back there. She might like to talk to someone."

LISA: "Oh, she has some speech. She'll be okay."

MS. WEBER: "I haven't heard it yet."

LISA: "They always have some speech. They always use their voice with me."

MS. WEBER: "It's one thing to have speech. But it is another thing to have speech that is intelligible. And she has to be able to understand the other students. Have you noticed that our deaf students don't even understand each other in here? You need to get back to the auditorium."

End of conversation.

I glare at Lisa until she slowly turns and walks out the door.

My ears are roaring with tinnitus. Too much coffee? Stressed out? I don't know. I sit for a few moments, watching the sun peek in and out of the window. A fake plant jitters on top of the vent.

I twist a pen with my hands. The wall of a portable classroom and a wire fence closes the far end of the inner courtyard. I think: *Well, at least I get my own backyard. And this cramped, cluttered classroom is the only place in Regina that I can be Deaf, sign my way through the day, and where exchanges with students and teachers might be interpreted when necessary. Better than nothing. It's the only place in the universe where deafness is not a malicious, unwelcome guest snickering at my ineptness.* I think: *But the garden is a desolate and empty place.*

Murray looks up with inquiring eyes as I plop into the couch, hardly able to speak. After several stilted starts at conversation, I finally say, "Those kids do not share anybody. They want undivided attention from me or the interpreters. Even though they patiently wait their turn, I get the feeling that they are resentful for not having me to themselves all day."

"How do you know that?"

"They won't talk among themselves. They won't converse in a group. They all wait for one to one conversations. I think I'm exactly the same way. With you, Anna, and Paula, I mean."

"That's because those kids are just young. Naturally they want undivided attention."

My chest tightens: "It's a deaf thing, Murray." I can hear the impatience in my own voice, as it says: "It has nothing to do with maturity."

Later that evening, I lie on the bed, brushing away the fringes of a crocheted afghan, a hideous orange, purple, and red affair, as I read. Murray lifts, his eyebrows high again with inquiry, but I burrow more deeply into the bed.

But he snaps on another lamp.

His voice is low. "Anna, . . . " I lean over to catch his vowels, "wants to go to a party tomorrow night." The dimmed lights make his face look like a fading photograph.

I ask: "Well, what did you tell her?"

He says: "I told her that I'd talk to you."

I hook my fingers through the loose stitches in the afghan. I'd rather not say anything, in case I say something wrong. I think: *Why couldn't you have said yes to Anna?* The fox wife answers: *Ah, but he doesn't want you to accuse him of controlling you by not consulting with you in the first place.* I find myself tongue-tied. This is such a simple question. I tell myself: *Yes or no.* The fox wife says: *Except that Murray would want to analyze all the pros and cons, how much homework, housework, and computer time Anna has been doing lately, who else is going to the party, whether the parents would be at home and whether there will be alcohol. Talk, talk, talk, talk, talk.* I tell myself: *Say yes and be done with it. Too much discussion. Why couldn't you just make the decision and spare me the painful deliberations.* I blurt: "I really can't be a part of this family, this *Hearing* family."

Murray rolls his eyes.

MRS. DEAF: "I saw that, Murray. Mr. Wonderful Communicator."

His voice is firm. "We have a decision to make. Together."

MRS SULLEN: "The only thing left for me is to do everything on your terms."

MR. WONDERFUL COMMUNICATOR: "You're jealous of us, Joanne. Get over it."

I tighten my arms around my waist and say: " . . . " I think: *He might be a teacher of the deaf, but he still doesn't understand Deaf.* And bitterly: *He's Hearing.*

MR. HEARING: "Joanne, I want us to be a family. I don't know how you're going to do it, but you can be in both worlds. I thought signing was important to you, that having Deaf friends makes you feel normal. Now you can teach deaf kids."

MRS. SULLEN WITH HER BACK UP: "It's about your fundamental orientation toward me. I have a Deaf body and you have a Hearing body. There's one hell of a difference."

MR. KEEP FAMILY TOGETHER: "Joanne, this is not about you. I am tired of being made to feel guilty that you can't hear. I don't want our daughters to grow up with that kind of guilt."

MRS. OH-HO!: "Guilt? Is that what you think?"

MR. THINKER: "Joanne, don't you see? They want a private life apart from us. They don't want us to know anything about what they're doing at school."

MRS. MOM: "That's just teenage stuff."

Murray throws up his hands in exasperation.

PAULA AND ANNA'S MOM: "They're not telling you anything, because they don't trust you. You've been away from them for nine years."

PITIABLE DEAF WOMAN: *(Adds)* "And they're not talking to me because I'm Deaf."

MURRAY TEACHER THERAPIST: "Many teenagers try to be adults without learning the skills and responsibilities."

I claw the afghan off my body, thinking: *There are to be only harsh solutions to this business of being Deaf in the Hearing world. Either I shut up, put up, take all responsibility for communication breakdowns, relying on my defective hearing to be a part of things and smile through it all, or I become a crusty, angry bitter woman who has found the great promise of being able to speak and hear to be profoundly lacking, no delicacy is possible with this, no gentle bursting of flowers, words, or shoots of green leaves,* and I say: "I just want to be connected, I don't care how, I don't care if I have to use sign or speech, I just want to be close to someone without being yanked away by deafness."

MR. HEARING WITH THE LAST WORD: "But you don't seem to try very hard to be close to anyone. You know that I thought you were married to someone else all those years, your lawyer put you down as being married on our court papers, that's why I didn't come around, I thought you wanted me out of your life, so don't blame me if you didn't bother to proofread what your lawyer wrote."

Murray's large bulk throws a shadow over me. Through it, he softens and says: "That's in the past. We can't do anything about it. We need to do what's right for the girls now."

I say: "I need sign language with the girls. For God's sake, Murray, they're going to think it's a bloody hobby and not worth the time, because they can communicate with me just fine, one on one."

He offers: "Then give them time to understand your deafness."

FOX WIFE WITH THE LAST WORD: "What about us? The girls won't trust you until I can trust you. If you know it all, know everything that's going on with the girls and hear everything they say, then what do I have to offer them?"

Jane Eyre doesn't marry Rochester until he is sufficiently humiliated. And, our daughters don't sign much. I can only communicate to them through speech and residual hearing. Murray signs passably, to me, but speaks to the girls. There are two languages, and English is the primary one. *This is a house of Babel. Perhaps I should just adapt. Let Murray do all the thinking, talking, and giving.* He has more information than I do. I have sign language, but I can't even immerse my family in the Deaf culture or the Deaf community because the community in Regina is dying. There's not much going on. Darts in a bar once a week. The yearly banquet. It wouldn't be fair to expect teenagers to abandon their social lives to come to whist games and socialize with old Deaf people.

I look at the foot of our marriage bed. At the four or five baskets of clean laundry. At the quilt nailed over the window because I am not sure if I want curtains, not sure if I want to stay. *I want a Deaf house. Where sign and speech are not wasted. The two flowing back and forth into each other. Driven by silences.* But there is a different silence that belongs in neither place, Deaf or Hearing. The silence that suggests tombs, churchyards, and a letting go after great pain. I don't want even want to think about the strange secret garden at the back of my classroom with its perennials, growing with no effort from a gardener, in silence.

Six

THE RESOURCE ROOM WITH ITS OLD furniture, fraying carpet, fluorescent lighting, and ill-fitting curtains is an easy place, even in its shabbiness, reminiscent of a cabin at a lake. In the mornings, I am relieved as I enter the classroom at seven thirty, sink into my old velvet plush chair, and drink coffee while I survey my domain, but at the end of each day I have to walk down the great school hall toward the double doors where Murray is waiting for me in our car. Today, as we speed on Ring Road toward our house in the pelting rain, I suddenly wish that our house had an indoor swimming pool, and think: *Might as well let water into the house. I can't worry about everything.*

He is seventeen years old. Already a month of classes has gone by and he's attended less than half the semester. He's six feet tall, First Nations, with sharp black eyes that brim with tears, as he struggles, "I hate school. I don't want to have to take Grade Ten English for the third time."
Earlier that day:
LISA: "Nolan doesn't take care to sign carefully and his fingerspelling is atrocious. He can't spell."

MS. WEBER: "I wonder. Why can't he pay attention to your interpreting?"

LISA: "He pays attention just fine."

SOPHIE: "No, he doesn't. He doesn't understand the signed English we've been using."

LISA: (*Her mouth tightening*) "He just doesn't pay attention."

MS. WEBER: "At any rate, he has missed school four days this week."

LISA: "He often goes home to sleep during noon hours and just doesn't come back. He doesn't realize that all he has to do is show up and he'll pass. His English teacher promised him that if he showed up during the last week of classes last spring, he'd pass that class. Of course, he stayed home." She shakes her head and stoops to pick up her sheaf of papers from her desk before heading out the door.

I stare at the closed door. I've seen Lisa somewhere before. Long ago.

I think: "—?"

Then I remember: *The woman with the small dog in her arms! The house party after the presentation in Regina. The one who must have everything she wants.*

MS. WEBER: "Sophie, what do you know about Lisa?"

SOPHIE: "She has a deaf son, Luke. Actually, he's her sister's son. Her sister got multiple sclerosis and Lisa took him in."

MS. WEBER: "And they use Signed English, of course."

SOPHIE: "Well, she wasn't popular with the Deaf community."

MS. WEBER: " . . . "

SOPHIE: "The school board was desperate back then. She is a single mother, very smart, worked hard to set up the program even though she had no university education or formal training. She learned sign language when Luke was about seven or eight after trying to teach him speech."

MS. WEBER: "Well, that's a bit late in the game. Learning languages is more difficult after seven."

SOPHIE: "But she wanted her son to be oral. She tried so hard." *Silence.* "Then she trained other interpreters."

MS. WEBER: "But then they relied on her, a Hearing person, to train and evaluate other Hearing interpreters. There were Deaf parents in that program. What about them?"

SOPHIE: "They were Deaf."

MS. WEBER: "I know them. They both have university degrees from Gallaudet."

SOPHIE: "Doesn't matter how smart and educated they were." Sophie's signs are blunt and hard. "Lisa won every battle. They had no power."

I have seen or heard of this before, these familiar scenarios now tumbling furiously into my brain like children smashing into each other at the end of a waterslide: mothers interpreting for their deaf children at school, mothers learning sign language from books or videos while avoiding Deaf adults, mothers advising school boards, mothers sitting with their deaf adult children at job interviews, and . . .

I startle out of my reverie: *Her deaf son who ran around ignoring me.* "I've heard about him in the Deaf community." The Deaf shook their heads about him, wondering why he was not allowed to join them, to participate in their curling teams, to join the storytelling at Deaf socials, to travel with them across Canada to the Deaf Olympics.

Sophie nods: "Lisa wouldn't let him be involved at all with the Deaf. Even though he can't speak at all, and needs to sign, he can't be with the Deaf."

I remonstrate: "That's ridiculous, he is an adult now, isn't he?"

The door bursts open. Melissa scowls as she crosses the room and throws her books on the table with a resounding thump.

Lisa follows and seats herself at her desk, preparing to sort her papers. Melissa slumps in her chair, raises her foot and crashes it on another chair.

MELISSA: "I feel like a freak. They stare at me. I'm not going back to class."

JW: "Well, you *are* a freak in this place."

Lisa rises from her chair, her eyes round in alarm. She stands behind Melissa, her face stiff in uncertainty.

LISA: "What Melissa means is . . ."

JW: "I . . . know . . . what . . . she . . . means. Melissa, there is a place in this world where you don't have to feel like a freak. You don't know ASL, so I'm going to help you along. Watch me carefully. I won't sign the way you're used to."

I drop the initials in my signing — those stupid, tight little handshapes I've been struggling to remember. Instead my lips blow, chuff, and tighten into a flat line. I perform the actions accompanied by emotions, raw and unrestrained, a theatre where there is no ambiguity in the body's language. Blunt. An edge. Where one is sure to fall or cut oneself. This theatre contains spaces, vast regions, small claustrophobic boxes, or hilly terrain, or a map of the body.

Melissa laughs outright.

I stop short. I seldom hear laughter like that in my classroom. Even Nolan can't laugh.

I look up at the staff interpreters who appear shocked at my use of this contraband sign language. Lisa comes to stand beside Melissa, performing her signs in the awkward stiff manner of the Hearing. She makes the sign for "deaf," swooping her index finger from her ear to her mouth in an awkward, frozen semicircle.

I think: *She is seeing this sign as the word is printed on a page. The Hearing sign in frozen, stiff handshapes, because then the signs are like words arranged on a page. This is the way the Hearing like it: words that have crystalline shapes, which are finite.*

LISA: "You look Deaf. Your face is different."

MS. WEBER: "It's a part of me, I guess." I think: *I haven't signed in American Sign Language for nearly five years with the Deaf community, but sign lives in my muscles and the sinews of my hands, arms, and face. It is roused out of its hibernation. English erodes around it.*

MELISSA: "Can we do more of that?"

JW: "Not now. Maybe tomorrow. We have to finish your homework."

I think: *My short outburst has been enough to plant a seed in Melissa's mind and suspicion in Lisa's. But now I know what I must do with Nolan.*

Sophie smiles behind Lisa's back when I take Nolan to the conference room across the hall.

Nolan settles into a black leather chair, his eyes blinking in the dim light.

"What if I taught you English myself?" I ask him, "That way, you stay in the resource room. No interpreter. We'll use ASL. After all, I'm an English teacher and have an honours degree in English literature."

Nolan swallows hard and nods.

The next day, Lisa says: "He'll need to know the literary devices, the elements of the short story, and how to write essays. English language."

I nod quietly.

I think: *Language of the eyes.*

꩜

I was five years old and the sun was shining. I plodded down two flights of stairs and rushed out the apartment building and across the street to the paddling pool. It was crowded, and as I gathered from the open mouths of the children splashing everywhere, very noisy. My mother had no concerns about me drowning; she stayed at home in our apartment across the street while my baby sister napped.

She warned: "You must be extra careful because you won't have your hearing aid on."

I took my hearing aid out. In silence, I swung a towel over my shoulders and padded barefoot across the hot asphalt road. Soon I was swimming among the ankles of the swimmers, dodging their steps while I blew bubbles around their feet, the water carrying me to a place of another silence, far away from people, cradling me in its arms, whispering: *Come to me. You are safe from the Hearing. I am taking you to a place where there are no half noises, no muffled sounds, and no broken sentences or phrases, nobody is watching you.* I dreamed in that underwater place of leg forests and fish girls and bubbles scurrying past my eyes, then out of the pool, I dreamed as I walked across the street, until a car stopped within inches of me, and a man jumped out. I couldn't hear him, but I saw how the anger twisted his mouth, his wild gesticulations, and watched how he slammed the door to drive away in his car. I stood in the middle of the road, stricken, thinking: *I've made someone angry, so angry because I am walking somewhere in a dream, in that underwater place where deafness doesn't matter, but now I deserve to die, that man seems to say so.* I rushed up the stairs to our apartment.

I said: "Mama, ak see dent. I die."

My mother said: "No, you are all right. I watched from the window. But you weren't looking, it's a good thing he saw you."

She hugged me. But I lay down on our chesterfield.

I said: "I die."

My mother said: "No, you won't. The man . . . angry. He wants you to . . . "

But I was shaking so badly I couldn't hear the rest of her words. I lay on the couch, watching her move about in the small kitchenette. Then I tasted blood in my mouth. I thought: *I am being punished for leaving the water place, and for not looking both ways on the land, for not trying hard enough, for dreaming. I will die.* I tried to focus, but my eyes hurt with chlorine. My mother walked slowly in the small kitchen, as if she was underwater too. Her face appeared muddy before my chlorine eyes. Soon, her body became a grey, shapeless, insignificant blob. I was in that underwater place, pulling my favourite blanket, the leopard spotted one, up to my face, thinking: *Why is the man making me die? How can his anger reach inside of me and make my mouth bleed?* I watched, my eyes just above the blanket, and I thought: *Mama cannot save me, she doesn't know what really happened and I can't tell her because she thinks she knows. I want to go back to the pool. I want to be underwater. If my mother is going to be grey and shapeless like her words, I want to be back in the water, where I don't have to hear anything anyway.* But she came to me with a wet facecloth, and brushed my lips with it. Then she reached inside my mouth with her finger and pulled out my tooth. I looked at the blood smeared across the back of my hand, and at my mother's kind eyes and her smile. Everything was so clear again. Except I still didn't know how that angry man made my tooth come out.

꙼

My mother gave me a large green ledger folder filled with letters from the John Tracy Clinic and a small green journal filled with her observations of my early progress. There are copies of tests on my hearing, intelligence, speech, and language, under the age of five.

The papers have faded over time: uneven, typewritten. My mother's journal entries range from detailed notes to hastily scribbled lists of words I've mastered. She has even entered diacritical notations of my speech in order to remember just how I've pronounced a word. In the back of the green scribbler, she has to-do lists to approximate the Montessori training that she knows she cannot fully provide. I shuffle the papers in my hands, searching for a word or a phrase, something that might indicate why or how I cannot be close to my husband and daughters, some malfunctioning of the brain, perhaps, some deep-seated personality disorder, or just a difficult temperament, but the letters and tests from the John Tracy Clinic are sunny. I sift through the exchange of letters between my mother and the speech pathologist at the clinic. She carefully explains the etiology of my hearing loss, how and where I got my first hearing aid, and how I, at the age of three, am not making any words except "up". And how the speech pathologist says nothing much except keep working on it. Keep on keeping on. Amongst all my mother's detailed descriptions of my speech and language development, I pause at these words:

Our more immediate concern at this point is her drinking apple juice to the exclusion of other foods. We can't seem to persuade her to eat any other foods or to drink milk or even water. Is it typical of deaf children to exercise such restrictions in their diet?

Otherwise, there is no vein of sadness, frustration, or despair. Every professional assures my parents that my future is bright.

The Japanese houses I've been researching in the library are famous for their judicious use of space, the *genkan*, for instance, an entrance through which one must remove their shoes, put on slippers, and walk through a set of short curtains brushing the shoulders, the world of the street or the wharf left behind.

Genkan, the preparation for entry into a new world. A Japanese house is measured out in mats, according to traditional sized mats used under the feet, the kitchen, bathroom, and toilet along one side of the house toward the back, while the *i-ma* or the living space, is enveloped by *rouka*, long wooden passages alongside the house, and any of the rooms can be used for any purpose, just like I can use the space in front of me to represent anything in sign language: a mountain, a house, a road, open sea, or even the inside of an engine. In Japan, people sleep, eat, converse, study, and work in the *i-ma* in any way, there is more than one room for baths, a toilet room, a sink room, and a room with a tub. Washing with water is ritualistic, ceremonial even, one must wash hands from a spout in the corner of the toilet room after squatting over a hole, then wash hands in the sink, then wash the body with a wet cloth from a bowl of water in the sink room, and finally one must draw water from a heater — usually with pails — and fill a tub in the room, soak, and watch water ripple out from one's body. I think: *The Japanese have made the use of water into a ritual form as it is the lifeblood of the house, a singular vein running throughout the spine. And I am worried about keeping water out. All I need to do is keep water in the right places!* I strike myself lightly on my head. In the Japanese home, every thud, footstep, bang, and accidental clash of teacups has a measured meaning. People with no privacy must communicate with the lifted eyebrow as soon as one's back is turned. Swiping the air with index fingers, peeking around a sliding door, watching the shadows through a screen. Less is spoken, more is animated, presented to the eye if one is careful and observant. In other words, sign language! I feel a growing sense of excitement. This will be my Deaf House. An ecosystem of silences. An economy of words and signs in which nothing is wasted.

Seven

There is something in the way Joanne runs to me when I come back from golfing with Sue. Something strange in how she moves her arms, her elbows twisting from side to side, and in the flapping of her open red coat, as she bursts between the low gates in front of our house, nearly slamming into me, running over from the neighbour's house, and I remember something about Tommy, how he was discovered wearing his sister's clothes, and I resolve never to let him babysit her again.

We are both distracted. Joanne twists around in her chair, knocking her glass of milk over on the table, and I just sit, letting the milk drip onto the floor. I am unable to think of what to do next, if anything happened next door with that boy, how much can she remember, without language, how can she even think about it? She is only three years old.

Later she puts her bear in our bed, scolds it, picks it up lovingly, and lays it to rest once more. Then she backs out of the door, still scolding, shuts the door tightly, opens the door, scolds the bear, this time leaving the door open a crack, then she backs down the hall, pretends to listen, and scolds. She refuses to allow the bear to be removed from the bed the rest of the day.

"Is the baby asleep?" I ask her.

She points to the bedroom. "Ma ma."

My heart sinks. She remembers everything. She must remember the time we left her in the hospital for two weeks because of a severe bronchial infection and after two days of looking through a glass window, watching her being manhandled by that nurse, I couldn't bear to watch her scream, standing in the crib, clutching the bars. We stayed home for two weeks, dishes often left unwashed on the table, and wondered how we could ever explain the doctor's decision, that we loved her, that we were coming back, hoping she slept in that tall crib, instead of gazing all day through the bars. But she'd wake to that nurse and her brusque hands, ripping the sheets from under her, whipping the blanket off to inspect her diapers, and I could hear her screaming again and again until she slumped against the bars of her crib, exhausted. When we came to pick her up, on that winter day, the nurse brought her out, limp as a rag doll. She turned her face away from Ed as he took her into his arms, and refused to look at me. She looked waxen, as if she'd been drugged. Her lips were blood red. Her hair was matted with sweat.

For the next twenty four hours, we tried to play with her, talk to her, coax her to eat, but she lay on the couch, under her blanket. I held her hand, but it slid out of my palm. Her eyes smouldered, like the peat fires on my father's homestead up north. The next day though, she came to life, began to walk about the house, looked at the Degas prints of ballerinas that hang on our bedroom wall, picked up her puzzle board and began to fit the pieces into their slots. I thought: *She is going to think that the world is a frightening and hostile place.*

~☙~

In the evenings, my father pulled out his saxophone and I ran eagerly to get my costumes from the box in the living room. My favourite was a lavender silk tutu with petals over a stiff ring of white netting. The music was already flowing when I shot out from the long hallway into our living room like a cannonball. I leapt to the high notes of the saxophone and shimmied to the ululating notes as my father tapped his foot to his big band music. I attempted to claw up into the air, pointing to the ceiling of our old house. Amidst the dying notes, I ran into my bedroom to change into another dance costume. Now in a filmy skirt, I pirouetted, lifting my leg and arching my foot. As my muscles rippled under my skin-tight bodice, I wanted to shed my body, rise in the air, slither along window panes, and wrap myself around my mother's neck. I floated round and round in dizzying circles, wanting my skin to spin off my body, leaving behind bone or muscle as I flew upwards, but I danced like the stiff bare branches of the small tree potted at Easter, feeling my arms weighted by Easter eggs. There was a rabbit cake at the base of the tree, with pink paper ears. I wanted to be lovely just like that, a tree, upon which I could fasten my broken vowels and pin consonants to my words. Afterwards, I lay on the floor, my head spinning among the dying notes of my father's saxophone, spinning in my own loveliness, the beauty of myself apart from having to hear, listen, and form the letters properly, and the relief of not having to wear those heavy headphones and to imitate my mother's voice day in and day out.

∽

Green Journal

Just returned from Saskatoon today. Our visit with Dr. Alvin Buckwold has me reeling. I can barely collect my thoughts and emotions after hearing what he had to say about Joanne. I'm quite surprised to hear his emphasis on cognitive development, especially the development of abstract thinking. He is particularly pleased with what I've done with Joanne so far, using the Montessori ideas, and assures me that Joanne will perform at the same rate as her peers, even though her speech is still far behind. He warns me, however, to be strict with her, and not overindulge her. So many children with disabilities are ruined, he says, and cannot cope with future demands, because their parents pity them and give into their every wish and whim.

Joanne isn't giving out as many hugs as she used to. She doesn't do much with her teddy bear or dolls anymore, either, but spends many hours making marks on a piece of paper. Most likely she prefers thinking about things to touching things, but Ed and I need more education in order to teach her. The Tracy course is very helpful, but the letters from the clinic are so brief. I still don't understand the connection between imitation and memory. Joanne survives by imitating what is expected of her, but does she understand what she is doing and why she is doing it? Perhaps Minot State College in North Dakota can help answer these questions. They've been providing deaf education classes for many years now. Perhaps this summer.

My mother always had books with her, books with no pictures, not at all like the books that she gave me. Her books were always high up on the dining room table. She pushed the books aside when she set the table, but I climbed up on the table and flipped through their pages while her back was turned in the kitchen.

I thought: *No pictures.*

I ran to her with *Chicken Little.* I wanted to know how the sky could fall in. My mother could never explain anything to me, but I wanted to know right now. *Does it fall like a blanket down around my shoulders? Those wisps of clouds in the sky must be very soft. Let it come down around my shoulders,* I wanted to say to my mother, but I couldn't say anything. Instead, I repeated after her as she read in other books, "The horse says neigh, the cow says moo, and the cat says meow," because she wanted to me say these things. I would rather say other things, but I couldn't.

At least, I could move my body. I looked through my father's magazine, *Sports Illustrated,* and saw a man with a stick high up in the air. There were many pictures of him moving that stick. I traced the stick with my finger, watching it rise above the man's shoulder and down in an arc toward the ground. I ran to my mother, "Loo," and raised an imaginary stick to show her. My mother quickly cut out the pictures and pasted them into a book for me to look at every day.

I sat with my books, paper foothills stacked against my knees. I had papers spread out in front of me, and several coloured pencils. I hunched over the papers, and painstakingly made a tiny mark with a blue pencil, and then I used a green pencil. Soon, all my papers had many tiny marks, in all colors of the rainbow.

When my parents read to me, as they did several times a day, I began to see the marks in the books swelling on the pages, becoming longer and rounder. The voices of my parents swirling around my head became one voice inside my head reading to me as I slid my finger along the words on the page. And the voices of other people, broken, fragmented, and confounding, coalesced into a voice inside my head as I read, telling me that what was described in those pages was the only life that was real.

Green Journal

Joanne is practically never in the house these days although she's willing to sit and be read to when the opportunity presents itself.

But she is still not talking much. Some small pimple in her outer ear made me refrain from allowing her to wear the aid for about two weeks. She's now quite choosy about wearing it, and often refuses it unless I tie in the presentation with a book or record. I think she's self-conscious about it now, because so many people are seeing it for the first time and asking questions about it, while staring at her as she clutches her red jacket to cover it up. And clothing is a real sore point. Joanne always knows exactly what she wants to wear and if it isn't what I have in mind, it takes brute force to dress her. Finally I leave her dresser empty and hide her clothes in the basement.

Nolan is taking an International Baccalaureate art class. His marks don't qualify him for full entry into the IB program, but the art teachers agree that his work deserves attention and further development. He is given a thick black notebook. He is to research art movements, develop his own art practice and an approach to his own artwork. At first, he doesn't understand what this means.

"It's a journey. You need to find out what's inside of you and why you are interested in certain forms of art and not others."

Nolan shrugs. He continues sketching cars with flames licking the doors, hoods, and roofs. I've seen those flames — on skateboards and T-shirts.

I try: "Maybe it's a certain kind of car you like."

Nolan shrugs again. He continues to draw coupés with flames.

I try, again: "Well, what is it about those coupés?"

He signs: "I don't know. They're nice cars."

The interpreters and I circle him for the next two months, eager to look at his research book, but behind his back we cluck and shake our heads.

Clucking Women: "He's still drawing cars. He's not going anywhere with this research. He's not reading anything. Just cars. He can do so much more than just cars. We've seen that drawing of his father, that painting of his mother, why can't he get beyond the cars?"

Nolan wants to write too. He gives me drafts of stories and screenplays he has written. At first, the plots are intense, full of action, and mostly about the relationship between robots and humanity. The names are strange: Halo, Neo, Trinity.

Lisa sighs: "Has anyone seen *The Matrix*? He's just taking bits and pieces of the plot and rearranging them. They're just plot summaries of movies he has seen."

Joanne counters with: "He's told me that he has really made this up himself."

Lisa persists: "Nolan's done that before." She turns to Catherine, "Remember two years ago? He came to school with a bandage wrapped around his arm? Said he broke his arm?"

"Yeah, we phoned his parents." Catherine says, "They said that there was nothing wrong with his arm. It was all a charade. He doesn't know the difference between reality and fantasy."

The mistrust in Catherine's eyes makes me feel uncomfortable. I persist: "But why would he do such a thing?"

Catherine explains: "He's seen nothing but movies. He plays video games far into the night. He doesn't know anything else."

I sink into the dirty velvet plush chair at my desk. Why are there answers that stop discussion and answers that invite more exploration? On a hunch, I begin to type "Deaf artists" into Google. Soon, I'm arranging images of their work into a PowerPoint presentation. It might be a waste of time, because I have to help other students with their Math, English, and Science homework, but I direct Lisa and Catherine to do the tutorials with the students so I can finish the presentation.

The next day, I'm ready. First I show Nolan Susan Dupor's *Family Dog*. The Deaf family member sits on the floor, his eyes bright, his tongue hanging out, while the Hearing family members sit elevated on the chesterfield, their arms folded, their faces obscured, looking down at him. I sneak a look at Nolan. His face remains impassive.

I try this: "I've always thought being deaf in the Hearing world is like being a fox."

His eyes slowly focus on me. "What do you mean?"

I unfold my idea: "It's like being chased during a fox hunt. Hearing people run after me and demand that I be like them. They want me to imitate everything they do. People are always watching me, to see how much I am like them."

"It's like being in a fishbowl," Nolan nods.

I rush on with: "My foxholes are bathrooms, libraries, bedrooms, kitchen sinks, closets, and cars. I often give people the slip."

Nolan comes back the next day with his research book opened to a page. He beckons me over to look at it. He has drawn his own portrait: only his head, inside of a fishbowl.

I ask: "What does it mean to you?"

"People are always watching me," he says and flips open to another page. He has drawn himself, a full body this time, but as a child against the backdrop of tall people, black and grey in their clothes. His coat is red.

He says: "I can't see those people. They don't exist. They don't have any colour to them. I can only see myself."

I sit down before him, arrested by his drawing, unable to move. Lisa comes up behind Nolan and looks over his shoulder at his research book. He explains to her what his two drawings mean.

She frowns. Then she signs to him in her impeccable English: "Why don't you start around American politics? 9/11, for instance. Sports, maybe. This stuff here . . . I don't think anyone is interested in it."

From that day, Nolan turns his interest toward three dimensional art. He constructs a miniature of the White House, with the flag of the American eagle, skirted with debris. His art teacher reluctantly passes him and he is still in his basement bedroom, his walls painted black, playing for hours on Xbox, incommunicado.

⁓

Green Journal

Joanne doesn't have many more new words, only about twenty so far. Although she listens carefully and seems to understand everything we say. I hope Joanne is starting to forget whatever she went through with Tommy next door. She never looks at him and he turns the other way too. Is she remembering? But how can she remember without being able to talk? Doesn't memory rely on language? I'm sure you can't remember feelings without having language first. And the speech pathologists insist that she can't think or reason without language. I'm not so sure about that. I clipped an article about Montessori today from the *Saturday Evening Post*. It says something like if a child perceives through the senses, then those perceptions are stored in his mind somehow, and contribute to building the intellect. Yet, Joanne has to understand what things mean to her. That's where the language comes in.

Eight

ANDY AND CASEY ARE TWO LOLITAS, hand in hand. They rely on their parents, or the men they've slept with, to wake them up in the morning, because they will not use special alarm clocks for the deaf. After they've pulled their tightest pair of jeans over their hips, and donned their faded black hoodies, they'll come to school around ten, clutching coffees, with hair meticulously arranged to cover the cochlear implant processors hooked over their ears and twinned to a magnet placed over another magnet inside their skulls.

Today Andy raises her cup as she walks into the classroom and announces: "Robin's Donuts is the best." Before she pushes her sleeve down, I again notice faded cuts on her wrists.

Casey's words are unintelligible.

Andy nods: "Yeah, she got a hair in her donut from Tim Horton's."

Coffee shops, Walmart, the assorted men that come and go, and the spirits that flit in and out of their house, translucent globes hovering over their dead dog, pictures that they took on their cell phone cameras, I shake my head. And friends! Every criminal within a fifty mile radius of Regina, every victim who has died and every person who has wielded a gun or a knife.

When they disappear for days at a time, they say: "It's because we're grieving." Hours on the internet, researching the lives of every serial killer, every convicted murderer, and every sexual predator, their excuse: "We are traumatized. That's why we can't come to school often." Every distant relative who's killed or the friend of a friend of a friend who's now in jail, an intimacy with so many people, most of them in gangs, or dealing drugs: predators. The two girls are savvy to their evil, even though they're trying very hard to become pregnant with any man who will sleep with them. In their dream plan for their family, there's no father, no husband, and no lover. Instead, they will live together in the same house and raise their babies together. They just need a man or two who will spend a couple of nights pumping his sperm into them while they look at the wall.

Research says that approximately fifty percent of deaf children are sexually abused.

This is how far we get: the fight they got into with a group of girls, and the knife in their friend's locker. Casey's speech is so poor that Andy often steps in to repeat what she's said. The language of twins. Andy won't talk about sexual abuse, so Casey can't even bring up the subject.

They're never without each other, except on the day Casey comes to school alone and announces: "Andy is with a guy today. He works nights, so they have to do it during the day."

I shrug. I am teaching "The Highwayman". I have a yardstick. Tucked under my arm. I establish that Bess, the landlord's daughter, and the highwayman are romantically linked, and that the King's Men have tied Bess to a bedpost in full view of the window where she can see the Highwayman galloping down the road. I point. I say: "Read this line out loud."

Casey reads in a quiet voice. I can't follow her "She twisted her hands behind her; but all the knots held good! She twisted her hands till her fingers were wet with sweat or blood!" at all.

I ask: "What is Bess doing?"

Casey shrugs.

I hold the yardstick under my arm and grimace. I hook my finger into an imaginary trigger.

"Okay, Casey." Steely-eyed, I raise the yardstick at her: "What am I doing?" I aim it at her. Casey's eyes widen. I ask: "What is this, Casey? What do you think this is?"

Casey blurts: "Da gun, see wan him as he come dun ta roa." She giggles, then stops, her hand over her mouth.

I stop too, wondering if I haven't gone too far in renewing the violence they can't seem to get enough of in their own lives.

Lisa signs to me sans voice: "Now, you'll have to go back and teach this in the way her English teacher does. You have to find all the literary devices in the poem."

I sign: "Not today." I show her my back. I turn to Casey and ask: "Why don't you write me a paragraph telling me how you think Bess feels being tied up to the bedpost?"

Casey nods quietly, and takes out a sheet of foolscap from her binder.

Lisa lobs a grenade: "No, that's not the assignment from her English teacher."

I lob back: "I am doing just one unit with her. As Casey isn't doing well in English, she doesn't comprehend the material."

Lisa gets down to it: "But what will *I* do?"

I get down to it: "Work with me here."

Lisa purses her lips and turns away.

I sink into my chair, my cheeks burning with anger. *Why is Lisa so upset about this new arrangement? Can't anyone see that*

Casey and her sister have been easy victims because of their deafness? Who is going to give them a voice to say what really happened?

Then it dawns on me: *Lisa is worried. About not being visible in the rest of the school. About her job becoming obsolete as I pull more and more kids out of their English classes to deliver the material myself.*

I argue with myself: *Can't she see that I'm doing more than just teaching?*

Myself: *But she is hired to interpret and take notes. If she isn't in the classrooms out there, how can she keep her job?*

I think: *But if Casey doesn't talk about what really happened, how can she think about what's happened?*

❧

I'd just turned six. My mother insisted that I write in a diary. Every day. One or two sentences about what had happened. Today.

Why? Everyone already knows. Why do I have to write it down? Why do I have to remember anything that has happened to me?

The real reason soon emerged. The diary became a battlefield over grammar, for verbs in past and present tenses. My mother wanted to fight this war, but I was a most reluctant soldier, only ferocious when provoked. After she changed my sentences, I waited until she turned her back, then erased her firm printing and slipped in my own phrase: "I jumping on box." My mother came back and erased it again. She demanded that I write it properly. I was grateful when we forgot the diary at the end of my First Grade year, but I picked it up a couple of years later, and wrote whole paragraphs in the remaining blank pages: grammatically perfect paragraphs; detailed descriptions of who I was with, what I wore, what I did, even the smell of the yellow vinyl purse I got on the day my father took me to *The Sound of Music.*

I flipped through the pages. There was the memory of my friend Margie and I jumping inside the large cardboard box in our living room and landing on the carpet.

I realized: *The diary gave me memory.*

At age seven, I was allowed to go swimming at our local pool in the summers with my best friend Laura, or by myself, at least three times a day, for swimming lessons in the morning, for the afternoon swim, water ballet afterwards, and, on some days, speed swimming, and for the evening swim until the pool closed at nine o'clock. I didn't wear my hearing aid for most of the day, because I was so happy in that silent place, that said that the only thing that was real was me. All the communication I needed was in the wet, slick bodies of children bouncing around me, swimming between feet on the concrete pool floor, ripping off the swimming trunks of the boys I liked, shocked at the paleness of their bums in contrast to their sun-burned bodies, and all that time in the water did not consist of the past, present, and future. Water took me to a place outside of time, toward a destination that I did not know. Time-water ran in my ears when I tried to finish hearing what my parents said before they went on to another topic at supper. I didn't know if I'd finished hearing what a person was saying or whether I'd started a new path, gathering vowels just as a river gathers twigs, leaves, pebbles as it rushes headlong to a lake.

Green Journal

I'm relieved that we don't have to move to Saskatoon after all. I don't want to enroll Joanne in that new special class for the hearing impaired in the Saskatoon Public School system. Dr. Buckwold is so impressed with her progress, and says that Joanne got the best possible education in preparation for entry into a regular school. We even took courses again at Minot during June and July, just to make sure we'd done all we could to prepare her for Grade Two. All the testing at Minot in June confirms that she's nearly on par with her peers. I now drive Joanne to a speech therapist in Unity every Wednesday in lieu of art class. Mrs. Burrill has Joanne reading a lot of poetry out loud. It's strange to hear Joanne practice reading poetry.

Murray's son Ben phones us one evening to say that he'd been in the basement of our house earlier that afternoon to pick up some boxes he'd left there.

"Everything is soaked, Dad. You and Joanne better go down and check."

I never visit this room in our house. It's full of old furniture, and Murray's tools, which he forgets to put away, old paint cans, rags, computer magazines, vinyl records stacked on shelves of a bookcase, a mattress leaning against the wall.

I complain as I bag mouldy cardboard: "Where is all this water coming from?" Murray tips a heavy bookshelf on its side. Mould is already growing on the bottom shelf.

How long has the water been sitting in the room? How could we have missed it? We've been so busy. The girls sang at three concerts this week, and Anna acted in the school play.

Murray grunts as he drags the wet mattress across the floor: "The walls aren't wet. I think it's coming up through the floor."

"You mean there's some sort of an underground cavern somewhere?"

"There must be." He leans the mattress against the wall

"It's not the sewer, is it?" I speak to his back.

Murray turns around. "No, the water is clean."

I think: *Clean enough to swim in.*

❧

Shadows began to spook me in the middle of the night. I woke up with a start at four o'clock in the morning, thoughts going round and round in my head like a manic carousel, Caroline, the girl I met in Regina when I was twelve, now the gorilla in *Stranger at Green Knowe*, who grunted and lowered herself to the floor, her buttocks firmly planted in the corner, her eyes large and sad as if to contain every grief that clung to the straw scattered across the floor, *Green Knowe* whispered its secrets to me: *To live in this house, you must endure many hours of boredom, pretend to understand, lest you make others uncomfortable with your constant need to know everything that is going on. You can't know everything and no one will ever know what happened to you. You'll live with fragments, bits and pieces of things, puzzling over them long after everyone has said goodbye and gone home. A certain rage will move in you like sludge trying to move through blocked pipes, but you won't know about any of these feelings because you'll be frozen, like Judas in Dante's hell, embedded in a lake of ice, shards of ice in your eyeballs so you can't look at anything with interest anymore, and the people who live with you will know nothing of this. You've been relegated to the attic, forced to sit on newspaper, and eat bananas and fruits, and furtively roam the neighbourhood in the night.*

❧

Green Journal

Joanne is beginning to have difficulty, now that she has entered the upper elementary grades. She misses a lot of school. Her last report card indicates that she was sick for a total of one month of school (on and off), because of all those stomach aches. I have no idea about why she keeps having stomach aches, or the whole lost month. Simply no idea, since I am so busy looking after her sister Ruth, and then David, who takes so much out of me, he is so stubborn. Her marks have plummeted, even math. Fractions, decimals, percentages, geometry. She wants to get her ears pierced. We say no, but she keeps badgering us about it. We dress her in the nicest clothes, buy her the best of everything. But pierced ears? Joanne says that every girl in her class has them. I hope that Joanne will want to stand apart from such silliness, but she can't get the notion out of her head. She even writes "pierced earrings" on our grocery shopping list. We know that it's a sort of membership requirement for Joanne, if she wants to belong to a certain group of girls, but it'll take much more than pierced ears for her to belong to anyone.

I wonder if she notices that her friends don't come around anymore. I asked Sue yesterday about why her daughter Laura doesn't visit. Sue hemmed and hawed and said something about how Joanne can't keep up with the communication. Prepubescent girls just want to talk.

∽

Lisa interrupts my session with Nolan as I am in a passage from the short story, "Penny in the Dust". She says: "You're going too deep. You don't need to explain that much."

I stand still, shocked.

Nolan looks away, embarrassed.

I think: *But this is why I am using ASL with Nolan, to get at the deeper meanings that Signed English can never touch.*

I've seen Lisa's Signed English interpreting and I can't understand much of it, even though she delivers it in beautifully formed handshapes and in an easy rhythm. Nolan carefully hides his inattention at her bowdlerized explanations, rushed concepts, and assumptions of certain English idioms and phrases.

I begin to sit morosely in coffee houses in the evenings, rushing out of the house without explanation, without indicating when I'll be back, even darkly hinting that I might not even come back. In my classroom, I continue to worry about Andy and Casey. I fuss over them and rant to Sophie about how the twins will not make their own appointments by telephone, because they refuse to use a teletypewriter that will allow them to read what the other person says to them. Instead they will text their mother, instructing her to make an appointment with the doctor. They will not take buses around the city. They rely on family members and the boyfriend of the week to drive them. They will not use an FM system to augment their cochlear implants, insisting that they hear everything just fine, then they rely on me to reteach the material that was covered in scheduled classes. Then they begin to skip classes, until I offer to teach those classes in my own room, then they come every day, because they now can ask questions and ask for clarification, but they have increasingly insulated themselves from the Hearing world. I throw my books on to my desk with a bang.

Sophie signs: "They are not our children."

"But their parents think that Andy and Casey are just fine. Remember, those girls can have basic conversations with anyone, and all you need is about five hundred words for that. That's all most people can see when talking to a deaf or hard-of-hearing person. People are satisfied with so little."

Sophie signs: "No one wants to know what we know. Nobody asks us what we see in those kids." She turns back to her herbalist manual.

I nod, morose, inconsolable, and turn to the garden outside my window. There's a dirty rust stain bleeding down one of the walls forming the enclosure. I haven't seen that before. How can I expect to see things if I don't look closely enough?

Then Casey flings the door open to the classroom, tears streaming down her face.

She says: "Something's wrong with Andy. She's in the bathroom."

She's lying on her back in the girls' bathroom, with a tea towel wrapped around her wrist. I shout: "Andy, wake up!" I pat her face lightly and shake her shoulders. Casey is sobbing on the other side of her.

I shout again: "Wake up!" I tap Andy's cheeks, arms, and hands insistently, while a plan is unfolding in my head. I know that the two school counsellors are away today, that their offices are empty and locked up on the second floor.

I tell Casey: "Go get Mrs. Wapass. She's in the Resource Room." I think: *Sophie will comfort her while I try to keep Andy from slipping away from me.*

Sophie comes back, her face draining as she sees me kneeling beside Andy on the floor.

I give orders: "Go call 911. And take Casey back into our room, so she'll be close by for questioning when the ambulance comes."

Andy remains passive as I increase the volume in my voice. "Andy, listen to me, it's Ms. Weber, you must wake up." I unwrap the tea towel around her wrist but there's very little blood on it. I look for the cut, it is near her knuckle. A small, insignificant cut.

It seems I am alone, interminably. A secretary comes into the bathroom to see what's wrong.

I say: "Sophie has called 911."

She walks out, leaving me more alone than ever.

Andy's face is white, her lips slowly turning purple. Her hair tumbles around her ears. I wonder if she has her cochlear implant turned on, and am about to check when a red bag plops down beside me. The paramedics have arrived. Sophie stands in the doorway.

"Where's Casey?" I demand. "They have to talk to her now."

Sophie's face reddens. Is it anger or embarrassment? I have never seen her look like that.

She signs: "Lisa sent her upstairs to guidance. She didn't want Casey to upset the other students." I stare at her: "You mean she is wandering upstairs by herself? Alone? Go get her now."

Sophie turns to leave, and I am heaving suddenly, realizing I can't understand the paramedics. I need an interpreter and there is one, sitting in my classroom.

Sophie runs back in with Casey and begins interpreting for me, when she realizes that the paramedics are speaking to me behind my back. I'm now able to answer the rapid fire questions and also comprehend Casey's garbled responses.

Casey sobs and Sophie interprets, listening very carefully: "She started passing out when we were walking over the bridge. I had to drag her, half carry her here."

Andy is strapped into the gurney and wheeled out to the front doors of the school. A paramedic quietly asks: "She's taken some kind of a drug?"

"Don't know", I say, "but you have to talk to her carefully, she's deaf."

The paramedic shoots me a knowing look as he grasps the edge of Andy's stretcher. I shrug, knowing that he expects drugs, suicide, and abuse, a messed up family, anything that will explain Andy lying unconscious on the bathroom floor. But not deafness.

I receive a phone call that afternoon from the mother: "Thanks for helping Andy. She accidentally cut herself and passed out from the bleeding." I raise my eyebrows at Sophie. I think: *That little cut near Andy's knuckle?*

The next morning, I let myself into my classroom, eyes still swollen from crying. Andy and Casey don't know what's happening to them and I can't tell them, I can't tell them about their deafness because they think they are fixed with those cochlear implants, they think they can hear everything, because the implants pick up every little noise, even the rustle of paper on a desk, what they don't realize is that they don't understand the human voices very clearly, that they have to strain to decipher the sound that comes off everyone's lips, if they don't think about how they struggle to hear, and always attribute their poor vocabulary, low reading and writing skills to being "dumb," as Andy often says, how can they know they've been sexually abused as well?

And I can't dislodge the sullen lump of anger at Lisa who sat in my classroom protecting my other deaf students from Casey's tears, sending her out alone like Jane Eyre on the high heath, wandering.

I'm grateful for the darkness of late November mornings in the car on our way to work. I can't breathe until I reach my classroom. Instead of telling Murray what's going on, I tell him about Mary of Egypt, a prostitute who sought out men, desperate enough to say she'd do it for no pay.

"That sounds like a male fantasy," he says as he clicks on the left signal, the headlights from onrushing cars light up his face.

"Well, not really. She tried to enter a church, because she was curious about the mass that was being held, and was physically pushed away from the door."

"Well, of course, church people would turn away a prostitute."

"Well, no," I say, "that's not it. It was an invisible force. Something wouldn't let her enter the church."

Murray responds: "Hmm."

I : "She realized what held her back. She went to confession, renounced her life of prostitution, and went back to the church door."

"She went in?"

"Yeah, then she fled to the desert, never to be tempted by men again."

"What on earth was she doing in the desert?"

"Looking at herself, examining herself thoroughly. It is the way of desert fathers and mothers. Stripping away all illusions."

Murray carefully noses the car into the parking lot, "I'm afraid I don't understand why she had to go to the desert to do that."

A long forgotten dream suddenly comes to me, a recurring dream I had before leaving the Deaf community in Saskatoon to work in North Battleford. I am trying to lead Deaf people through a scorching desert plain dotted with mesquite and cactus. The safety of the mountains looms ahead.

My stomach lurches. I think: *This desert thing is silly. Why is everything I think about related to something I've read?* After a quick hug and kiss, I clamber out of the car and run into the school, the classroom key in my hand. I pull the drapes open to the courtyard. It's now ghostly white in the winter snow. The boughs of the trees are bent with snow and hoarfrost. The courtyard refuses to say anything to me.

I say aloud to the empty classroom, and to the waiting garden: "I'm tired of keeping secrets. I'm tired of always speaking in literary code."

Nine

My friend Laura's parents went to Switzerland for a month, so we played Switzerland by getting old pantyhose and braiding the silky nylon stockings into braids. We pulled the elasticized waists, bums, and crotches over our heads and carefully tied bandannas around our foreheads on top of our wigs, tucking the ends at the nape of our necks. We read *Heidi* and practised the lines. No one wanted to be Charlotte in Frankfurt, so we took turns being Heidi. There was no Peter, but everything else Swiss was fascinating: the chocolates, the cheese, the mountains, and the fir trees whispering through Heidi's window, Grandfather calling Heidi over the meadows, the goatherd, Peter, blowing his horn. Every day, Laura and I donned our vests (hers a real one from Switzerland, mine a dove grey vest decorated with a bit of braid, which my mother had sown for me) and in our backyard we swung high into the air, our imitation braids flapping down our backs as we pumped our knees, the air rushing up our long, full skirts feeling like mountain air as we ran through imaginary meadows.

Our last time together was the afternoon we played one of her older sister's records. She was out for the afternoon, and we sat on the couch, listening to Paul Simon's "I am a Rock", moodily knitting scarves, while shadows reached into the living room. Laura told me what the words were to the refrain that played again and again on the turntable, something about not needing friendship. But pain and the need for friendship followed me as I went out the door after the long afternoon, trudging home in the purple snow. I was too naïve to realize that this was the last time I'd ever play with Laura, that she wanted something more from me than imitating characters in a book.

After that day, I tried to talk to Laura on the phone, but I couldn't hear very well, and her mother told my mother that Laura was just so busy these days. I turned to reading, working my way through the *Green Knowe* books, until a new girl in the neighbourhood, Glenda, came by on her banana bike, a pudgy kid with wavy hair sloping down to her eyebrows, ridged by oil, who walked like a boy. Her strong arms swung a bat effortlessly, as I ran for her grounders, and when I played kick the can, she could outrun me and the neighbourhood kids, even though she was quite overweight. But these weren't the first things I noticed about Glenda, she didn't like to read and she didn't play imaginary games, so I slowly began to put away my books, because I imagined, somehow, that she'd protect me, and teach me things that no one else could.

Glenda had pictures of David Cassidy from the Partridge family all over her bedroom walls. I looked at them with great curiosity. I couldn't understand why there must be so many pictures of one person. She had quite a stack of magazines on the floor beside her bed too. We leafed through them, and then went out to ride our bikes. I now wanted a banana bike, because I saw how Glenda reared up in hers, as if she were reining in a wild stallion.

My parents said: "No, your bike is good enough." They also said: "Glenda is not good for you. Find a different friend."

But I turned away. I refused to look at their mouths. Laura was gone and there was only Elsie, whom Glenda refused to play with, because Elsie was German and poor, but Elsie was always faithful, a hanger-on. We wore identical coats, brown fake fur with a dark brown stripe down our backs, we jumped together in a large cardboard refrigerator box, and when I was over at her house, we ate cold chocolate cake.

She told me: "I eat it for breakfast every day."

I was not envious, because when Elsie's mother bought her ice skates, she purchased the skates five sizes too big, so while I whirled on the ice, Elsie was clinging to the sides of the rink, her feet encased in five layers of socks and skates that extended three inches past her toes. Her parents worked at the meat market all day, cutting up meat, and they always had blood on their aprons. Her mother smiled and talked at me in her broken English, her face worn with work. Elsie was always quiet when we were in the meat market.

Glenda didn't like Elsie. Elsie was shorter than Glenda. But Elsie had started to develop breasts. Her hips were round. Her arms were soft. Her hair was cut in a bob, with bangs straight across her forehead. Her face was so German, with broad round cheeks and large brown eyes.

Glenda took me aside. She whispered: "Look at her chest," and laughed.

I looked too and laughed. I didn't know what else to do. Glenda's laughter slowly erased memory after memory of my days with Elsie, how we jumped on the box together, rode our own bikes, knitted our scarves, played with jacks and my favourite game with elastics, where we tied full lengths of elastics into a loop, stretched them across two chairs six feet apart, then pretended to be acrobats, pulling down the lines with our feet, twisting, turning, and jumping in and out of the varying geometric patterns we created with our ankles, calves, and hips.

Glenda began to openly taunt Elsie about the size of her breasts. I stood beside Glenda, and joined in.

Elsie was so desperate that she wrote a letter to my mother: "Joanne and the other girls are making comments about my advanced development."

I realized that someone had helped Elsie write this letter, most certainly not her mother who could barely speak English. "My advanced development," a phrase so courteous, so abstract, so painfully put by an adult into Elsie's life.

My mother took me aside. "You must stop this friendship. Glenda is not good for you, and Elsie has always been a good friend." But I continued to play with Glenda, pretend my bike was really a banana bike and that I just hadn't learned how to make it rear up like a wild stallion.

I snarled at my mother one day after several futile efforts to draw a house for an art project. My ruler lines were always at the wrong angle. Little shavings made with my eraser, rolled across the page.

I announced: "I'm going out to play with Glenda." I bounced the ruler off a stack of books on the dining room table.

My mother called: "Wait, Joanne." She sat down beside me and drew a line with a ruler on a piece of paper, and then drew another line freehand. She asked: "Which line do you think is the best?"

I pointed to the impeccably straight edge.

Then my mother asked: "Which is the most interesting line?"

I stared at the two lines and something ancient and familiar flooded into me: *The best line doesn't always point to its expected destination. I pointed to the freehand line my mother had drawn.*

➶

Murray's chest is rising and falling in great heaves. We've just made love, and I lie awake twisted in our sheets and blankets, my mind unable to stop the frenzy of its own movement, thinking: *Why am I with him, what is the language we share? I'm only with him because I'm such a good lip-reader. Hearing people like that. There isn't much effort on their part. They merely have to talk. My mind whirs like a computer program, putting every possible sound I've heard to good use, making educated guesses.* I think: *What would happen if I became tired, distracted, or overwhelmed? It'd amount to a computer malfunction.*

Signing with Murray is like sinking down into the leather seats of a Cadillac humming down a new black asphalt highway. The beauty of his words thrum in me, his body, his touch, his voice, the way he moves, opens a tunnel of light between us, a tunnel I want to travel, and of course, I can sign with him, his eyes follow my hands when I need them to — when I want to be Deaf. But all the reasons my heart knows dissolve in an underground lake of anger that sends its sulphurous fumes through every crevice of my being, especially my mouth and hands, resulting in the vitriolic attacks against him. I belch fire, and Murray stands there with his shield of love. It's too much. I think: *I am an impostor. A faker, a cheap imitation of a Hearing person. Murray will find me out, I'm sure he already has, he sees what a poor single parent mother I've been in North Battleford, leaving Anna and Paula to themselves while I worked frantically on my business contracts in my home office, taking breaks only to feed them, admonish them, and to answer the phone, those long days at daycares, in the homes of my sister and my parents, those strange thumps upstairs that I managed to ignore for three hours one evening only to emerge from my basement office and find that Anna had moved Paula and all her furniture into her room because she'd decided that Paula and I should stop sharing a room.* I think: *They were small gardens going on without me to tend to them, able to grow without me knowing any of the details.*

Murray and I have this conversation many times:

Murray: "This is what I mean. Anna has been bullying Paula all these years."

Joanne: "But Paula is very manipulative."

Murray: "Yes, but with an older sister who must manage the affairs of her Deaf mother, what can you expect? They're CODAs, Joanne."

Children of Deaf Adults. Interpreting for the police at age seven, interpreting for the bank at age ten, answering the phone, interpreting at funerals and weddings. I had prided myself on not relying on my daughters in the same way. I think: *Ouch.*

Murray adds: "But they've had to grow away from you at such an early age. They've taken charge of themselves and their lives, knowing that you can't hear well enough to understand what goes on between them. They've developed roles between them because you don't hear them. Now they hide most things from you."

Then I remember. Their backs turned, heads bent together in whispering, mysterious thumps in the bedroom, phone cords wrapped around their backs as they speak into the phone, the careless comments shouted upward to the top floor, the calls from the basement.

I remember the daycare worker say: "Your girls are wonderful, please don't move them to another daycare, we love them here. They are so good, they behave so well."

And the teachers: "I wish that the rest of your daughter's class was as attentive and well behaved as your daughter. Paula needs to work on her spelling, that's all."

Teachers, daycare workers, friends, and colleagues all think I have two darling daughters. No one would ever know that my daughters are CODAs. Not even Anna and Paula. The three of us managed to fool everyone by approximating what was expected of us.

Except Murray. He isn't easily deceived by my ability to imitate how others live, to have two high achieving daughters, and to pretend I am morally superior to Hearing people by engaging in hard work, a life of reading, and by withdrawal from frivolous conversation.

I wore bell bottom jeans, tight shirts to show off my own breasts. I found a purple bubble shirt that wouldn't show too much of my hearing aid jammed between my breasts, but would still outline my own burgeoning figure. Glenda and I were smoking at the end of the school yard with Scott and Tom, in a little dugout fitted with a roof. Even though I couldn't bring myself to inhale the disgusting cigarettes, I watched with fascination how Glenda was able to exhale the smoke out her nostrils. These small rebellions seemed so much better than reading books, because, finally, I belonged, I was a part of things without having to hear or talk too much, all I had to do was smoke a cigarette and rebel against my parents for absolutely no reason that I could see. I thought I might be able to participate in sports because Glenda swung a bat with those muscular arms and she ran like a boy, so I signed up for the basketball team, the volleyball team, and the cross country team, and began travelling with Glenda to the small towns around Wilkie, playing games at Unity, Cut Knife, and Biggar.

My father was quiet. As the principal at McLurg High School, he knew every kid that swirled past me in the hallways. He also knew that I was not athletic at all.

Late at night, Glenda and I sat in the back seat of a car, riding home from the basketball game. I watched the moon move in out of the frames of the car windows, imagining it chasing us home, when Glenda slid her arm around my shoulder. I remained immobile, wondering if anyone else was noticing. Then she bent her head close to mine, I told myself: *This is not going to be a little girl kiss. This is something else.* She pushed my head down, and her strong arm became a bough, where I could rest my head. We remained in this position several minutes, until I could feel her face coming closer to mine. I moved away from her, leaned forward away from the arm-bough that promised to shield me from loneliness, from no friends, from awkwardness.

The next day at school, I stood alone at my locker and turned away when Glenda came down the hall. I looked for Elsie, but she had turned away, too, to talk to some other girls. I thought: *She knows I'm there, but she will never talk to me again.* The knowledge flashed in me like a swallow that shoots across a lawn from a tree bough, flying too fast for me to notice the colour of its wings or the tilt of its head: *I've missed a chance at genuine friendship for a belonging that I thought to be found by engaging in small rebellious acts that would pre-empt the need for conversation.*

Glenda took to hanging around with a heavier girl, June, whose breasts and hips were the most voluptuous I had ever seen. Her legs even rubbed together, and I could see the holes in her pants near the crotch when she carelessly opened them. I turned away.

I walked past a table where I could see a piece of paper hastily dropped by Glenda and June as they clopped down the stairs ahead of me out of the library on the top floor of the school. Their laughter and squeals were punctuated by furtive looks at me at the top of the stairs. I turned back to the table and picked up the paper scrap.

In my hand was a list of names of all my classmates associated with a sex act, including fellatio and cunnilingus (although I didn't know what it meant), like "Sidney wants to know what's under those panties," then I came to my name: "Joanne, the virgin, will scream when her cherry is popped. Ha ha, like that will ever happen."

My face flushed, the paper was a burning coal in my hand, I wondered how others had thought about my sexuality before I could even conceive of it, on the weekends, while other girls in my class were giggling under the doe eyes of David Cassidy on their walls, I was watching musicals with my family, with my mother scribbling down lyrics to love songs as they were sung by Julie Andrews, Audrey Hepburn, and Barbra Streisand, and I read into the night because Glenda ignored me and Elsie refused to look at me, turning her back to me as I walked past her in the hallway, and I stood alone at my locker between classes and came to school nearly late, so I didn't have to stand around by myself when the bell rang. I stopped wearing jeans. It was the seventies, and everyone was wearing bellbottom jeans, but I didn't care, it was now Fortrel pants for me, the ones with a seam sewn down the middle of each leg. I started to sew my own clothes. I chose patterns that were loose and gathered, even though I checked myself in the mirror every day to make sure that my stomach was flat. I was grateful that the platform shoes I wore made me seem tall and willowy. It was time to lose myself in a house of fabric, to hide my curves and lines. In the summer, I stopped swimming. I didn't want anyone to see me in a bathing suit, and I was uncomfortable with the lifeguards walking around in their swimsuits. I took down the pictures of the doe-eyed David Cassidy from the walls of my bedroom.

My parents said nothing to me about Glenda's disappearance in my life. I wondered if they'd even noticed. They should have at least congratulated me for having figured out what Glenda was about. I wondered: *Maybe they don't care.* I thought: *Doesn't matter. I can rely on books to live in the world, to peddle my knowledge as a passport to the land of the Hearing. It's the only honest way I can be superior to the Hearing people, not by imitating and pretending but by reading.*

Suddenly one late winter evening, this scene:

MURRAY EXPLORER: "Let's take our renovation savings and go to England."

The snowflakes are flying thick and fast outside the large window in the living room — another late snow, another refusal of the winter to submit to spring.

MRS. SENSIBLE: "Don't you think we should focus on the repairs? The rotting sunroom that's pulling away from the back of our house? The mouldy showers? Another tile fell off this morning when I was taking a bath."

TANTALIZING MURRAY: "Joanne, hasn't it always been a dream for you? To take the girls to Europe?"

BAITED FOX WIFE: "Yeah, but . . ."

I drop my head toward my lap, not wanting to lipread Murray any further.

I think: *There goes my chance for a real home, a home I can be proud of, where I can confidently invite other people instead of apologizing for the peeling sidewalk, the tangled dog leash that inevitably ends up on our front steps.*

But Murray knows as well as I do, that our urge to travel is always stronger. The need to know, learn, and discover is greater than the need for a posh house. England will elevate me somehow, fill my head with important things, console me with images, written words, and historical data, so that I can sit through future spontaneous conversations with my family and not bother to embark on the futile chasing of their words flying in the air, and I think: *Coffee shops, where I write furiously in a journal, are no places for a Deaf wife who should be at home with her Hearing husband and children. Or travelling in England.*

⁓

I had never seen a grade eight teacher wear so much purple. I thought: *Miss Johnson must have a very limited but imaginative budget, since she duly shows up in purple slacks and sweaters varying only in hue and texture.* I secretly liked her, especially when she told us that we must compile an anthology of two hundred poems, although I heard the moans and thumps, slams of books in retort to an impossible assignment, especially from the farm boys and hockey players in my class. I sat in the front, reading the steady stream of emotion flitting across Miss Johnson's face, as she fielded the objections from the back of the classroom. Finally she ran out in tears, and I stole a look at Dwight sitting across the aisle from me, her only other sympathizer. Dwight's moistness poured off him like a melting iceberg. Each time he touched me on the shoulder to show me the page in order to follow a schoolmate reading aloud, he left an imprint on my blouse. His eyes brimmed often with almost tears, his hair was damp around the crown of his head, and his shoes squeaked like sodden sponges. I cringed each time he flipped my book to the correct page and laid his finger on a word, soaking it into a small dot of oil and sweat. I never lifted my head during the times when Miss Johnson hurried Dwight out of the room. I thought: *Perhaps he waits until the last possible minute to go to the bathroom and must be hurried out before he wets the floor.* Everyone raised their heads, listening to the noises outside the classroom, but all I could hear were muffled thumps, so I returned to my book.

I continued to ignore Dwight. I didn't want to encourage him, because he now shuffled behind me as I hurried down the school's marble steps and into the park. The dirty white cenotaphs blocked my backward glances at him. I thought, *Perhaps he hides behind them*, but I often caught sight of his arm, or a leg, scuffling through leaves and sending pebbles of the gravel path to roll near my own scurrying feet. When his shadow crossed mine, I looked up at his reptilian skin and the greasy hair stacked over the collar of his dirty white shirt. His jaw was so tight, it even looked wired shut. His eyes suggested all that is wrong with religion, because they shone, a kind of shining that I didn't like. I wanted to tell him to stop following me, that the park was my home, a life of reading had created vast regions within me now, the spaces I inhabited must be larger than the house I lived in with my parents and my siblings: an English moor spiked with purple heather, the Russian steppes waving with wheat, the prairies, where the pungent smell of canola rose from the yellow flowers in the hot summer, the park, a house where the evergreen trees forming the quadrangle were my walls, that allowed in gentle breezes and filtered out the furious sun, the cool steps of the cenotaph, even though hard and angular, my divan, where I sat to gaze at the mown lawns and carefully tended flowerbeds where not a single soul was in sight, and broken branches with sad green leaves glittering in the sun after a storm and sparrows darting across the empty benches. When Dwight's shadow caught up with mine, I could feel tiny claws scraping the back of my throat, the dying twitches of a small animal, as I forced it down with hard swallows. I wanted to tell him to stop, but every time I turned around, he smiled and nodded, always careful to keep a few steps behind me. The wind lifted my hair and a whine began in my ears. The tinnitus said: *Whizz, bang, ring, ring, whine, whine, whine, tit, tit, hiss.* Some days it was harder to hear over the noise in my head, but today I could hear the wind sighing in the branches. Dwight looked straight ahead.

I thought: *He's afraid of me.*

But he caught me looking at him and his face lifted in joy. I said nothing and dashed out from the lane of evergreen trees down the street to my home.

During typing class in the last week of June, I was pounding on the typewriter keys until I felt a thud behind me, as if a bowling ball had been dropped on the hardwood floor beneath my feet. The clacking of typewriters ceased, and a strange thrumming began under my feet. I paused in a moment of indecision.

I decided: *Okay, I will look.*

Over the shoulder of the crouched teacher, I saw the grease stiffened hair sticking straight up from Dwight's forehead, the whites of his eyes, and saliva bubbling from his grey lips. It came to me in the roar of my ears: *Dwight's adoration of me is simply a neurological misfiring.*

I felt the flurry of movement behind me as the ambulance workers came. I thought I heard Dwight moaning, but I didn't want to check to see if I was right. I thought: *His desire to be close to me is nothing more than the strange machinations of his brain. Dwight is kind to me because I'm deaf. His kindness is merely a bargain. All disabled people should stick together. That's what he thinks. But I'm not disabled. Rather, I'm more intelligent and capable than most of my Hearing peers because I read, read, and read.*

At noon, I ran away from the school into the new rain. The drops on the greasy grey sidewalk bloomed in jagged petals the minute they hit the surface, I could feel them between the hairs on my scalp while the trees galumphed in the wind, their green boughs outstretched for more rain. I lifted my face and the rain ran in delicate lines down my cheeks.

One summer morning after reading *Jane Eyre* deep into the night, lying in the tent warmed by the early morning sun, I paused to think of the paper that was dropped on the library table by Glenda and June.

Was it because of my deafness? Was I that loathsome?

I remembered running to the mirror in the girls' bathroom after hastily crumpling up the note and throwing it in the garbage, watching my lips move, over-exaggerated, listening to my hollow voice, for the first time, how my tongue twisted to the right side of my mouth as if it had a life of its own, worrying that deafness had deformed my body, set me apart, unworthy of a fire between my legs, or a man's mouth on mine, that deafness had made me into a virgin.

I crawled from the tent on my knees in that pink cream nightgown, stumbled onto the wet grass with my finger between the covers of *Jane Eyre*. The great meaning must be in the spiralling staircase where Jane can peer down at Rochester walking into his office after blowing her a kiss: *"Farewell, Jane!"*

Indeed, I was the strong, plucky Jane loved by ugly Rochester, admired for what I could do with my deafness, but not loved by normal or ordinary people. I thought: *Only Dwight loves me.*

Once I stopped breathing heavily, I went into the house. My mother was stirring one of her homemade soups. I watched her chop onions and celery. I breathed in the smell of the steamy chicken broth, but I knew I had to leave this warmth. I thought hard. Where would I go?

❧

I balance the coffee shop tray as I head toward a table — empty except for a litter of cups and used napkins. I whisk them to another nearby table already overflowing with dirty dishes and sit with my back to the windows so no one can see me if they're walking by. The afternoon is already wearing away, with my last glimpse outside I see a grey pallor falling over the street, the faces of the people scurrying by are pinched with cold. I sit, grateful for the steaming windows, the warmth of the coffee cup in my hands, my open journal on the table, and the Hearing people who surround me with their words, noises, and sounds that I'll never comprehend, I look at the room around me as if I'm peering through a pane of glass: their mouths move, noises fly everywhere, meaningless. I think: *It's what I am used to.*

But I wonder: *Who are these people? The truck drivers that come in with their smeared coffee travel mugs. The man who reads his Bible in the corner. The heavy women with poodle hair and sweatpants.* And I think: *There is an air of aimlessness in the shop, people slowly coming and going, the chink chink of the till, the hot coffee pooling around cups on the counters. But reading makes me feel not so alone.* Jane's sharp, astringent voice hisses in my ear: *If you're reading, then why sit in a coffee house?* I imagine her pursing her lips, folding her hands together just above her belly. I see her pulling her shawl more closely around her. She says: *You are a snob.*

I pack my journal in my bag and stumble out the door, scurry to the car, sharp spears of the first November snow ping against my cheeks, I want to purge myself of my deafness and my need for sign language, I think: *Now. I want now to happen. The now that's been lying in wait for me. Time's bloodhound crouched at the exit of all my tunnels and escape routes!* I drive too fast, stop the car with a jerk in front of our house, wildly look up at the rising moon, and down again at the glitter on the light covering of snow, the découpage of frozen leaves on the road, trip and fall by the split tree at the front of the house, a meal of crushed leaves worked into the faded grass between the exposed roots bringing a faint metallic smell to my nostrils, and I think: *The fall air has arrested the decay. It will begin again in the spring.*

In the house, Langley Hall, bookcases line the walls. I think: *Why haven't I noticed their heaviness? Books and papers. Books stacked sideways against books stacked vertically. The bookcases lining three walls of the living room and extending far into the dining room. Something is gnawing my stomach. A small animal is nestled inside me. It has begun to masticate my innards.*

Our bedroom too, is lined with bookcases from ceiling to floor. Atop a row of books, I have stuffed a brassiere, and a T-shirt. A towel hangs on a nail hammered into the side of one bookshelf. I think: *There is someone or something unwelcome in this house. It must go from me. Either I must leave this house or it must go.* And I think: *How do I make it go? Must I leave my husband, and take our two daughters? Again?* Out the window, clouds like scraps of torn black lace claw their way past the moon.

Mad fox wife howls: " . . . !"

I think: *I don't know how to talk to my daughters. Especially when Murray is in the room. I've never been good with small talk, the world seems polluted with it, the endless jingoism, the right smart sayings, the pithy comments, the foolish giggles of teenage girls, and worst, the bright words, the words that suggest happiness, optimism, quick intimacy, a solution for every problem, a platitude for pain.*

Mad fox wife howls again: " . . . !"

I try to coax myself, sternly, even though my mind feels drained of words: *Make up stuff to talk about. Talk about the weather, the neglected garden at this time of year, how the tulips are now bedded in the soil, waiting for spring, and the yellowing grass around the lake.*

Within a few minutes, a wordless stupor comes over me, a slow beckoning to dullness amidst the chatter of my daughters and Murray at the supper table. I eat, sinking in the irony of having learned to speak and to hear with my residual hearing, but not hearing enough to participate in a conversation. I inwardly snarl at deaf education professionals who attempted to clean my English language ability simply with the soap of grammar, their promise that good speech, no matter how faulty my hearing, would provide the ticket to the world at large, the ticket to jobs, family, love, and happiness. I still remain a Deaf woman who hovers in the shadows.

﹏

In my classroom, Nolan approaches me, a book balanced on his outstretched hands. I suppose that he thinks that the worship of a beautifully bound book can lead him to literacy. If my aboriginal deaf students were all living in pre-contact times, they would've had their own literacy. They would've wrapped their blankets around their necks and read the tracks in the fresh loam, watched the stars at night, built caches of stones to warn others, and painted marks on skins of tipis. That knowledge is dying with their elders. Their elders are libraries disintegrating with old age. I think: *This literacy involves keen observation, experience, and deduction based on visual clues alone: the Deaf have access to it.*

The students watch as I finger the golden whorls on the cover of Nolan's book and caress the silken endpapers. Slowly, I weave the narrow red grosgrain ribbon through my fingers. My hand runs lightly over the gilt-edged pages fanning outwards from the red leather binding. A map of Odysseus' travails is in the back. Essays on Homer's work are interspersed like islands throughout the pages.

Nolan tells me: "I paid one hundred and fifty dollars for this book."

I want to say nothing, and nod to preserve this sacred ceremony of this book. Surely the silence of our deafness is enough to make the book holy. But I think: *Why pretend, Nolan, to read books you cannot read? Even if you could, you'd still be very alone.* I also think: *Give him his essay. You've marked it. It's sitting right there on your desk.* I say, continuing to slowly flip the pages: " . . . "

Nolan snatches the book away from my grasping hands. The air is bright, sending the faces of the silent students into shadow as he pushes the book back into its gilded case. Silence follows him like an unmarked trail as he hastily leaves my classroom. His paper remains stacked against my books. I have given his essay a narrow red zero for plagiarism.

Ten

I HAVE NO PATIENCE WITH MARY of Egypt. She chooses to become helpless before the God she professes to love, she chooses to lie in the desert, parched, baked, and feral; without a consistent supply of water, food, or shelter, she has chosen to confront the harshest of all landscapes. I click my tongue with impatience at a picture of her prone body, her arm across her eyes, shielding herself from the sun. *Why doesn't she run to a shelter, to friends, or to family, where she can be at home, where she can be cared for, and where she can care for others? What on earth makes her stay in the desert, where there's nothing but rocks, stones, prickly cactus, camel trains sliding in the shifting sands, and dangerous animals that prowl about at night. Why do I think she has something I don't have?*

⁂

It was my last month of high school. I asked myself: *Is it a low pitched whine, or a moan?* I was sitting in my grade twelve biology class. It was the last period of the day, and I had to sit for another hour yet, oblivious again to all the talking that was going on. I'd just sat through four hours, polite, smiling, nodding, keeping my eyes open and trying to look alert so I could convince my teachers and classmates that I was indeed a part of this class. I stared

straight ahead, my eyes fixed on the clock, the foghorn playing its
unceasing moan in my ears. Except that sometimes it was a sort of
a whine. Sort of. I was trying to figure out the rhyme or reason to
this tinnitus. I wondered: Did it play according to my moods? If I
heard a cluster of snakes about me, hissing as I bent my head over
my books, did it mean that I was in an altered mental state? Am
I a cobra ready to rear up at any moment if provoked any longer?
*Was the noise in my ears a remnant of another language, something
I've heard before?* Yet, the foghorn was the most common sound. I
asked myself: *Is it the long song of boooooooorinnnnnnnng or is it that
I am most aware of the noise when I am bored or restless?* I glanced at
my teacher, Mr. Scotton, in his white lab coat, rubbing his beard
with his hand. He had such a pert sound to his voice, he sounded
excited, animated, alive. I could only hear his vowels sliding up
and down. I tried to attend to the vowels, trying to parse them
into something I could understand. Instead I slid back into the
whine inside my ears. The vowels outside my head; inside my
ears, the moan. I cast a glance around the room. Everyone else
seemed motionless. Papers remained piled neatly before them,
books were unopened. I thought: *If only I could read my biology
text right here and now, the moan in my ears might abate for a while.*
But I couldn't open up a text book and read right there in front
of Mr. Scotton and everyone else too. I thought: *It would be rude.
I'd be chastised for having bad manners, for being anti-social. Worse,
yet, I'd get reprimanded for not paying attention, for not listening.*

I looked longingly at the biology text as the moan increased
in my ears and I thought: *I'll have to spend a couple of hours in the
evening, going through the book, making notes, charts, and diagrams,
to help myself learn the material. Too bad I can't do it now, so I can
relax, read a book, and listen to some music in the evening.* I shifted
restlessly in my chair. Mentally, I sang to myself, trying to fit words

to the long moan: *Down in the valley, valley so loooooooooooow, hang
your head over, hear the wind blooooooowwww.*

Suddenly, hands snatched at their books and papers. Chairs
were pushed back from their tables. Mr. Scotton had turned his
back to the class. I realized: *Oh, class is finished.* I never heard the
bell, the loooooooow tone I had heard on countless occasions, the
tone I longed for at the end of every class.

In the last days of the final semester before high-school
graduation, I was dreaming of university: pristine white halls,
freshly mowed green quadrangles, and window seats in old
buildings. I thought: *I will bathe in a sea of words that will splash
its bright and vivacious vowels and consonants. I will begin a life
with people at last. It will be nothing like the whispers, giggles, and
boisterous shouts of my classmates in high school. There will only be
dignified speeches.*

My father said: "The best thing about university is you'll get
to live in a dorm with other roommates. You'll get cooked meals,
and you won't have to worry about housekeeping."

I scanned my mother's kitchen counter: a rubble of opened
tins, torn cereal boxes, dirty cups, and vegetable peelings. Red,
yellow, orange, and purple, the hill of clutter made a noise in my
head, a series of sharp quick hisses, a station not quite tuned into
its bandwidth. I thought: *In my new home, everything will be spare,
white, and clean.*

During the first week in September, I went to the Shannon
Library at St. Thomas More College in Saskatoon, and stacked
my books on a table, claiming my end as I saw the other students
did, went back and forth between classes to sit at my table,
looking over at the students whose heads were bent down, intent
on their books and papers.

My mother urged me: "Go to the cafeteria on the lower floor, eat the terrible chili on Fridays, and go to Mass every day." She continued: "Eventually someone will stop and say hello."

Instead, a girl from my high school class in Wilkie came rushing up to me in the cafeteria with: "I want to quit, I hate this place."

I looked behind her at the cafeteria, the heavy stone pillars that marked off every ten feet, and the blue Arborite tables arranged in long, snaking rows between the pillars. I said: "You've only been here a week."

I had attended a couple of parties with her in the twelfth grade, yet all I could remember is her sitting on her boyfriend's lap, downing a beer. She must miss him. It never occurred to me to quit, even though I hadn't spoken with a single person for the past three weeks — other than the girls at St. Paul's Residence.

It was a long wait.

In the meantime, my thoughts behaved like bored birds, pecking listlessly at the ground, then flying off before I was able to grasp them. I couldn't remember where I'd put my keys anymore. I had to rummage through my backpack every night in the dorm hallway in front of the door to my room.

In psychology class, I finally leaned toward a girl sitting next to me, who looked pleasant enough. I said: "Mind if I photocopy your notes? I can't make good notes at all."

I didn't want to tell her that I'd heard nothing of the lecture, that I was deaf.

She smiled and nodded. She said: "I'm Janet. Your name?"

It was a start. I didn't say much when we exchanged notes, because I wanted to hurry back to the library at the Catholic college I'd came to inhabit like a timid wren, occasionally putting my head out and up over my table to look around.

Late one evening, I guided myself surreptitiously through St. Thomas More College. I peeped into the chapel, an auditorium, a cafeteria, and the Murray room, a multipurpose room where small intimate masses were held on Wednesdays. I opened the doors at the back of the Murray room and climbed the spiral staircase. There was the Chelsea lounge for receptions. A grand piano occupied a corner. Windows on all three sides looked out onto College Drive, and the campus. The Basilian Fathers had their own living quarters just off the lounge. I peered through the grilled glass window in the door at a black jacketed priest crossing the hall from a room to another room. The massive stone building brought to me memories of muffled voices, the slamming of doors, and the sudden snuffing out of lights. I whispered: *Jane, this is Thornfield Hall.*

Green Journal

Parenting Joanne during her first university year was difficult. She brought home a skirt she had purchased in a store, half price, a gorgeous rich red and gold diamond pattern with a band around her midriff decorated with strings of beads. I could see why she bought it. It was truly bohemian and a work of art, but she missed looking carefully at the back of the skirt. Right about the bottom area of her bum, the pattern dissolved into a huge red blotch. I told her that the skirt made her look like she's had an accident with her period. She went silent, but then she came home the following weekend still wearing it. I was mortified.

And I had to snatch a volume of Plato from under her arm as she was preparing to go out for a walk around Wilkie. I scolded her about developing affectations. She wanted so much to be viewed as an intellectual. She wanted everyone to know how smart she was by flaunting her philosophy text at any old farmer who might be driving down the road. I was more concerned about her ability to live in the real world than she was. She really didn't have a sniff. The way she carried on about the Saskatchewan Junior Citizen of the Year Award, one might have thought we were dragging her to the dentist for a root canal. I could understand why she might not want to be singled out because of her deafness, but she could have taken *some* sort of pride in functioning so well in the world.

She came home with a paper that had been given an "A" by Gladene Robertson, a professor in the Special Education Department at the University of Saskatchewan. Robertson's comments included a sentence about Joanne's remarkable ability to synthesize knowledge from a variety of sources. I saw a quiet sort of smile grow on Joanne's face as I read that comment aloud. Clearly Joanne was pleased which meant more to her than any award she received for being so well integrated in the world. Come to think of it, that ability to synthesize must had come from those matching sets Ed and I made, all those attribute blocks, even the Montessori principles I tried to implement. Dr. Buckwold was right: developing cognitive thinking was more important than getting Joanne to articulate properly. Funny, as her vocabulary grew, even at university, she still mispronounced many words.

During the day, professors appeared before me and disappeared into offices and classrooms, or walked down hallways, laden with briefcases and books, deep in conversation. I could easily imagine what they were saying if they were talking about Plato or Virginia Woolf, or James Joyce's *Dubliners*. If I read the same things they read, then to a certain extent I could predict what they would say. A plan formed in my head: An educated imagination was a means to enter those conversations before I faded away into oblivion, whereas my inability to decipher a spontaneous conversation rendered me invisible and alone, but I was only in first year, already scowling over the poverty of my knowledge, even though I was earning reasonable grades. I asked myself: *How could this be possible? I couldn't hear the lectures. Did the professors suspect that I was deaf and take pity on me?* I thought: *God forbid.* Perhaps I was the only person who reads textbooks.

By the end of the first semester, I realized I could churn out the papers and write the examinations just by reading the assigned textbooks and the hasty notes scribbled by classmates. By late March I could no longer sleep. It was difficult to keep track of sound and time. I had a shower in the morning, the water pellets flew off my skin and down into the drain between my feet, and I thought: *Was sound and time like water, always flowing away from me? I was no longer sure of anything.*

It was English class and the professor was droning on. I leaned over to watch a classmate scrawl note on her clipboard, but she was left handed and had rounded her arm and fist to cover most of the paper.

PROFESSOR: " . . . Arthuria . . . leg . . . sour . . . "

I deduced: *Chaucer drew from sources such as Arthurian legends? Must check the preface to the text.* I heave a sigh of relief. I am getting better at guessing.

PROFESSOR: "O . . . wi . . . baa . . . boody . . . "

I deduced: *Bloody? Bawdy? Old something . . . Wife of Bath?* I'll have to reread it.

PROFESSOR: " . . . Pig . . . a mush . . . trava . . . "

I deduced: *Pig in a bush? Travel? Oh, the travellers went on a pilgrimage.*

" . . . Seven . . . motif . . . "

I thought: *Seven motifs? Are there seven motifs in Chaucer?* Never saw anything amounting to seven of anything.

My classmates furiously scribbled in a rarefied air of diligence and high seriousness.

There was no angry rebel skulking at the back of the room and if he exploded, I wouldn't hear anyway. Only the occasional clank of the radiator in the small room startled me.

I thought: *It is hard to live with so much nothingness. If I was in a large building, at least I could occupy rooms in my mind. In this small cramped classroom, I can't even read anything on my table without seeming rude.* The professor tapped my table. I wondered: *Is this his way of alerting me to something he's said? Dear God, does he know?*

I was not sure what the damn tapping meant. I looked up at the wall but there was no clock. I was not even sure of the time. When I was stuck in a place like this, I could always take out a book so that time will cease to exist. But now time swelled like a bud of water clinging to the lip of a faucet.

PROFESSOR: "Shivaree . . . nigh . . . ady . . . "

I sighed and steeled myself to wait: *ten more minutes and this boredom will be over.*

That evening, my mother phoned me, taking care to enunciate every word. Another drama ensued:

PLEASED MOTHER: "Joanne, you will receive an award for being the Saskatchewan Junior Citizen of the Year."

SULLEN JOANNE: "Why on earth would they give me an award?"

INSISTING MOTHER: "They, Joanne, is the Saskatchewan Weekly Newspapers Association. You've accomplished so much with your deafness. All the volunteer work you've done, sports, and your marks."

DEFIANT JOANNE: "Well, I am not going. I don't want to receive an award for being able to endure boredom."

EXASPERATED MOTHER: (*Audible sigh*)

JOANNE: " . . . "

DETERMINED MOTHER: "You are going. We're picking you up tomorrow on our way to Regina. Ruth, David, and Carol are coming with us. We've booked a hotel, and the ceremony is the next day."

The drama continued in Regina. I slumped on the hotel room bed, ignoring the excitement of my siblings as we prepared to attend a tour of the newspaper offices and the Legislative Building. My sister, Ruth, wanted to interview the Lieutenant Governor of Saskatchewan and dignitaries from provincial and federal governments. I wanted to talk to nobody.

EXCITED MOTHER: "We will meet Kevin Hamm, the editor of the Unity Press, you know, our friend from Unity. He will navigate us through introductions with people from the Saskatchewan Weekly Newspapers Association and Pioneer Life Insurance, who are also sponsors of the event."

DEAF DAUGHTER: *(To no one in particular)* "I just wish they would let me live my life."

My mood did not improve when I met the other recipients. Agnes Powalinsky was being honored for her work with the mentally handicapped in their family-run special care home in Kinistino. She wanted to be a doctor. Jim Werbicki was a Ukrainian dancer, who achieved top marks. All that practice, determination and focus! David Herbert and Michael Fenrich saved somebody's life, for God's sake. Diane Wassill and Ken Schneider were normal people with individual talents and achievements. But they wanted to give me an award for just being deaf! For sitting through five hours of school every day for twelve years in sheer boredom, understanding nothing, and I still couldn't hear a damn thing in my university classes. The best I could do was to look interested and smile and laugh at the right time. I thought: *I shouldn't have to receive an award for doing that.*

The final scene: My parents dropped me off in Saskatoon on their way back from Regina, and I slammed the door to the car before going up the steps to the residence at St.Paul's Hospital.

As the winter months stretched into dirty spring, there was nowhere to go. After seeing the words sprawled on the concrete path leading up to the College of Agriculture: "Drag your scrag to the Ag Bag Drag," a dance to beat all dances on campus that year, I couldn't imagine being among drunken farmers, squealing blond girls with pouffed hair and tight jeans, or the band music throbbing in my ears. *How could I follow what anyone said when they were moving their bodies? Heads had to be stable before I could lipread what anyone said. And there was so much shouting, banter, joking, teasing, and the liberal pouring of beer down the front of shirts and pants. How could that possibly mean anything?*

It became harder to live with so much nothingness. Dullness seeped into my brain, eroding consciousness, leaving me to wander among fantasies and half-formed thoughts. Dullness said: *My ability to cope with my deafness in the Hearing world is a powerful opiate for everyone around me. I should be mollified with the idea of being part of a family, a community, a something. Surely, someday, I will. After all, I'm almost Hearing, and will arrive in the Hearing world, that blessed place, I hope, soon.*

At daily Mass, I liked to watch motes of dust dance in the stream of light from the stained glass windows, the flowing vestments of the priest, and the backs of people hunched in prayer. While the priest mumbled the rituals, I was already making a bed for myself on the altar. I would clear out the pews so that I could create a comfortable reading room with soft sofas and pillows. The kitchen would be in the vestry. With the soft light of the saints in the stained glass windows caressing my shoulders, I would sleep warm and safe, and my beliefs, patient blackbirds, would come to sit on the clipped green church lawn, having flown in sometime during the night.

❧

According to legend, Mary of Egypt survived on a few greens here and there. I wonder: *If she never met anyone during all those years, not even a Bedouin, didn't she go mad? She must have reached an oasis from time to time in her wanderings; humans cannot survive without water.*

So I ask Mary: *How were you able to stay in a harsh and unyielding landscape for over forty years? Didn't you have a friend?*

Mary says: " . . . "

❧

I watched people come and go in the library. There was a tall woman, large boned, who always wore dresses underneath a black blazer, her name was Lillian, I found that out. Her look was disdainful but intelligent and alert, like someone from another century, a medieval noblewoman, somber, quiet but with an eye for mischief as she winked at me when walking by my table, I decided that the only way I was ever going to meet her was to give her a poem I'd written, in which she was Lady Lillian. I invited her to my home for a poorly-cooked meal, relying on cheese and crackers for appetizers, and I found a soup I could warm up. I thought: *There isn't much else I could do on a hotplate.* But she arrived at my door with her rucksack full of books as we planned to walk back to the library after supper.

The evening went passably well. My instinct about her was sharp enough, that she was pleased with the dreamy Lady Lillian poem I gave her. After that meal, we were friends, and with her encouragement, I became the unofficial poet in residence that year, handing out poems to people about themselves. Boosted by this new confidence, I began now to greet people and stopped to chat with them in the library, hallways, and classrooms, scribbled out many bad poems and began giving them away to people between studying, visiting, and swimming in the university pool. I didn't write a poem for a young woman always rushing about in a plaid jumper over a white blouse with a huge bag strapped over her shoulder, because she came up to me and introduced herself, Dorene.

She said: "I've seen you around here a lot."

She invited me to her suite on the top floor of a large house and offered me pills from her vitamin bottles on a table, and a pair of jeans.

She said: "These belonged to my brother who died last year."

Her bag was slumped over to its side. A wet facecloth, poppy seed rolls wrapped in plastic, a couple of blackened bananas, a plastic drinking cup, and a book spilled out on to the floor.

I said hastily: "No thanks."

She reached into her fridge and whisked out a paper plate shrouded in a napkin. *Cookies.* I reached stealthily for a cookie, but as I opened my mouth, a high pitched "eeeeeeeeeee" erupted into the room. My earmold had become dislodged by my bite.

Dorene nodded knowingly. She said: "I have a sister who's deaf. She's a student at Walter Murray High School."

I took another bite of my cookie. I thought: *No wonder she speaks so clearly.*

"My parents found out that Janice was deaf when she was five," she said. "For the first five years, they thought she was mentally retarded." Dorene shook her head. "Then I persuaded them to let her move to Saskatoon so she can go to school here. She's living with foster parents."

I nodded in sympathy, but inwardly I wondered: *How did this sort of thing still happen? It was 1978. Even I knew that there were good hearing aids, behind-the-ear ones, for profound hearing losses. I'd just acquired one. What a relief not to wear a body aid tucked between my breasts, with a heavy cord pulling down on my ear.*

I didn't know what I could say that would be of any use. I changed the subject.

Soon we were shopping every Saturday. Dorene had a great eye for sales since she left a small southeastern Saskatchewan town, with fifty dollars in her pocket, for Saskatoon upon her high school graduation, determined to attend university that fall, and knocked on doors, asking to live with people and to work for them in their homes. I knew that we were not thrown together without reason; despite my privileged middle class upbringing and her life in poverty on the farm, we both knew how to beg with a certain dignity. This friendship became an oasis in the endless stretches of boredom between waking and sleeping.

I am a desert mother, stumbling about in the sand, far from everyone but Murray, who reads horse stories by Dick Francis. I want to tell him: *This is what it is like to live with so much nothingness. This is how I must live with the sheer indifference of the desert, that inner and outer landscape that threatens to devour me.* Instead, I say: "Another tile fell off in the bathroom this morning."

Murray lifts his head from the newspaper, nods and says: "We'll redo the whole bathroom, but first we have a trip to plan."

I slam the door to our bedroom and fling myself on our bed. *A trip? I want a home where there is a balanced economy of silences and languages. I don't want to wander overseas, especially with Murray and the girls. I don't want to live in any more temporary homes. I want to live and die in the same house.*

Eleven

I COMPLAIN TO SOPHIE ONE DAY, looking out the window at the lone evergreen tree skirted with fresh white snow: "It's like we're all locked in ice in here."

Sophie offers: "Well, it's cold outside."

I nod slowly, then retreat to my desk. I look over the classroom and sigh. Every one of these students seems locked into their own frozen state. They are individual statues walking about in the room, unmoved by each other.

I ponder: *How will they ever learn to live in a community, to be active participants in a group? But they are not fretting about it. After all, they've operated in dyads all their lives. Mother/child. Interpreter/ student. Teacher/student. An older sister/deaf sibling. Hearing friend /deaf. Helper/ helpless. Powerful one/weak one. One to one. One on one. One for one. One by one. Two in one.* I shudder.

❧

Melissa signs: "I don't need interpreting. I have a cochlear implant." She rolls her eyes in impatience at my inability to appreciate what the implant does for her.

I sign: "But you don't even wear that processor most of the time. You don't like to use your voice."

Melissa turns away, stony faced.

I tap her arm: "It's great that you have a cochlear implant. But don't you think you need to develop your speech skills and listening skills?"

Melissa informs me: "I can hear perfectly."

I inform her: "You mean you can hear sounds and voices, but can you understand what people are saying?"

Melissa says: " . . . " She drums her newly manicured fingers on the table, red nails, each with a green dot in the centre, sending the small beads jumping away from the leather piece she's been working on.

I think: *How can you sign when those nails are nearly a half inch longer than your fingers?* I want to shout: "It's not part of Deaf culture to have such long and colourful nails! It's too distracting to watch!" But I check myself. *She isn't part of any Deaf community.*

Melissa merely shrugs.

I leave her with the Hearing girls, who are laughing as they pick up beads with their needles. She'll come to me later in the afternoon and complain about feeling like a freak because she's sure that the Hearing girls are laughing at her and I'll have to reassure her that the girls wouldn't likely talk about her because they just wouldn't care enough about her to do that, and I feel an overwhelming weariness.

✺

The signs of American Sign Language are like explosions of a Japanese haiku on a page, a shower of images in which I can stand and pluck the fruit before it falls to the ground, heaping detonations of light, movement, and colour, the grimaces, the flashing of eyes, the rounded lips, the finger tracing a trodden path. Most Hearing people would stand oblivious through it all.

I sign to Melissa: "Don't you think that Hearing people sign in a messy way, that their hands are so awkward and their faces are so dead?"

She shrugs and signs back to me: "They sign just fine to me."

I want to say: No. *The hands of the Hearing are birds with broken or deformed wings, creatures that flap in a crude and rudimentary manner. Their signs are defective visual noise, just as Melissa's deaf speech is defective and painful to listen to.* How can I tell her that she sounds like Donald Duck?

I say: " . . . "

I get up and turn my back to Melissa and stand before the window, my eyes blinking over the field of ice diamonds in the afternoon sun in the silent courtyard, thinking of names of businesses, organizations, fundraising events or even games: *Silent Hands, Silent Painter, Silent Barber, Silent Walk, Silent Volleyball. Ugh.* I turn to Melissa again. I ask her: "What do you think of this business of always talking about silence in association with the Deaf? You know, 'Silent Walk' for instance. You went on one last year to help raise money for Saskatchewan Deaf and Hard of Hearing Services."

Melissa shrugs and says: "It's okay to me."

I want to say: *But there is no silence in the Deaf community. Objects float in the air around me as I sign. My signs disappear rapidly after being anchored in an invisible place. My lips twist, puff, stretch into a grimace, indicating size, texture, number, intensity, and thickness. I shape my face into masks of emotion that I never thought existed within me. There is no silence in my hands. They are the wings of a bird. There is the sudden dip, the lifting of a shoulder, the folding of the last feathers on the end of a wing. As I take flight, my thinking changes. I order ideas in my head in terms of visual relevance. Like*

when I turn on the TV, the picture bubbling up on the screen tells me
more than its accompanying sound.

I look at Melissa's head, bent down over her homework. She is
struggling to decipher a paragraph that is written at a grade ten
reading level. In a few minutes, I'll have to sit down and explain
the whole paragraph to her in sign language, because there is no
time for her to figure it out. I'll soon have to rescue her from the
desert of words because she can't understand the structure of
English.

·ઍ·

I think: *Murray will pick me up after school, as always. As I climb*
into the car, I'll have to turn my head, to lipread him, while he'll
say something like, "How was your day?" What else do people say
after they've been apart for a day? I can nod to indicate that I have
understood his question, spoken quickly while driving, with hands
firmly gripping the steering wheel. He'll be sure to ask what the girls
are doing after school. Ballet? Riding? Vocal lessons? Piano? I have
their schedule memorized, so this part will go well. But the chances
of appearing like a slightly addled child will increase, as Murray will
want to regale me with stories about his work, his brother, or his older
sons. I close my eyes and think: I'll not think that far ahead. But I
know that the spoken words will relentlessly come soon.

MURRAY: "Joanne, do you remember the list of things you
were supposed to do yesterday? What about the groceries?"

JOANNE EYRE: "Pardon me?"

MURRAY: "Don't forget the list of jobs and to get the groceries."

JOANNE EYRE: "Groceries? What about . . ."

MURRAY: "Yeah, we're out of milk."

JOANNE EYRE: "I forgot about it." I look down at my hands.
"I'm so sorry."

When it happens, a muddiness seeps into my thoughts and I'm unable to concentrate. I hear the edge in Murray's voice, the signal I've been waiting for. He's getting tired of me and my sudden fits of anger. Perhaps he has had enough of making love to a Deaf woman. I've heard that many Hearing men seek out Deaf women for the sounds they'll make or not make, for the added sensuality that will somehow pour out through their fingers because they are cut off from sound, for any innovative postures and techniques that might well up from the deprivation of sound. I think: *Is the appeal of making love to a Deaf woman like the appeal of making love to a virgin? Is there something virginal about silence?* I think hard on it. *Silence sets the Deaf apart, virginity sets a woman apart, a virginal silence, all that deprivation. In other words: unmitigated boredom.*

I think: Hmmm. *Virginal Silence* might make a title for a book someday but that's about it.

I say: " . . . *(Sigh)* . . . "

I know: *I have become a hateful creature. I am slipping away from him, away from the beauty of his face and his large hands into a dark well where the rhythm of words, metaphors, symbols, similes rushing in and out of my heart, once tireless in their coming, going, and returning now feels like foreign blood in my body.*

My mother once said: "All women must learn to be virgins during their marriages. 'Virgin' means 'to be set apart from everyone else.' Husbands must learn to see their wives as set apart from all the other women that cross their lives."

I realize: *Virginity is not only about wearing a satin nightgown and reading far into the night alone, rolling on a nylon sleeping bag in a tent. It's about accepting that I've been set apart because of deafness. I've been sent by deafness to the desert, although not of my own volition.*

Not yet.

Twelve

EASTER VACATION. MY COUSIN LIVES AT Sylvan Lake, in a cabin two blocks from the shore, a squatter, the last in a row of otherwise gleaming aluminum-sided white houses. Its dirty stucco is a reminder of a once genteel lakeside community in the early fifties, a house now stubborn in its refusal to improve its image. Murray's hand in the small of my back feels protective as I walk on the sunken stone path to the door.

Inside, the overwhelming smell of dog saliva and dander fills my gorge, a dachshund and a basset hound sprawl on the floor like tossed bolsters before a four-by-four television screen, the VCR and DVD player blinking like silent spaceship consoles, Len, in dirty shorts and T-shirt, on an L-shaped sofa, where all four of us arrange ourselves. Every inch of the countertop is covered with dirty dishes, emptied fast food containers, and drained beer bottles, the two dogs come up to me and lick my leg, perfuming me with rank dog odour, while Murray chuckles at something on the screen, his head nodding in agreement.

I could ask Len to turn on the closed captioning so I can at least comprehend what's being said, but I know that Hearing people don't like to see ribbons of text running across the screen, and I haven't come all this way to watch television, I want to have a conversation. I twist my head behind the couch toward the kitchen, trying to stem the tide of indignation rising in me, and think, *I could go for a walk along the beach alone,* but inertia weighs down my bones. The endless stream of images on the monstrous screen urges me to surrender and sink into the black hole of the worn sofa. The girls are nodding occasionally at things Murray and Len say, now several empty beer bottles sit around Len's and Murray's ankles, while the television screen bears down on me with an overwhelming benevolence, its images of food — a cooking show glistening, vegetables fried up in gleaming saucepans. Overcome with the close smell of dog, the cigarettes, and beer, I tap Murray on his leg. I sign to him so that Len can't detect any frustration in my voice: "Can I speak to you for a minute? Outside."

Len turns his gaze back to the screen, while we let ourselves out the screen door. Outside, I slide down the crumbling steps, careful not to trip on the toe grips. It is a little family drama:

JOANNE OF EGYPT: "Murray, I need to go."

MURRAY: "Joanne, what's wrong now?"

I exhale. I have my eyes trained on the forest at the edge of the yard. The sudden flight of blackbirds rising from the meadow beyond the forest startles me.

JOANNE OF EGYPT: "Nothing really."

MURRAY: "All right then."

I turn to go back inside. Murray's hand is upon my shoulder as I cross the splintered threshold.

Over the next two hours, this new resolve to endure the visit for Murray and our daughters' sake dissolves slowly like a hard sugar pill in water. I think: *I have an extra car key in my purse, nestled among Kleenex, old bills, and my wallet. If worse comes to worst, I can bolt and breach the front door to our car.* I poke Murray again: "Put me on a bus back to Regina. I'm getting really angry."

I'm careful to make my signs large and clear and my face pleasant and impassive. I don't want Len to see the anger in my face, and I know that he won't understand the meaning of claw hands scraping across my chest.

Murray's puzzled face prompts me to slow down.

The pretence of pleasantness hardens my facial muscles. My jaw is locked into a spasm of cheeriness.

Murray is clearly exasperated, and jerks his head to indicate we should step outside again.

Somewhere a bird caws. To my left, a magpie alights on the small, fraying lawn. Carrion birds. I feel a tap on my shoulder.

Murray says, with his voice: "You're being so disrespectful to Len. Get a grip on yourself."

I try to soften my voice: "I don't think you understand what's going on."

Murray's lips say: "How do you think Len feels about your carrying on? Stop being so dramatic."

My voice hardens and I feel as though my skin is being ripped, like old worn fabric ready for the rag pile. It says: "I don't think he cares." I draw in a jagged breath. As I let it out again, it says: "I need to go somewhere. I'm too isolated."

Murray's lips say: "How does that help? Leaving me and Anna and Paula here helps you feel less isolated?"

My whole body says: "Being among strangers feels more honest."

Murray's whole face says: "Joanne, get a hold of yourself. You always say these things and then you say you're sorry the next day."

I shake my head and turn to go inside, the living room now darkened in the evening hours, and sit beside Anna and Paula still curled on the couch, mesmerized by the shadows cast by the flickering screen. Finally I ask, ever so politely, if the closed captioning can be turned on. I think: *More reading as usual.*

I read somewhere that prisoners who, are left in solitary confinement for extended periods of time, do not cope well after release from prison. Often they will literally recreate the environment by living alone, and take on the same weird behaviours they developed in the darkness of their cells. Just so that they can feel that they are in control of themselves.

Thirteen

ON THE DAY AFTER EASTER VACATION, I sign to Sophie over the oral students' heads although they're not the least bit curious. And Melissa's okay with all the wooden signed English shooting forth from the staff interpreters' hands, a cochlear implant she rarely uses, and beading with Hearing aboriginal girls who are always talking, giggling at something, Melissa pays attention to no one else but them in the school and while she remains oblivious to me and Sophie. In these small snippets of signing to Sophie, I sense the return of my Deaf mind, igniting the small synaptic explosions in my brain, as I synthesize my body, hands, and face into a fleeting series of postures and gestures coloured by several shades of intensities. Finally I turn to Melissa and my other students: "I have a Deaf body, you have a Deaf body. There is one hell of a difference between a Deaf body and a Hearing body." I'm desperate to tell them of the other world waiting for them, a community of hidden people who are alive and vibrant within their own language and culture, but the oral deaf students say nothing and Melissa waits impassively too, and then I sigh and go on, with the curriculum I must cover, with Shakespeare, novels, plays, and poetry, even though my students are semi-literate, even Steinbeck's *Of Mice and Men* is too difficult for them, listless in their dyadic worlds, depending on me to help them graduate with a grade twelve diploma clutched in their hands, that says they have received an education equal to that of their Hearing peers.

సౌ

"Cochlear implants, who can argue with that?" I tell a teacher on our staff during our lunch break: "But very few people know about the cochlear implants that have failed or the kids who are implanted but need sign language anyway, there's no backup plan, no alternatives, sign language is not presented as an option." I pause: "And they can't read very well."

But she says: "They're not that much different than their classmates who are not reading either."

Before I can protest that *it's not the same,* my colleague nods politely and waves briefly to me as we part in the long, wide hallway. I return to Sophie, who is quietly reading at her desk.

I break the silence with: "I'm tired of not being able to use my professional training, knowledge and experience with these kids. By the time they come to me from elementary school, I can't do much. The damage is done."

Sophie signs: "Joanne, we can only do what we can. We have no control over anything."

Not mollified: "But even if we were to espouse the oral route entirely, these students still have terrible speech, there's hardly any speech therapy available at the high school level, and they aren't reading enough. How can anyone say that this program is working?"

Sophie looks up. She signs, stone-faced: "It's audism. The Hearing want the deaf to be like them. They are prejudiced against people who can't talk like them."

But I'm not finished. I must rant again like I've ranted every day since I arrived in this room: "But it is not only about sign language. It's that we are a low incidence population. Nobody cares about a handful of deaf kids who can't function well in the hearing world. No one gives a shit."

Sophie shrugs into: "The parents of those deaf kids think their kids are doing fine. And that's all that matters. If they're happy, then we're doing our job."

I slump angrily into my chair. Sophie's sarcasm only succeeds in making my gorge rise again, and I sign: "It's a matter of perception. The deaf kids who can't live up to the oral promises are stranded in their home communities, maybe live in their parents' basement for the rest of their lives. They deserve just as much of a life as anyone else."

Sophie sighs: "Joanne, you're getting too tired and frustrated. Find something else to do."

I sign: "No one is going to do anything for a few kids scattered all over the province. Even those deaf kids will say they're doing fine. Wouldn't you say you were doing just fine if you had someone taking care of you all the time?"

Sophie says: " . . . "

I finally drop my hands into my lap and sit at my desk.

I feel a tightness in my chest these days, as if I'm locked in a garbage compressor. Plastic bottles, tin cans, and cardboard boxes pop, crackle, and explode in my ears as the walls come closer together, then the grinding, crushing, and whirring closes in on me. The tinnitus is becoming more and more deafening. I think: *I have to deal with this. I have to be able to solve problems and teach my students to solve problems if we are to get anywhere. I* remind myself: *If I am to get anywhere.*

～

A Classroom Drama:

JW: "Now we have to learn to take control of the conversation. Not let it control us. You see?"

MELISSA: "But . . ."

JW: "You just sit there and let it go on and on without you. Interrupt for God's sake, make a comment, ask a question, and the focus is back on you. Go ahead, you try it."

MELISSA: "I can't slide in that fast. I have to be sure of what I think is going on." (*Melissa twists in her chair, motioning at the door*) "The bell just rang."

JW: "Yeah, I know." (*Aside to Sophie*) "It's hard to believe there's a heaven if you've never seen it." (*JW waits until she hears the click of the doorknob, satisfied that Melissa has closed the door behind her, and has merged into the stream of Hearing kids rushing headlong to their classes. She is no longer JW*).

JOANNE: "Who am I kidding, thinking that I can teach Melissa to politely interrupt a conversation with a group of Hearing people who don't know sign, and request that they focus on her?"

SOPHIE: "It's called assertiveness. Many Hearing teachers of the deaf seem to think it's the answer to deafness."

JOANNE: " . . . "

Sophie shrugs.

⟩⟩

Murray is reading *Grimm's Fairy Tales*. His grey whiskers shine in the lamp over our bed, and he swallows in concentration. I can't resist any longer.

I say: "Murray, why are you reading those?"

He looks over the top of his reading glasses. He says: "They're interesting."

Later that week, I tell my students, two of them teenage boys, that my husband, now in his *fifties*, is reading fairy tales. They just stare at me, uncomprehending. I tell Gillian, our school librarian the same thing.

She says: "You and your husband must have a lot in common."

             sa.

Billy chokes out his words, mentally preparing himself to include every vowel and consonant, speaking in grammatically correct English, at a very slow pace, because he tries to form the words in his head first before pushing them out of his mouth, he is like a stutterer without a stutter, he is deafer than I am and his cochlear implant, that he's had since age two, doesn't help him that much. He has spent his allowance on his dreadlocks, hoping that they'll fetch a friend for him.

I beckon Billy to come over to my desk. He shuffles up, his hands encased in the folds of his sleeves.

I say: "Here's a pencil. I want you to break it for me."

Bob Marley Wannabe clarifies: "You want me to break the pencil?"

I affirm: "Yes."

As he takes the pencil into his hands, I rise from my chair with a roll of masking tape in my hand and walk to the other end of the room where the pencil sharpener is. I put long strips of tape in an X-formation over it and turn to Billy, taking care to enunciate carefully to him.

I say: "The pencil sharpener is broken. You have to take one half of the broken pencil and find a way to sharpen it without using the sharpener. If you need any tools, you may ask me."

I return to my desk, and stare straight into my stack of papers, because I do not want to see this pitiful creature struggle. Sophie shushes up the other students who are eager to offer him their solutions. Out of the corner of my eye, I watch Billy sit at the table, holding the broken pencil.

Billy sees another pencil on the table and picks it up. He asks: "Ms. Weber, can I use this pencil instead?"

I answer: "No, you can only use the broken pencil."

I notice only a finger and a thumb protruding from the mass of cloth bunched at the end of his hands as he turns the broken pencil over and over. I put my finger to my lips and warn the other students: *Do not help him.* They bend their heads over their own books and papers, but they are watching. Finally Billy stands up and walks around the room. He sees another pencil sitting on the file cabinet.

Billy Marley Wannabe asks: "Ms. Weber, how about this pencil?" He swallows nervously.

I answer: "No, you need to figure out how to sharpen the pencil I gave you."

His lips tighten in anger as he turns away from me. His blond dreadlocks begin to shake silently. I look down at my desk, now unable to concentrate on what I'm doing. I casually move papers around on my desk to create a semblance of order. Other students are peeking at him out of the corners of their eyes.

Finally, Billy walks up to the jar where I've jammed a pair of scissors with several markers. He opens the blades and begins to scrape. He comes to me, holding out the pencil whose stump barely reveals the lead. I look up at the tall fifteen-year-old boy and smile.

He writes in his notebook: *This is the hardest problem I have ever solved in my life.*

I find myself staring out into the silent courtyard often these days. I don't like this enclosed space, I decide, so I pick a fight upon returning home to Murray.

JOANNE PROBLEM SOLVER: "You're monopolizing the girls. I don't have that connection I had with them before we moved to Regina."

MURRAY PROBLEM FREE: "I'm not your enemy, Joanne. This is not about you or your deafness. Anna and Paula are teenagers and they don't think much of anybody right now."

JOANNE SNORTING BULL: (*Shaking her head*) "It's not that simple, Murray. They do find it easier to communicate with you."

MURRAY MATADOR: "Well, should I then poke pencils through my eardrums? At least you have a very good excuse for being angry all the time. I can't blame any of my foibles upon anyone but myself." He chuckles as he squeezes my hand.

I remain silent, unsure.

I think: *There has to be a way to correct this ecological imbalance, where communication between the Deaf and Hearing is a series of misses, near misses and occasional connections*, as I flip through the pages of the picture books I've collected for my Jungian retelling of fairy tales to my deaf students. They will just not read for enjoyment, and they can't extract the main idea from a textbook. Yet. I ask: "How many of you have books at home, bookshelves with books at least?"

They all shake their heads.

So I ask: "Do you remember being read to as a child?"

Again, no.

I ask: "Do your parents read?"

They shake their heads again.

I grasp at straws: "How about newspapers?"

One student raises her hand.

So I'm reading *Little Red Riding Hood* illustrated by Beni Montresor, now long out of print, to my grade nine and grade twelve students, and showing them the pictures — this is a most disturbing picture book. I ask my students: "What do you see in the picture of the Wolf, dapper in a suit and a top hat lurking behind a tree, leering at Little Red Riding Hood?"

Billy enunciates the word, "pedophile" very carefully.

I think: *What the hell? Sexual abuse? Has this kid endured sexual abuse?*

I become even bolder and jab a finger at the illustration of the wolf's stomach in which Little Red Riding, swallowed whole, floats in bliss. I ask the class: "She's being swallowed up and looks pretty happy about it, doesn't she? What does this picture remind you of?"

Melissa says: "Too much alcohol?"

I want to add: *Yes, and being swallowed up by the demands of the Hearing world.*

Instead, I listen carefully to what they say. They say: "Drugs make me feel like that," and "When I'm drunk, my head spins and I lie down just like that," and Casey: "I don't think about the sex when it happens."

I think: *Dissociation occasioned by drugs, alcohol, and sexual abuse. Their knowledge is deep in their eyes. No wonder they can't even think about the Hearing world swallowing them up, demanding that they live in a zombie state, always controlled by Hearing people. They have issues that are even more pressing than deafness.* I turn the pages even more slowly. I think: *These students don't even have fairy tales or myths embedded into their consciousness because they can't, won't, don't read, and their parents never read to them when they were young, yet they seem to readily grasp the metaphors in these* pictures. *The images unlock something in them perhaps for the first time.*

✥

I ask: "Billy, do you have your math homework done?" His blond dreadlocks jammed under his hat give him a slightly angelic look.

He answers, sort of: "I don't have a pencil."

I grin, thinking: *He knows enough not to borrow anything from me by now, having lost all my pencils that I lent to him, having gone through three sets of school supplies, and it's only March. He relies on the goodwill of his classmates, continually borrowing their pencils and erasers and, of course, losing them as well.* I say: "Billy, I'll lend a pencil to you if you can give me a guarantee that I can keep while you're using it. What about your hat?"

Billy vigorously shakes his head: "No."

I try again. "Have you got any change?"

He shakes his head again. "No."

Again: "What about a shoe? You can get it back when the bell rings."

He shakes his head again. His eyes become darker.

Again: "Well, then you think of something." I return back to my papers on my desk.

A few minutes later, he returns to my desk, holding out a math textbook in his hands. He asks: "Would you accept this?"

I admonish: "No, Billy, that textbook is mine. If you don't give me the pencil back, you've got nothing to lose. The exchange has to include something personal, something of importance to you so that you will take care of my pencil and return it to me."

His eyes darken even more, and he walks away. Out of the corner of my eye, I watch him take off his shoes and place them by my desk. His voice breaks as he struggles to form the words properly: "Ms. Weber, I need the pencil." He sits in a chair, with the pencil in his hand, and begins to weep.

I say: " . . . "

The other students glance at him. They walk quietly around him. I motion to Sophie to leave him be. He continues to shake and weep with anger in his chair.

Then he throws the pencil across my desk and slips his feet into his shoes. When the bell rings, he comes to stand by me.

He asks: "Is my face okay?"

I ask: "Are *you* okay?"

He says: "I was very angry because you should never take anything personal away from anyone. It's wrong."

I explain: "It's a way to teach you to value your own things, and to value other people's things. When you borrow something from others, you need to return it."

He says, his nostrils slightly flaring: "It's wrong to take personal things away from me."

I think: *Why didn't you negotiate?*

But I know the answer: *negotiation requires too much talking and he's too used to people solving his problems for him. It's easier for him to get what he wants without entering into an exchange of any kind.*

Fourteen

I TRUDGE TO THE BASEMENT, WHERE various boxes stand piled high in the storage room. The air is close in that room. We haven't opened the windows since we've moved in two years ago. I pull at the box of photographs and lug it back upstairs.

Anna and Paula giggle over our first family photograph taken at Walmart, a rushed sitting during Christmas season. Murray has just had a haircut, and I look like a middle aged matron with no-nonsense, closely-cropped hair. Anna and Paula, young, fashion conscious, and wearing makeup, are the most pleasing people in the photograph. Otherwise the picture is painful to look at.

Anna points out: "Mom, it's not that bad. At least it's only from our waists up."

I ask, suddenly suspicious: "What do you mean by that?"

Anna recovers: "Well, you know, Mom, that you look fine from the waist up but from the bottom down . . . well . . . "

I demand: "Well?"

Paula giggles: "You've got such a big bum and hips."

Anna adds: "You should always wear dark colours on your bottom. Forget those brightly coloured skirts you like to wear."

I ask: "How do you know all this?"

Anna shrugs: "I just look at my own body, and at what other people wear. I think about the cut of clothing and how it flatters my body."

I am about to say: *You're a teenager!* But I stop myself.

Paula asks: "Are we hanging that family photo up anywhere?"

I snap: "Of course not."

I think: *What else am I not seeing?*

What I don't see, I've seen already. I realize: I must grow into my own story. In the meantime, I patch my way with bits and pieces of other stories, waiting for it all to coalesce, gather inside my Deaf body. I look at my hands. *I've always been here.* But others don't want my story. I don't want it either. *Not yet.*

I am three years old. It is summer. We are at Minot State College, where my parents are taking classes in deaf education and I am going to the Language Nursery School. *I am walking across dry grass, its blades are needles prickling the soles of my feet, my father is studying in the big chair far away from the house near a group of trees, it is dry and hot and I have no shirt on, just panties and my leopard print blanket, my mother is in the big house, on the first floor in the house of many rooms, the house where something bad lives on the top floor, mama cooks and reads in that house, and writes on paper every night, my father comes in too and spreads his papers on the big table, we only stay in the bedrooms off the kitchen, sometimes I roam in the living room, but I don't do that anymore because something bad lives up on the top floor of the house, I know because one day I go up many stairs, up to one floor, and then up to the next floor, and finally I walk down a long hallway with doors on either side, my blanket licking my heels as I drag it behind me, and the window at the end of the hall*

is bright, beckoning me, even though I have just been outside playing with my gun and cowboy hat. I take few more steps and there is a box to my right high up on the wall, something is thrusting out of the box, like a tongue out of a twisted face, the box has wavy curls about its face and a trapdoor for its mouth, I turn and run, my blanket flying in midair behind me, that night, my father has to spank me so I will stop screaming and go to sleep, finally I lay quietly in my bed, half asleep, thinking of the face that lives upstairs, the face that has a tongue that sticks in and out, the tongue that is like mine, which is supposed to move around in my mouth in the right places, to stick in and out at the right time, and it will follow me all the days of my life because somehow I have done something wrong because I went upstairs, to places I should not go.

Last summer, Murray and I and our daughters stopped in Trois-Rivières in Quebec and entered a museum featuring an exhibit on the ogre that ate children. Outside the exhibit were child sized capes hanging on a row of hooks. A sign nearby invited us to don a cape and enter at our own risk, into the home of the ogre who, according to a television reporter on a television set right outside the exhibit, was responsible for the disappearances of many local children. The pictures of the missing children were posted outside the entrance to the exhibit.

Anna, Paula, and I walked past the rack of cloaks to the doorway where we must part the hanging vines to step into the ogre's home. I looked behind me and saw that Murray had the cape on, hood drawn over his curls. The length of the cape only reached his lower chest, since he was six feet tall. He looked like a hobbit.

As I walked over the threshold of the exhibit, into the ogre's mouth, the terror of Hansel and Gretel descended upon me, in the form of a sickening, familiar claustrophobia. As a child, I had begged my mother to put away the picture book whose cover featured an old woman with an evil grin towering over two hapless, rosy-cheeked children. The boughs of the trees in the dark forest around them seemed to reach out for the children, shielding yet obscuring them from the rest of humanity who could save them. My mother urged me to take a rational approach.

"Joanne, these fairy tales are not real. They're just stories." Nevertheless, I begged her to put the book away up high above the kitchen cabinets. That book vibrated with a power that I could not understand, tectonic plates shifted within me every time I saw the cover of that book. This was the one book I could not abide in my growing preschool library collection. Boomy noises accompanied me through the innards of the ogre's house where I saw what he had devoured for lunch. Were they the sounds of his stomach gurgling, I wondered, or someone just talking through a microphone? I walked through the ogre's large, outstretched mouth and into a small octagonal room with mirrors on all sides. The mirrored door closed behind me and I saw myself everywhere. I searched for a handle on the pane that would let me out. There were no handles.

I began to sweat profusely. *The Phantom of the Opera.* The room of mirrors that nearly drove Christine's lover, Raoul, mad. Finally, I pushed on the mirrored panes. Suddenly a pane opened behind me and Murray stepped in with me, his cape still drawn over his head, grinning with a camera in his hand. The mirrored door closed behind him.

"I need to get out of here," I signed to Murray. "There's no way out."

"There's always a way out." He chuckled and took a picture of me in the room of mirrors. Together we found the one panel that pushed out into another looped path through the exhibit.

Now I am six. I am in Grade One. Every day I come down the stairs to our basement, the dark walls, the cold cement floors, the dusty boxes, the washing machine, and the stairs leading up to the kitchen, my father has left a small square of carpet underneath the stairs where I can crouch and fold my doll's clothes carefully. A small swing hangs from the rafters just beside the stairs. When I'm done folding my doll clothes, I sit on the swing, where my heels lightly tap the deep freeze before I lean backwards, trying to swim with my legs leading out into the small basement room lined with shelves storing suitcases, boxes, and canning jars. I think: *Basements are not good places.* One day, I notice a light, a small light that bounces off the ceiling as I swing toward it, I twist my head around to look at it, the light is not coming from the sole light bulb screwed into the socket in the centre of the room, I leap off the swing, and the bones in my feet shiver as I scramble up the stairs as fast as I can, I am screaming, trying to tell my mother, there is someone down there with a light, someone trying to find out where I am.

I sob: "Lik . . . lik . . . lik . . . "

My mother's puzzled face bends over me, her arm around me, trying to console me.

I think: *Perhaps it is someone who doesn't like me and is shining a light to search me out.*

My mother firmly grips my hand and pulls me down the stairs. I cling to her legs as she walks up to the deep freeze. She points to the window over it. I look closely at the small basement window, masked in grey dust, my mother's finger traces the path from the window to the light that has settled on the wall opposite the window, sitting, waiting, silent. I see her mouth moving, she is trying to tell me that the light is coming from the outside, this small circle that is gold, purple, blue, pink, is coming from something beyond the window. I want to say, "But how can it have so many colours?" but all I can repeat is: "Lik . . . lik . . . lik." At least, I am no longer screaming.

I never play in the basement again, because it is a bad place where things I don't understand are hiding and waiting to get me because I've done something wrong. I'm sure I've done something, although I don't know what it is.

⋙

At the end of my third year of university, I wrote poem after poem every night, inserting nursery rhymes, fairy tale characters, and theological imagery anywhere I could. I wanted to be mysterious, indecipherable, hiding under a façade like Dame Edith Sitwell, wearing heavy velvets and silks, and I briefly considered wearing a turban. I hadn't worn jeans since my first year. Instead, I migrated to bohemian clothing, the world of long skirts, socks, blazers, and scarves. I was in love with anything that was different than what my sisters wore — those pink tracksuits, those white Reebok runners. In my mind, I had left the prosaic world behind. Instead, I was most preoccupied with developing an identity that established me as incomparable. I would be in a class of my own. This aggravated my mother greatly, I knew, but Dorene was most encouraging. My parents wouldn't think of me taking a year off after earning a Bachelor of Arts degree. I had it all worked out in my head: *I was going to find a job somewhere. Work, maybe travel.* My mother looked at me as if I was cracked to form such a notion.

She asked: "How do you think you're going to get a job with no skills?"

I answered: "I'll get something. Lots of people take time off from university."

She asked: "You can't afford to do that. You must get some training to get a job." She added rather darkly: "You don't know how things are going to go for you in the job market."

I told her: "I want to teach. I want to change the world by encouraging students to break out and be themselves."

My mother and father, both teachers, shook their heads: "Impossible. You won't be able to hear well enough to manage a classroom."

Mom added: "Besides . . . " And silently looked up and down at my clothes.

Finally we settled on librarianship. Grudgingly. I could understand the reasons. Libraries were quiet places. Communication would be a lot easier.

My mother: "One to one." She pointed out: "You don't have to deal with a lot of people."

Quickly: "But I don't want to hide in a library. I can't see myself working in a library. Shelving books, signing out books, a spinster with a home cluttered with poems and a cat."

And to myself, although I dared not admit it to anyone: *I wanted to be noticed. I wanted a following, of some sort. I wanted to be a writer, a passionate artist who would confound everyone with words whose meanings flashed like fireflies in the dark.*

But I saw the worry in my mother's eyes and entered the University of Alberta that fall in the library science graduate program. My mother gave me a briefcase for my birthday in October. I sent it back. I was still walking with Dylan Thomas in the October wind whose frosty fingers punished my hair, and I certainly did *not* want to carry a briefcase that the wind would slap against my hip.

The students enrolled in the library science graduate program seemed to be exactly the people I wanted to avoid. There were too many: briefcases, pens tucked in pockets, pleated pants, pinstriped shirts. They talked about: modems, computers, databases, information retrieval, and cataloguing. I sat in the classes, unable to comprehend: any of it. The textbooks were: unspeakably dull and uninspiring. The only class I looked forward to was Children's Literature. I could explore Hans Christian Anderson's fairy tales. Catriona de Scossa, a refined looking woman taught me History of the Book, another class I attended eagerly because I had found textbooks featuring photographic plates of illuminated manuscripts, tracing my fingers over the swirls on shiny pages. I discovered Marshall McLuhan. Otherwise, I sat in a river of voices, bubbling, rushing, racing past my nothingness. At least in English literature at the University of Saskatchewan, I read and reread literary texts while the professors lectured. In library science, deciphering a cataloguing problem involved input from the entire class. Words swirled about my head. We all crowded around one computer, while a professor typed in commands and explained what to do. I stared at the back of his head. I thought: *Precise details, concrete facts, procedures, stray bits of pertinent data quadruples in the classroom and the assignments.* I took refuge in Children's and Adolescent Literature, History of the Book, and Storytelling. Anything where there was a reasonable chance I could bullshit my way through. Yet I kept scoring "A"s and "B"s in all my classes, not only the ones that I felt reasonably competent in. Instead of feeling pleasure in my achievements, I became increasingly anguished at receiving "A" after "A". I thought: *There has to be a mistake. How could I earn a graduate degree without the faintest idea of what is going on?* I scolded myself: *You're simply adept at hiding how little you know and hear. As if reading fairy tales provided you with all the knowledge you needed. You're trapped in your daily nothingness, sallying forth to class, saying as little as possible. You are an imposter.*

I could see that my professors were kind, so the problem had to be within myself, I had fooled them somehow. Desperate, I began attending Mass every day at St. Joseph's College. It had a sparse chapel, with no pews except along the sides. The open green-carpeted expanse before the altar invited people to sit cross legged on the floor. It was always packed on Sundays. I sat on the floor with others, seeking meaning in this otherwise meaningless existence. Somehow, I was noticed without having to say a word, or engaging in any word play in order to convince anyone of my intelligence but by merely sitting in a chapel, oblivious to sermons, having to rouse myself out of my reveries in order to kneel, stand, and move my hands according to ritual practices.

I sit moodily in a coffee shop, pen poised over my journal. Why didn't I teach Anna and Paula to sign? I sign all the time now, despite the pain in my wrists. I do it for my students, why didn't I do it for my daughters? I shake my head. I know why. I don't want them to become CODAS, to interpret for me, to struggle with doctors, lawyers, police, and insurance people. I am proud enough of what I already know. I don't need their help. And I wanted to spare them the CODA guilt that would surely descend upon them when they became young women. The guilt of taking advantage of my deafness to escape the house without me hearing the door close, making secret plans, mumbling into the telephone, meeting people I disapproved of, laying with boys in some field or car. I shake my head. Such magical thinking.

I worry about Anna the most. I am her Demeter, she is my Persephone. Somehow, she has been taken away from me by my deafness, the Lord Hades. I know it in her eyes, in her silence, in her refusal to talk. Deafness has tucked her into an underworld of bewildering voices too old for her to understand. I argue with myself: *How can she be a CODA if she doesn't sign well?* Easily. She phones. I don't answer because I don't hear her. I am not at home where she needs me because I am too busy proving my worth to others.

Hades comforts her, coaxes her into crouching alone by an underwater lake, its sulphurous fumes feeding her anger.

∽

Mark interrupted me while I was reading a newspaper in St. Joseph's lounge after mass. He was a large man, muscular, athletic, with thinning hair on top, but with a kind face. He was quite nervous as he asked me where I was from, what program I was in. It turned out that he was taking theology and philosophy, similar to the classes I took at the University of Saskatchewan.

He came to my dorm room for early morning jogs. I became sick with love. We lengthened our walks around the campus. We hid in empty corridors and college classrooms, holding hands and kissing. He broke away from me suddenly when someone came into the classroom or around the corner. Soon we were hiding in his room, in my room. We no longer went out anywhere. We sat at separate tables in the library. But whenever we could find an empty classroom, a lone corridor, or an abandoned stairwell, we were groping like starved children.

I dwelled: *Why this new need for secrecy? Is he ashamed of me? Is it because I'm deaf? Am I too wild looking? Too bohemian? He did ask me if I was comfortable in my low flat shoes and the thick socks that I wore with my skirts. That was a hint, wasn't it? He doesn't like my clothes.*

I began to struggle into the tight jeans discarded by my younger sister. Still fascinated with colours, I bought red, gold, and cornflower-blue jeans. I even got a jean jacket. I reminded myself: *It's the eighties. The bohemian look is out.*

But the secrecy continued.

I wrote poems, sick with longing. Between the stacks at the college library, I began to read books on marriage, sexuality, the history of married saints, and monasticism. I read Thomas Merton, Jean Cocteau, Baudelaire, and Balzac. The history of Heloise and Abelard had me weeping. I thought: *Is Mark not driving me into a cloister with this secret love to be buried under the guise of celibacy? Is my life to be spent in hiding?*

When Mark pretended that I was nothing to him, as he walked casually past me in the hallways of St. Joseph's College, I rebelled against his rule of secrecy and donned my bohemian clothes again — my nun's habit. I thought: *I don't care what anyone sees in me. I don't care what anyone thinks. My bohemian clothes ensure that no man will approach me. They will even protect me from Mark.*

Yet, when I felt Mark watching me, I struggled into the tight jeans, but when he turned away from me for days at a time, I pulled on my skirts, socks and shoes, because wearing those jeans put me in a class of women trying to attract men with tight clothes and sculpted bodies, secretive women, as if I was trying to help him to peel off those jeans with his imagination in order to lure him past the heavy hearing aid that sat on my left ear.

This schizophrenic existence continued for four years. While Mark earned a degree in philosophy and theology, I struggled to finish my library science classes and began to take upper year English classes at the University of Alberta, studying the novels of Thomas Hardy, the poetry of Dylan Thomas and G.M. Hopkins. An elderly lady in one of those classes, Madeleine, invited me to her home in an apartment across the High Level Bridge for tea, a rare moment of peace in her sunlit living room in quiet conversation about books and writers. I walked slowly back over the bridge during rush hour traffic, with my hearing aid shut off to block out traffic sounds. I thought: *How weary I am chasing a man who essentially doesn't want me.* I thought: *Something is dreadfully wrong with me. Something went wrong a long time ago.* I thought: *The little girl in a red coat.* I resolved: *Enough hiding. Enough of Mark's secrets that I am not privy to. Hiding under the cover of darkness, in the middle of the night, at St. Joseph's College, in corners, empty classrooms, his residence bedroom, and the auditorium in the basement has to come to an end.*

No wonder I didn't like basements.

✍

Our staff interpreter Lisa's eyebrows are high on her face: "Isn't Nolan going to the pep rally?" Her voice hits the exact note of innocence. Even I can detect it. "Shall I interpret for him on Thursday?"

It is not an innocent question. I think: *Nolan is eighteen years old, over six feet tall, built like a football player, and doesn't have a friend in the school.* He misses school on the pep rally days. He misses the days before and after the pep rally, too. At this pep rally, all the students will sit as usual in a darkened gym peering over top of each other's heads to view the antics going on at the front of the gym. The program will be augmented by strobe lights, screams from the audience, and candy flung out over the heads of the students. This time, though, Lisa will be ready, with the pep rally program propped on a music stand, to interpret for Nolan, the only deaf student in a high school of nine hundred people (Melissa has to go to a doctor's appointment). And: *Lisa will stand at the front in full view of everyone, a tidy aside from the wild antics on the stage, and Nolan will be made to sit with the grade nines, corralled into the front of the gym.*

Catherine sees my hesitancy. She shakes her head and says: "Nolan should go, he should be part of the school. He should not hide in this classroom, away from everyone else." She adds: "Nolan has to do what the other students do. There shouldn't be any special rules for him."

I say: "He'll just stay home." I think: *Dear God, when to hide, and when not to hide? I think: If I had an answer for that question, perhaps Lisa wouldn't be so uneasy.*

Lisa gives her opinion: "Well, too bad for him. He doesn't value his education enough to come to school. He's just hiding from everyone. Just think, he could've graduated last year if he didn't play such games."

I say: "It wouldn't be so bad, if there was someone to go with him."

Catherine volunteers this: "I'll sit with him." Her dyed hair seems unnaturally bright at the moment.

I think: *Did she get a new dye job or have I just seen her in a new light?* Her eyes are dark. Worn with care.

I say: "I think he won't like that."

Lisa remarks: "He is so spoiled. So overindulged. He'll just manipulate people into bending rules for him just because he's deaf. He needs to learn to be a part of things instead of creating his own world to suit himself."

I say: " . . . (Sigh) . . . " I think: *Lisa's right. Nolan's parents have parked him in front of the TV set ever since he was a toddler. Now, he plays for hours on his Xbox in his bedroom alone and watches every new movie released in the year. He has no friends in this school because no one his age signs, and he does no homework, so he's jeopardizing his chances of earning enough credits to graduate.*

In her lined face, Lisa's wisdom flashes out at me, like a jolt of electricity. Then I realize: *This is what she is so upset about, this business of integrating deaf into the Hearing world. If the deaf remain sequestered, apart from the Hearing, how are they to be integrated? They must be pushed against their most natural inclinations, which is to be with their own kind or to be alone. Yet, sitting with an elderly woman in a darkened gym full of screaming teenagers or remaining in my classroom to work on Hamlet is really no choice at all.* I retort sharply:

"Entering a room of meaninglessness, even with an interpreter at your side, reduced to the role of a passive spectator. Would you choose it?"

Lisa's voice is just as strident as she says: "If I wanted to be a part of things, yes." She adds: "He'll be just as alone if he stays in the room with you."

I think: *Working quietly in my room, alone. None of these choices is acceptable.* I look steadily at Lisa. I sign: "No. Nolan will be allowed to choose. He is old enough."

Lisa signs back: "What about Melissa? She won't want to go if Nolan hides in the room during every pep rally."

I sign: "Melissa needs to go. She hasn't gone to a pep rally yet, since she's in grade nine and she needs to figure out how she can participate in a pep rally with other hearing students."

Lisa signs: "So now you are making rules for one person and not the other?"

I answer with: "Yes, I am. A deaf person must have as many choices as possible. But they must know what it is that they are choosing. Nolan is old enough to know."

I brush chalk dust off my sleeve and walk back to my desk. I know that inconsistency is my Achilles heel as I gauge each situation as it develops. Yet my intuition has created a labyrinth for Lisa to stumble around in. I cannot provide her with a clear set of guidelines.

↘

In early May, Lisa takes me into the corner of the staff room and signs in small crabbed signs: "I've decided to resign and to look for work elsewhere."

I study the diminutive woman before me: toothpick slim and topped with a meringue of moussed and sprayed blonde hair. A sadness comes over me: *I've failed to connect with her, to reassure her of her valuable contributions to this program, to laud her for her years of commitment to educational interpreting, and to praise her own dedicated work with our students. I've been too angry about how she skulked around the classroom, I only saw her guerrilla potshots at me as a frantic protest from a monstrous ego, after all, she wanted to be the authoritative interpreter relying on the mystique of being the mother who knew fully about deafness and being the only person who could sign in the school so the Hearing professionals around her would leave well enough alone, assuming that she knew everything there was to know about deaf education, even though she possessed only a grade twelve education, now I've come along, a Deaf teacher, fluent in American Sign Language, and she's no longer the revered authority, we could have made a great team if it weren't for our egos.* I think, bitterly: *With my need to prove myself as an authority on deaf education and her years of competent Signed English and as a mother of a successful deaf adult, we can't coexist in the same room.* I say:

"Well, best wishes for your future." I walk away.

Later, I'm confused at my own abruptness. I have no apologies, no words of regret, not even any words of kindness or appreciation for Lisa, and despite my failure to connect with her, my heart cannot help but swell in jubilation and relief. I see things she doesn't see.

Later, that week, another pep rally is scheduled. Lisa walks around in a tense silence, saying nothing when Nolan stays in my room. Another memory is throbbing in my veins, fractured by the pep rally's strobe lights, coloured lights roaming over gyrating bodies, and the thumping of the music, even though my hearing aid is turned off: *Every high school dance I attended, was the same. The same thumps, lights, and gyrating bodies. My spirit lifted high above the throbbing crowd and I was bewildered by the strangeness of the flashing lights and people moving in unison. I melted into the darkness along the walls of the huge gymnasium. But where else could I go?*

I awaken early the next morning and look out on the green lawn. At least fifty blackbirds have flown in some time before dawn and are now sitting quietly on the grass. I move closer to the window. A bird senses my movement and twitches her head, alerting the others. In a crazy moment, I see: *The blackbird is Lisa.* Quickly the bird and her companions gather themselves into a spiral and fly away from me.

Fifteen

THE PEAR ORCHARD SITS IN MY hand, after I've lifted it out from the box of books dropped off by Paul, the editor from Hagios Press. There it is, in my hands, its cover featuring two pears nestled together inside a twig bent into a circle. Finally, after twenty years of writing. Poems about leaning towards the love of Hearing men and then running away. *But it is more than that, I tell myself, there is always singing in my head and there shouldn't be, because sound is muffled to me, but in my head, there is a singing bird. All day long.* I turn phrases over in my head, wearing them to smooth melodies, stones that fit the palms of my hands. It is a small wonder that I've always wanted to sing but I obeyed my father who cautioned me not to sing loudly in a choir because I'm tone deaf. Yet somehow, I could catch music and fit it to the songs inside my head. At age ten, standing in the midst of an elementary school choir, I sang inwardly to a melancholy ballad that was reverberating all about me: *my wife was bare naked, bare naked as can be.* Those lyrics sounded better to me than the ones on the sheet music before me. And: *The poor man in my head, something had gone wrong between him and his wife.* Another strange ditty came to my consciousness as I stepped over the threshold to womanhood, a moment of ecstatic joy: *I looked down and saw I was golden with sunflower petals for a crown/mercies on me were high in loading, nay no longer could I weep to drown.*

Will Hearing people be able to hear the music in this book of my poems, *The Pear Orchard?* Instead of always being asked if I could hear their music, if I could enjoy music just like they do, will anyone be able to hear what I hear?

"Go litel book," as Chaucer would say, make your way in the Hearing world.

Jan was a physics major, an immigrant from Holland, working toward a graduate degree, but taking English classes to improve his English. I thought nothing of his attempts to converse with me or his insistence on walking with me to Lister Hall at the University of Alberta where we occupied rooms. I nodded my head frequently to his thick, guttural noises, and in my absent-mindedness, said "yeah" on several occasions.

After finishing part of the master's degree in library science, I moved back to Saskatchewan to room with Dorene. Jan wrote me a letter and charged me with tormenting him like Sue Brideshead in Hardy's *Jude the Obscure.* After the initial shock, my interest was piqued.

I thought: *He actually liked my bohemian clothes, my love of literature, and my intelligence, but he was furious with me for having said "yes" to his invitation to meet him for coffee, or to go to a movie with him and then standing him up several times, my heart must be cold and callous, I'd toyed with him especially when we were meant to be together, and would I just please admit that I loved him too.* I examined each angle of his copious letters. I exclaimed with pleasure over the flowers he sent me, and the cookies from Holland, where he was visiting his parents for the summer. His passion in his letters, his intense interest in the books I read, his appreciation of every small thing I wrote or said made me think: *perhaps a love affair based on written communication was possible.* But when I was *with* him, the guttural vowels of his thick Dutch accent poured over me like sodden lumps of gravy. Lipreading him was exhausting, because he didn't move his mouth in a natural way. I was used to the tongue being in certain places, the lips flattening and pursing, the mouth opening and closing in expected rhythms. His didn't. Yet in his words on paper, the music came through in his lamentations over my not returning his love. He told me of his sacrifices for me, how he had forgone dental surgery to buy me flowers instead. My response was " . . . " He wrote me of his sickness, of his love for me, *"this is happening to me, Jan, Jan Van Alst,"* and I was struck with the ringing of his name, the particularity of his being, this cry from his heart echoed in my head nearly all the time when I read his letters. It seemed preposterous to turn away a man truly in love with me only because lipreading him was exhausting, yet I decided: *I will not discuss this issue, my inability to easily comprehend his speech with him. Never.*

Jan wrote me his last letter, declaring that he could no longer contact me, as he was too tormented with the idea of not being able to hold me.

Sadly I filed his letter away in an envelope with these words written on the outside, *Jan, Jan Van Alst.*

❧

Sunday morning. We are going to church. Anna is driving. It is February. Langley Hall sits sullenly on the street, with snow skirted against her walls. The forked tree, with its three branches reaches to the sky in despair at this impossible cold. Anna is careful on the icy ridges in these streets. The radio is loud. I'm curious. A drama begins:

DEAF MOTHER: "What are you listening to?"

ANNA: "Oooshhsiii."

Anna turns the corner, the steering wheel slides through her hands, my mind is spinning, whirring like an iPod wheel with possible names of bands, trying to find a match for what she's just said. I think: *Perhaps if I just think about it, the word will come to me, that way I'll not have to ask her to repeat it.* Anna grasps my chin and pushes it away from her toward the windshield.

ANNA (*Shouts*): "Don't look at me like that!"

I lean my head against the passenger window and try to hold back the tears. I can't bring myself to leave the car once Anna has parked it in front of the church.

DEAF MOTHER: "You go on ahead. I just need a few minutes here."

ANNA: (*Her face stricken as she hands me the keys*) "I'm sorry, Mom."

DEAF MOTHER: "It's all right. I'll be right along."

Instead, I drive home to tell Murray what I always tell him: "I don't want to live here anymore, I don't want to live in a Hearing family, I don't want to go through years of meals at the table and not be able to follow a conversation, I don't want to be dismissed or scorned every time I ask a question they've answered hours ago but I've either not understood the first time, or have forgotten." And: "I want to leave, Murray, get my own place, have you guys come and visit, and when I've had enough, you all can go home. I can't do it, Murray. I just can't do this. Please respect that." The drama ends with:

MURRAY: "No, I will not respect that. We made a commitment to being married and we will work this out."

I slam the door on my way out of the house, armed with my laptop and swim bag. I think: *The only answer to this oppressive loneliness is to get out and get away from Murray and my daughters.*

I want to say: *I am not a pet, who must be told how to sit and move.*
I want to warn them. I am a dangerous animal. I say: "...!"

⚬

I sit in the Atlantis coffee shop on Victoria. Liz is coming. Murray's
words are reverberating in my head: *Yes, Anna corrects your speech*
and that's a power thing. Yes. They are too full of themselves. But for
goodness sakes, get more engaged with them. I think: *How?* I want
to scream: *HOW? When I can't be spontaneous, or play with them?*

I stare out at the flame lit in front of a restaurant across the
street, mesmerized by the way it licks the cold arctic wind. I wave
at Liz who comes through the door of the coffee shop, her face
reddened by the cold air.

Liz Warren is assigned by the Saskatchewan Deaf and Hard
of Hearing Services to provide sign language interpretations of
my poetry to Deaf and Hearing audiences. I've given her a copy
of *The Pear Orchard* so she can prepare for the poetry readings
throughout Saskatchewan. She is one of the best interpreters in
Canada, the daughter of two Deaf parents. Her first language is
British Sign Language even though she was born and raised in
Ireland. She can't remember much of it, having moved to Canada
as a young woman. She has a natural gift for sign language
interpreting; one of her prized qualities as an interpreter is the
ability to provide a translation in ASL with all the subtleties of
meaning of the English spoken by the Hearing person. For this
reason, she disappears when she is interpreting. After having used
many interpreters, I know that this ability is rare even among
children of Deaf parents who become professional interpreters
within the Deaf community.

In the coffee shop, we practice together. She signs while I read.
We stop to puzzle out ways in which the poems can be translated

into American Sign Language. It's no easy task. I've created a fox wife, Sylva, who in her human form is a Deaf woman. In Liz's hands, Sylva is alive and mirrors every thought I've ever had about being Deaf: the shame, the anger, rage, frustration, and fear of having to live with the Hearing. I watch Liz create a pear orchard with her hands, imitating the heaviness of fruit on a branch growing within her womb. Then she becomes Sylva, a Deaf woman, whose puzzlement and frustration appears on her face as she tries to grasp flashing lights from mirrors hanging from the branches of the trees. Sylva is unable to grasp speech in its entirety. Liz as Sylva makes me want to comfort her immediately, hold her in my arms, and say it is all right. Sylva gives birth, the labour pains causing her body to sway helplessly. With a tongue firmly embedded in Liz's check and a furtive look in her eye, Sylva becomes a fox-wife trying to navigate her way through a master-captive relationship with a Hearing man. Liz pulls up her hands as claws to her chest, in order to convey gathering chicken bones in her bed.

I wonder: *Who is this Deaf woman, Sylva, in Liz's hands? She is now someone I've never seen before, Liz's creation as much as mine. Somehow Liz is the Deaf woman in the pear orchard, not me.* I think: *But she is Hearing, not Deaf.*

∽

At supper, I am wary of Anna. *Should I just accept her perfunctory apology, although Murray urges me not to?* But I remember the stricken look in her eyes, and think: *Maybe she is sorry enough. Perhaps it's best that I be silent, accept her apology, although I want her to understand me, my deafness, and what it means to be a Deaf mother.*

That evening, I scurry alone through the exhaust of cars idling in front of Holy Rosary cathedral. I tell myself: *It's best that I be quiet for now. Let me think on these things further before speaking. Let me see if I need to speak at all. I am afraid. Of my anger, and the remorse afterwards, I mean. The vitriolic words I can hurl out and the remorse afterwards. Murray's: "You're so fierce, Joanne. Sometimes you can be so mean. How can you want to leave me and our children?" What is this thing that is so beastly and hateful within me? The capacity to destroy and discard relationships even though I am so alone. I've failed to connect with those whom I love. A misshapen creature lives in me. It mocks me: How do you think you can be close to anyone if you always push people away?*

But I am at Mass. I should not indulge in imaginary conversation. I stand with the rest of the congregation as the organ begins its drone. Then I hear "My Wild Irish Rose". I look furtively at my neighbour's hymnal. I read: "You are the voice of the living God". But the wild Irish rose song keeps playing in my head and I give up trying to follow along as the priest strides down the aisle during the recessional, I've never heard anyone sing it, but I've read it in song books, in novels, and once on a crinkled song sheet crackling against a bush after a late night campfire, and I keep hearing the phantom music as I step out into the dark street, lighted by the street lamps and headlights of cars leaving the cathedral. I hear a foot tapping and a young man singing in my head, "my wild Irish rose, the sweetest flower that grows."

Liz sits at the table in my classroom, sharing her lunch with Sophie and me as she tries out different sign glosses for *The Pear Orchard* reading coming up next week. The table is strewn with Liz's carefully prepared glosses. Liz pauses and mutters to herself with her hands while I try out possible combinations with my own. We are on the stage of ourselves:

LIZ: (*Suddenly looking up at me*) "How about this?" (*Signs*)
WOMAN FOX DEAF CRAVE HAND SIGN PRECIOUS.

DEAF POET: *Yes! Craving. Liz understands the hunger for communication.*

LIZ: "These poems are about my mother."

DEAF POET: "Your mother?"

LIZ: "Yes, she was an intelligent, easily frustrated woman who was not as content with being Deaf as my father was. She was well educated, a self taught reader, and tried to sign more in English than in BSL."

DEAF POET: "So, you had problems in your relationship with her?"

LIZ: "No. I was the baby. But my oldest sister had to take care of things and resented our mother's deafness. She refused to sign after she left home. I just loved signing and of course, as you see, I became an interpreter."

DEAF POET: "Your sister had to do things for your mom?"

LIZ: "Yes. Phone calls, messages, interpreting. Although my mother was very independent, there were just many things she couldn't do. I didn't have to do any of that for her, so she was just a mom to me."

DEAF POET MOM: "What about your sister?"

LIZ: "She was so angry for years. After she left home, she never interpreted for anyone and had no interest in Deaf culture or sign language. Deafness in our family became an off limits topic. But she never understood our parents' Deaf experience as simply another way to live, as "Deafhood". Instead, she saw our parents as disabled and just didn't want to talk about deafness and how that affected her while growing up."

DEAF POET MOM: "Are you saying that Deaf people shouldn't raise children on their own?"

LIZ: "Of course not. My parents had jobs and cared for us very well. There were things that they just couldn't do. Funny thing, it never bothered my father that he wasn't able to do everything that a Hearing person could. He was well liked, gregarious, and comfortable with who he was."

DEAF POET MOM: "But why was your mother having difficulty with her deafness?"

LIZ: "She was more Hearing in her thinking. She had much better English, read more, knew more of the Hearing world than my father. She was a Hearing woman trapped in a Deaf body."

DEAF POET MOM: "She was in both worlds. Or wanted to be."

LIZ: "Yes, and being Deaf and Hearing at the same time ripped her apart, I think."

I look at Liz's large blue eyes and her finely shaped nostrils, her full lips, and her long fingers as she shapes the signs before me. She sways from side to side as she signs, her fingerspelling slow and careful, her tempo even as she flashes her hands in a shower of images. Suddenly, I see Liz's mother, a Deaf woman long dead, a woman I've never met. And I hear in my head: "Oh, my wild Irish rose, the sweetest flower that grows."

Now I want to go to Ireland and Scotland. To the "thin spaces" marked by standing stones, Celtic prayers, and mythical beasts. Something I read long ago by Margot King but had forgotten, something to the effect of: The presence of Desert Fathers and Mothers in the deserts of Egypt, Syria, Israel and ancient Mesopotamia led to the development of Celtic Christianity. Perhaps this explains why there were more Irish monastics in comparison to other recluses in Europe. I think: *The "thin spaces" are places where the physical and spiritual interconnect, where there is a sense of timelessness, a profound sense of God. The Celtic saints often spoke of this thin space. Oh, I'm often in a thin space, with Jane Eyre and Mary of Egypt flitting in and out of my consciousness.* And:

My mother's family is of Scottish and Irish descent. They were border Scots who settled in the north of Ireland. I'll tell Murray we'll take that trip to the British Isles after all.

LIZ: " . . . "

JOANNE OF SCOTLAND: "I want to ask one more question about Anna. She's the oldest but she isn't fluent in sign. She just knows basic signs. Is it possible that she could resent the deafness in me?"

Liz's eyes are sad.

LIZ: "If you hate it in yourself, yes."

⁓

That night. In front of the mirror. Thoughts: *My mother is Celtic. My father is a son of German Russian immigrants who came to Saskatchewan at the turn of the century from Odessa in the Black Sea area.* Suddenly I *see* it. I see it in my small hands and feet, the quick and nervous gestures I make even when I'm not signing: *I have inherited my father's excitable nature and his passion for storytelling, his saxophone, and choral music. I've learned a dogged work ethic from my mother, a Protestant work ethic that survived her intense conversion to Catholicism, and her insistence on honesty and creativity run in my own veins, and is in the blood surrounding my damaged ears. The blood gives me music.*

JOHANNA

But who is really writing all this? Perhaps you've suspected that someone neither Deaf nor Hearing is making you privy to this travelling back and forth between two states of being.

I am here and not here, Deaf and not Deaf, Hearing and not Hearing, flashing like quicksilver, teasing, perhaps maddening with the behaviour of quantum particles: *not two, not yet one, and somewhere in between.*

I am Johanna.

I am an older woman now. I shut my new digital hearing aid off when street noises, engine hums, the hubbub of crowds threaten to overwhelm me. Technology is not advanced enough for me to want to wear it all the time. At times, it is too loud, picks up too much background noise, I am forced to listen to the *tin tin tin* of digital sound as audiologists tell me that the analog hearing aids have been phased out from the market. With people returning in droves to listen to vinyl records again, perhaps there will be a tiny revolution someday among those still forced to make the switch from rich deep tones of analog sound to artificial digital twitter. Until then, I walk up to salesmen in stores, sign without my voice and ask for paper to write on. They are happy to oblige. Why didn't I know that before? People are eager to practice their meager sign language skills with me as soon as they detect my deaf voice. I wear my hair short so everyone can see my hearing aid. Why hide it? Murray and I sign sans voice every time we shop, eat in restaurants, attend a public event. People glance disinterestedly our way. We are inside the house of love that sign language has helped to build.

Yet, in the Deaf House for many years, a language was scorned and dismissed, powerless people were doomed to live in the attic or the basement, and the house itself was threatened with oblivion, mostly through water and neglect. In this house, I was sometimes Deaf and sometimes Hearing, able to speak well, yet not hear very well, able to sign fluently in American Sign Language yet unable to live in the Deaf community. Where could I lay my head?

Now, love is building a house. Murray and I lie in bed late Saturday mornings when he pokes me awake, pressing a handshape into my back or shoulder. I roll over and he signs some more.

"We need to book our flight to Portugal today."

"Okay, why Portugal? Remind me again."

Murray shrugs, I turn away grinning into my pillow. He tickles me and I push his hand away in feigned annoyance. He sends the sheet billowing over us and I sink into a half sleep.

My life seems to be a series of crossings between faraway lands and my own home. This urge to travel, to pack, to be on the move never seems to leave me. Forty-nine times during my university years, the yearly move with my daughters to a new home despite everyone's protestations, and now the trips Murray and I take every summer. And how does Murray know my compulsive need to keep looking for something? Is it a longing to go on pilgrimages, as Chaucer would say.

Something now propels us toward Latin countries. First Spanish — as in Cuba — and now Portuguese. Passion, the color red, hot humid climates, and the Portuguese nun lamenting the indifference of her soldier lover having departed again to fight another battle. Her epistles hint at hours of secret passion in her convent house, her lover having sneaked past vigilant but weary nuns. Her letters would not be well received by a Canadian woman today: *Get over it, get a move on. So what if he dumped you to continue fighting in his stupid wars?* Ah but Mariana Alcoforado had no choice but to remain in a convent. She couldn't travel her way out of her heartache but lived and died among women. And historians still think today that her letters were concocted by a man. Why couldn't a woman in the fifteenth century write of her entrapment?

I am not as free as I would like to think and neither was Mariana. Her convent quarters became a harsh and unyielding landscape. Many hours of tears, boredom, and more tears. Boredom drilling its way into her skull like merciless sun on unprotected skin. In the end, what does she find, travelling in her cell? I think I know and I don't have to go to Portugal to find it. I don't have to travel anywhere, anymore, but I go to find the words to talk about it. With Mariana's help, I will explain it to myself one more time.

I turn toward Murray. He is sleeping again. I laugh. I turn over again to dream of a scorched landscape and a marriage bed in the midst of a dilapidated old house, with broken furniture, and walls partially torn away, where I must walk through a maze of rooms with torn linoleum, broken windows, scattered tools, to the bed covered with a shining white quilt, where the sheets are fresh and clean.

BOOK TWO

Sixteen

Simon and I had a five week trip ahead of us, an itinerary including Athens, Rome, Florence, Assisi, and Paris, and we'd just begun our first leg of the journey: Oxford. At twenty-five, I'd just warmed up to the idea of marrying this university professor. This strange, eccentric, lonely man who waved in such a funny way, arm at the waist, twisting his wrist in such an abrupt manner, who lived alone, stuffed every nook and cranny of his basement suite with plastic bags, and was months behind in marking his university papers but who was also the man who encouraged me to sing to him, who made up little ditties that we sang together while we prowled the streets of Saskatoon late at night, even if my voice was impossible and I sang off-key, our voices reverberating among the blue-black branches of trees lit by street lamps, who taught me "*confutati, maledicti*" from Mozart's *Requiem Mass* and the Welsh hymn, "All Through the Night". Simon had a BBC English accent, spoke Latin, Italian, and French, was writing a paper on the love between Penelope and Odysseus, and I critiqued his writing, delighting to find out that he thought of me as he wrote of Odysseus rising from the Ithaca shore, caked with brine, yearning for Penelope but fearing that she had not kept their marriage bed intact. He was that crazy about me, and I vowed to be his Penelope forever, though he was so sad, haunted, riddled by years of failed relationships with women.

Simon's hangdog eyes seemed sunken further into his head, his salad bowl haircut seemed even more impossible, I reached for his hand, but he let go of it immediately, conscious of our new arrangement, four days ago, we flew in from Saskatoon, to announce our engagement to his parents in Cardiff, Wales, and after two days of visiting with his mother, who declared loudly, that she loved me, Simon decided that he didn't want to marry me, thus:

PENELOPE: " . . . !"

ODYSSEUS: "I just don't know what happened. I just don't love you anymore. I have no desire to go through with this marriage."

Simon and I walked among the glass topped-tables showing illuminated pages in the Bodleian listening to a man singing a line of the Gregorian chant, pausing at each exhibit, the pages dappled brown with an enormous letter at the top, adorned with entwined gold-embossed loops, the gold leaf glittering, mostly in the upper left hand corner. We waited listening to haunting melodies rising from the glass tables nearby, Simon bending his head to me and whispering that he thought the man must be a musicologist, specializing in the plainchant and a bit arrogant to sing each line as it appeared on each of the pages under glass, and I looked around, and I thought: *No one seems to mind. We are all transfixed.* It was a moment of reprieve, it was an interruption to the long howl of fury and grief, that sonorous tone forever present in my ears.

Dragon Journal

The first time I saw a dragon was on a signpost announcing Cardiff in Wales. Dragons were everywhere, on flags, traffic signs, the corner bars. The dragons seemed to remind me: *again,*

I'm not loved. Simon is only impressed with my intelligence, my tenacity, and my success at overcoming my deafness. I collect jewels, intellectual gifts and knowledge, and hoard them and now he sees beyond my jewel-studded breast. He has reached the limit of his admiration for me.

I put down my pencil. I was a dragon? Dragons were greedy, with jewels embedded in their underbelly. In my more honest moments, I thought: *who was Simon to me?* Answer: *a university, an endless fountain of words. But hell hath no fury like a woman scorned.*

ॐ

Simon went to the Balliol chapel to pray, his eyes sunken with guilt, demanded that we attend mass every day, but I didn't want to, seeing that it was an useless exercise in atonement only to appease Simon's guilt. He was kneeling in the pew while I wandered restlessly in the back, until I found a door, and a spiral staircase up to the choir loft. High up in the loft, I sat on a wooden bench, and peered over the rail at Simon's head, that mess of loose curls, and the sweat blooming under his armpits and down the back of his shirt. A Dominican monk came sweeping over to me, tucking his hands into the great folds of his sleeves. Although we were sheltered by the heavy medieval stone walls from the sunny day outside, I could see beads of sweat on the monk's forehead as he shifted in his white habit.

SWEATING MONK: "Can I help you?"

Tears quivering in my eye sockets, me tilting my head upwards to prevent them from travelling down my face, me gesturing at Simon down below, unable to express the impotency to the monk before me, the futility of going through another failed relationship, and he glanced down at Simon, who was still kneeling.

MONK: "Come," (*Gestures*) "I have something to show you."

From beneath his robes, he took out a ring with several keys and unlocked the door to a dry, cool room on the same floor as the choir loft. The room was small and cramped, several old leather bound tomes lined the shelves. The monk lifted down one of the books, and opened to an illuminated page.

He spoke to me in a soft tone: "The miniature is from the Office of the Virgin. You know, the Divine Office."

Suddenly the rise and fall of the man's chanting at the glass-topped tables in the Bodleian filled my ears. *Phantom music.*

The monk said: "This is the visit between Mary and Elizabeth. Look, Elizabeth is reaching to touch the Virgin's swollen belly."

My eyes took in Mary's cobalt blue gown, the haloed heads of the women, holding hands as they talk, Zechariah, struck dumb, holding a crown high in the air behind Mary as if to name her queen of heaven, making signs with his hands because he refused to believe in the angel's prediction of Elizabeth's own pregnancy, angels striking him dumb, making him powerless, and the loop of the Carolingian script with crimson red and lapis lazuli flourishes, and the gold leafed initial adorned with baby's breath. The furious howling in me stopped. I realized: *I have come all this way, to England, for a page stored on the top floor in a medieval chapel. The page promises me life, beauty, and goodness beyond this difficult time.* I thanked the monk, marvelling at how he endured the heat, mopping his forehead to give me a glimpse of that page, and returned to the balcony to watch Simon grieve below.

At Perugia, I woke up crying in the morning. Simon reached across to the single bed I was in and shook my shoulder, and that made me feel even worse. The fading of our intimacy was complete. The light of the morning sun came through the single window of the hotel room, casting a soft glow onto the red-tiled roofs outside. Later that morning, at Assisi, I didn't want to go down to the lowest floor with Simon, to descend down the stone steps into the crypt of Clare below the basilica, but his voice was insistent: "Her body is perfectly preserved though it is over eight hundred years old."

Before entering the stone archway that led to the descending spiral stairs, I whispered: "Have you seen her before?" I could scarcely breathe; there was something morbid about viewing a body whose remains are entirely intact.

Simon said: "Yes, about five years ago."

I grabbed Simon's hand, even though I was not supposed to. I didn't want to see Clare of Assisi. I wanted to go up in the open air, feel the warm sun on my shoulders, and finally take this scarf off my head.

Simon pulled at my sleeve, and said: "Come."

I slowly walked past a glass case, where a woman lay in a dress covering most of her body. I willed myself to look at her head. It was partially covered by a wimple. Her hair was black, her skin a dark brown, dry as paper, but, nevertheless, skin.

I whispered: "Simon, doesn't she seem like she's breathing?"

He said: "Yes, but she isn't. But she looks like she's sleeping."

Clare's hands were folded under her breasts. I could see her knuckles twined with a rosary. The light in the crypt behind us mirrored my face in the glass against her body. She was one of the incorruptibles, one of the saints whose body had never decomposed. I stepped closer to the glass cage. Behind me, a line of people navigated the stone steps down to the crypt, captured by the idea that her body still had skin, bone, muscle, and hair, was a house whose spirit was still in the walls, floors, and foundation. I thought: *Morbid curiosity.*

I asked: "This isn't a hoax is it?" Simon said: "No, this is confirmed to be real flesh."

I said: "Let's go up, right now."

I wanted to be away from this woman who could not shed her own flesh, not even in death, I didn't care how holy people thought she was, I only felt horror at her flesh refusing to melt off her bones, suddenly I had no patience with the Catholic preoccupation with bones and relics and their triumphant promotion of several saints as incorruptibles, the whole thing seemed so unnatural, I thought: *Why hang on to our bodies? Who wants to remain in a wounded body, bloodied, torn, crippled, with heart and mind broken? Why not aspire to the realm of the spirit, or at least adopt a new body in reincarnation?* And: *The Catholics want to prove their own special point: Clare's body and the bodies of all the other incorruptibles are permanent houses, even though their spirits are gone.*

Then I was breathing in the open air of Assisi, and we were walking past the pink marble buildings to the walls of the ancient medieval town, and from a parapet I could see the rival town of Perugia in the distance. Simon was busy with the camera, working on a panoramic view of the horizon over the walls. I was breathing, this time with a certainty that I would survive this loss of love again. My breath animated my whole body, and I relaxed, as I tried to push out of my mind the image of Clare laying in that glass case in the crypt below.

I looked down to my breasts, lapping beneath my tank top, to the large, fringed scarf wrapped around my large hips, to my small, narrow feet interlaced with leather thongs, to Simon standing a foot away from me, his arm slack at his side, that, before our flight to England, was always twined around my waist, and I realized: *Simon's inability to form a commitment to me comes*

*from his own inner torments, however mysterious and puzzling they
are to me.*

But my body cried out these days, aching for Simon's touch. I
couldn't think, couldn't read, and couldn't sleep. I was overcome
with a profound sadness. All the men in my life had loved me
primarily for my mind, enthralled by my ability to live in the
Hearing world.

Leonard Cohen's "Suzanne" thrummed in my head, the voice
of a young Leonard Cohen touching Suzanne's perfect body with
his mind even as we travelled by train that night, where I breathed
in the sharp cold air of the Alps. In the morning, I awakened on
the top bunk of the sleeping car, watching two girls across from
our bunks prepare themselves for the morning stop in Paris. One
of the girls motioned at Simon sitting on the bunk below me, and
asked, in heavy, guttural English: "Are you with him?"

I shook my head: No. And to myself: *I am alone with this deaf
body, this imperfect house.*

JOHANNA

I should plant a garden this year. Even a handful of herbs if
nothing else. Murray offers to put our old pink bathtub out in
the backyard just in time for spring. I look at him aghast until
I realize that I missed the innocent lilt in his voice, his deadpan
face. I should know this by now, I chide myself, how he pulls my
leg, how I am gullible enough to take seriously his every gib and
jibe.

I'd like to blame it on being deaf, but I can't. It's not about
detecting those subtle inflections in his voice, it's about paying too
much attention to outward appearances. I understood that long
ago in Assisi when I saw Clare in the crypt. I got it, really got that
her body was her soul, that it was the house of her whole being. It
didn't even faze me to read, years later, that the leathery face I saw

was exactly that, a leather mask placed over her decaying skull. Rather, it was all about where to focus my attention.

Yet I figured that the body and soul were two parallel lines that eventually converged. If I bent the lines in forty-five degree angles that, dammit, they'd meet. Or if I could catch every subtle nuance, every syllable uttered in the dialogue between my body and soul, between the deaf and hearing, then the two irreconcilable parts in me would become one. Now I know better. There is no dialogue. Just silence.

Murray chuckles at me gently when I roll my eyes at the bathtub being carried out the front door. I should know him well enough to know that he'd do this, pull my leg, I mean, but he's so full of fickle and strange fancies. Murray is like quicksilver, not two separate substances, but not yet one. I have to pay attention to the silence growing in him and in me instead of relying on my faulty hearing. I have to travel between the *not two and not yet one* in him to find him as he is.

Seventeen

MY HEART LIFTED FINALLY, IN PARIS, as Simon and I boarded the train, as I looked through the windows at the racing trees and expected that they should be different somehow. *Perhaps their leaves are octagonal? Perhaps they should be purple? Perhaps the bark should be made of rubber!* And realized: *The world has changed since Assisi, but I'm not sure how.* Even Simon had noticed.

SIMON: "You are so much calmer now — much less angry and sad."

MAYBE CHANGED JOANNE: "..."

The train lurched toward Chartres.

~

Dragon Journal

I am now a mere collector of experiences, a tourist in search of shiny bits of knowledge, history, trivia, and facts. I am sitting on intellectual jewels. These are my treasures: Assisi, Clare in the crypt, the medieval plainchant at Oxford, and illuminated manuscripts. Now they are implanted into my chest like a shield.

~

I wound my way through the thick stone pillars at Chartres Cathedral, my neck aching as I studied the rose windows. The light was weak and the flagstones were cold beneath my feet. I was in sandals and jeans and a wool sweater against the damp. Delicate pools of light emanated from the tall panels and roses of stained glass: brilliant, rich colours; saturated hues of red, blue, violet, and green; figures on horses; people kneeling and weeping before a prostrate body, palms outstretched, somber eyes, and downturned mouths; all fractured by the thick black leaded lines separating the panes of glass.

Near the centre of the cathedral, I noticed a path on the floor approximately a foot wide. The inset stones formed sinuous loops. As I rounded a corner I saw that the loops were a circle. Its centre was inlaid with a flower of stone. I balanced carefully to keep on my path and held my breath. I remembered: *Floor labyrinths were put into cathedrals during the Middle Ages to accommodate those who longed to go on pilgrimages but were too infirm or poor to travel. Usually, the pilgrims would walk these stone paths on their knees.*

One loop promised to bring me close to the centre but suddenly veered away, taking me near the outside of the labyrinth, far from the stone flower in the centre. I thought: *How many times have I thought myself so close to the truth only to suddenly discover myself so far away?*

I saw a young man ahead of me on another loop and wanted to skip across to him because I thought he was Kevin. I studied philosophy with him in Saskatoon, he was the one who called me Johanna, *Johanna of God*, he wrote in his letters to me, and my asking, *Why do you call me that name?* and his answer: *Because it's the essence of who you are.*

We studied Thomas Aquinas, because we wanted to get to the bottom of everything, once and for all, attending classes in Professor McCullough's attic, because he preferred to teach us (four young men and me) philosophy in his home. Professor McCullough and the young men bowed their heads over their Aquinas texts on *prudentia,* and I, Joanne, sat beside the grand piano, in the attic, staring upwards at the polished wooden beams, thinking: *I thought attics were dirty, dusty places, crammed with boxes and odd-shaped objects, perhaps a fishing pole, oversized boots, and boxes of books read a century ago, but this attic is warm, clean, comfortable, and safe.*

There was only one problem with Kevin. He was too handsome with his aquiline nose, the finely sculptured body, his hair (reddish brown), his eyes (frank and searching), his mouth (perfectly formed). I became afraid. *My deafness is going to mar Kevin's acceptance of me. I am a rather plain woman, with a rather nasal voice, and articulation errors. It's only a matter of time until the soulmate bubble will burst.*

Then it happened. Kevin made a joke about how I was not able to hear something he thought I should have been able to hear. I fled. Away from him. Slammed the heavy College door in his face. I arrived home several hours later, after tramping along the river that snaked below campus. I found a new coffee mug on my desk, filled with chocolates and a hastily-scribbled note: *I wounded you in a deep way tonight, deeper than most people who are in your heart do. For I belittled you unknowingly . . . unwittingly I showed you all of your inadequacies that are the most painful because there is nothing you can do about them, O Johanna of God, Johanna the Controller, Johanna the Beautiful and Wise, Johanna the Defective and Incomplete.*

I stiffened at the word, "defective." He had left me with nothing to salvage. "Defective" was the final blow. I refused to speak to him again, despite his desperate entreaties.

Chartres. The sinuous loop brought me close to the centre again. The stone flower was on my left, pocked with age. I thought: *There he is! On the loop to the right! Kevin!* I reached out to touch his arm as he walked past. He turned around. *The face was not his.*

Embarrassed, I broke away from the labyrinth. Then Simon walked up to me.

He said: "Joanne, it's time to go back to Paris."

I glanced over my shoulder at the rows of somber stone saints on the outer wall of the cathedral, and silently said to them: *I will come back someday, to finish the pilgrimage I started on that labyrinth in the floor.*

Simon and I parted immediately after arriving back in Saskatoon. That year, I worked in the St. Thomas More Library. Each day, I walked to the university campus, thinking of the men I'd left behind: Mark, Jan, Kevin, Simon. And how I had to get back to England, Greece, Italy, and France. There was something I had to redo in those places. I did research in the library on how to get a PhD at Oxford. There, perhaps I would reclaim something I'd lost. I read *Jane Eyre* again. I heard the strange woman in the attic scream in the nights, and woke up tired. In the mornings, I swallowed a concoction of raw eggs and protein powder mixed with milk. I'd never consumed this unappetizing mixture before, but food seemed strangely irrelevant now. Soon, I forgot about lunch. Sometimes I came home and drank the same thing again.

The Greek peplos I'd bought in Athens now flowed over my body like a curtain. I moved to an apartment downtown to live alone, away from Simon's home across the river. In the early fall mornings, I walked toward the university bridge glimpsing, over the low branches of trees, the river running grey in the rising mist, shutting my hearing aid off so I wouldn't hear the heavy traffic thundering past me. Without my hearing aid, the bridge became a quiet stroll across the river Thames, alongside the spires of Oxford. I thought often of Clare, sleeping in her body, protected by a glass cage in the stone crypt below the basilica in

Assisi, with her hands folded under her breasts and her skin the colour of dark mottled paper. *She is who she is because of her body. Her body is her identity.* These thoughts slowly took shape in me while I dreamed of St. Francis beckoning me down a spiralling stairway into a crypt. I wanted desperately to go back to Assisi, where intellectual jewels formed a breastplate over my heart, protecting me from my failure to love and to be loved. I couldn't help thinking: *I am being greedy.* And: *The pilgrimage I took with Simon was an utter failure.*

The days moved slowly. I walked around the city, along the serpentine path alongside the river, and over the bridge to and from work. On better days, at night I quietly made myself a mountainous salad. I quietly watched my body fade, observing how its walls, floors, and foundation were crumbling.

Dragon Journal

Two months later. Something must change. I am too thin. Those graduation photographs from the University of Saskatchewan with yet another degree (!) reveal a morose young woman with eyes like burnt sockets. I can scarcely recognize myself. Although I'm grateful for the heavy folds of the graduation gown, my ankles are whittled down to toothpicks, as I stand bracketed by the heavier figures of my mother and grandmother.

I dreamt last night that I was entering the crypt of St. Francis, going down a spiral staircase below the basilica, in a cold sweat, afraid of what I would find. I think it is a sign. I must contact the Franciscans. Perhaps I am to join the religious life.

❧

I parked my bicycle at the side of the steps leading up to Ain Karim, a center of theological study and exploration established by two nuns in an inauspicious house in south eastern Saskatoon.

It was October, and the Europe trip hung over me like a diagnosis of a terminal illness. I hiked up the waistband of my jeans, now so loose, before ringing the doorbell.

A tall woman, clad in a simple long brown dress, with a wimple on her head, answered the door. She smiled with her eyes: *Welcome.*

Behind her, the living room was sparsely furnished. I had been here before with Simon, to study the theology of the body. At our first session, we'd received copies of a three inch thick book on philosophy, theology, science, literature, and spirituality, called *Theologies of the Body, Humanist and Christian.* Last winter, I had curled up in the giant chairs in the Education building on campus reading the thick tome. Simon merely tossed it on his desk in his office in the Arts Tower, already crammed with books and clothing. But I was not here to see Sister Sarah about the theology of the body. I wanted to talk about what happened at Assisi this past summer, about Clare and Francis, and about finding a way to a deeper life, to peace — perhaps through her order, the Franciscans? *I'm ready to join her order, since there's nothing left for me to do.*

Sr. Sarah pointed to a plate of Nanaimo squares: "Have something to eat."

We were in the kitchen breakfast nook, sitting across from each other over tea. I pushed the ever protruding ear mold back into my ear, knowing that every time I bit, the mold would become displaced.

My hearing aid: "Eeeeeeeeeeeeeeeeeeeeeee!"

I reached stealthily for a square, and opened my mouth but: "Eeeeeeeeeeeeeeeee!"

Sister Sarah asked: "Do you know sign language?"

I shook my head: "No." I paused: "No. I don't need it."

I bit into the Nanaimo square.

My hearing aid: "EeeeeeeEEEEEE!"

I fiddled.

SISTER ACUTE OBSERVER: "But you're Deaf."

JOANNE DENIAL #1: "Not really. I communicate very well."

PERSISTENT ACUTE OBSERVER: "You really think so?"

JOANNE DENIAL #2: "Yeah."

I impatiently pushed my ear mold back into my ear, anticipating another squeak, as I bit into the second Nanaimo square. Sr. Sarah scooted another plate over to me. This time, matrimonial squares. I realized how hungry I was, and took the matrimonial square, too. I licked my fingers before beginning.

JOANNE DENIAL #3: "Anyway, I'm here because I want to explore Franciscan spirituality."

Sr. Sarah smiled and leaned forward, with her elbows on the table and the sleeves of her habit pooling on the table like spilled coffee. She said: "St. Francis had a very difficult relationship with his father. He wanted him to become a wealthy cloth merchant."

I nodded: "Uh, uh." I thought: *She isn't getting what I really want to talk about.*

She said: "Francis kissed a leper. That was a pivotal point in his life. He chose to embrace poverty instead of the life that his father wanted for him."

An image came before me: *Francis pushing through strands of dyed wool hanging from beams in his father's dye house; peering through the steam rising from the vats of dye; men, women, and children standing, stirring silently in their grey rags; how he tries to take the wool strand away from the old blind man who is dipping it in a vat of blue dye. Francis leaps back in pain, having scalded his hands, not even aware that the dye is so very hot, how profoundly disturbed he is, as he climbs up the stairs to his mother, Pica, whose face is wreathed in an immaculate white wimple. She reaches out to him in tenderness.*

It was the Zefirelli movie.

PICA (*Extends her hand*): "What's wrong?" She looks at me closely.

JOANNE OF ASSISI (*Just sits there, is not sure*): *I have a wonderful relationship with my father, and with my family. Nothing is wrong.*

PICA: "Joanne, how do you feel about your deafness?"

JOANNE OF ASSISI: "Fine, just fine. No problems really. I communicate very well."

PICA: "No, how do you really feel about your deafness?"

I was not sure what to say. Sr. Sarah waited, her heavy cross clinking against the table as she shifted to a more comfortable position, she said nothing, though her face was expectant.

Suddenly I felt as though I was being lowered into a well: the shock of the cold water, the beating of air about my ears will drive me mad, the vapours rising from moss-covered bricks all inform me of an impending death, I must stop here, tug on the rope, have Sister Sarah pull me back up, away from the underground cistern, so I can run down the cobbled path, step into my coach, with an eye to my luggage, bark out the orders to the driver to take me to Thornfield Hall immediately, but there was one difficulty. There was no Rochester waiting for me. *There was only Francis and his difficult father.*

My eyes filled with tears.

Sr. Sarah pushed a box of Kleenex across the table. After I finished sobbing, she asked: "Why don't you learn sign language?"

"I told you, I don't really need it."

"You could communicate with other Deaf people."

"I don't want to." I sniffled.

"Why not?"

I struggled, looking at the remains of the matrimonial cake, its oatmeal buds trailing near the rim of the plate.

"Well . . . I find that Deaf people are not very well educated. They are rather uncouth."

Sr. Sarah leaned forward, perched her chin on top of her hands. "That sounds rather snobbish. Do you know any Deaf people?"

"Well, I have nothing in common with them."

"Why don't you read a book about Deaf people? That's not so scary." Sr. Sarah bit into a square, grinning. "You can do research."

"I guess so."

She said: "Remember, Francis kissed a leper though he didn't want to." Sister Sarah pushed back her chair and stood tall over me in her long brown habit and wimple. She said, softly: "You're very, very strong, Joanne." And: "You can do this."

I rode my bicycle back home in the dark. My bike light shone only two feet ahead in the dark streets. At home. I held up my fingers in the mirror. My fingers were small. Knotted. Each muscle defined. I studied the queerness. Of how I held my head to the left. All the time. Because I wore a hearing aid in that ear. How I worked my mouth in humming. Eyes darting everywhere. I gasped: *Dear God, I am Deaf. I've not been able to hide it.*

My eyes were now deep in their sockets. Smouldering. As Simon used to say. My cheeks were hollow. A cavity lay between my hips. Where a soft belly used to rest. But my bones were strong. I still had plenty of muscle. And enough energy to walk, to ride my bike, and to swim. I thought: *Sr. Sarah sees how I am strong, despite my cadaverous appearance.* I said to the mirror: *She says so, herself.* I thought: *Although she has seen the spirit that travels throughout my body, the restless, homeless spirit that sometimes lives upstairs in my head, and sometimes down in my belly.* I shifted in the mirror looking for it. Until I realized: *Sr. Sarah has invited my spirit to occupy me all at once, to go anywhere without restriction, willy-nilly, like water seeping through walls.*

Eighteen

SNOW CAME IN LATE MARCH, COVERING Saskatoon in white. My brother stood in the cramped entrance of my apartment, lifting his boots off the linoleum, looking for a mat. Snake-like strips of compacted snow fell from his boots as he pushed a parcel at me that our mother had sent. I wondered why he looked at me closely, until I realized he hadn't seen me for months. *He hasn't seen how hollow my cheeks have become.*

I said: "Come for a walk? I have to go to the university."

The evening was lit by snow-flecked streetlights, their necks bowing down toward us. I found it difficult to lip-read David, I kept sliding and slipping on the slush of the sidewalk, I could not read a face that moved, even if I was doing the moving.

David turned his face toward me, trying to enunciate his words carefully. His faint voice said: "I . . . ooohh, course . . . mark . . . ee . . ."

I thought: *Damn, my hearing aid battery is weakening fast.*

I nodded at David, to encourage him to continue his talking, and felt for the small, round pack of batteries inside my pockets, then my purse, and then my backpack. I twisted my back sharply in the slush, and almost lost my footing. David continued his barrage of words, which now felt like vomit spattered all over my coat.

I must clean up this mess. Was he upset? I'd never known David to talk this much.

My mind was racing with possible explanations. I'd heard the words philosophy, paper, and Professor Corrigan. I thought: *It's got to be about a mark he got on his paper.* But I was not sure. I nodded, hoping this would comfort him and convey a sense that I understood the heart of the matter that claimed his mind while I remain mired in silence, but I was a child again, *a child signing in stone, a silence of stone, signing in stone, signing silence.*

My eyes swelled with tears. I'd got my e.e. cummings mixed up.

I told Sister Sarah how I was chased, constantly out of breath, trying to find safety where I wouldn't be judged, evaluated, or measured how closely I could approach the Hearing in everyday speech, manner, and living. *It's a fox hunt,* I told her: *I am Sylva, the fox wife in the novel by Jean Vercors.* She nodded and pushed another plate of cookies at me.

SISTER VERCORS: "Your deafness is a gift, Joanne."

SYLVA: "No one else sees it that way. It's something that has to be fixed."

SISTER VERCORS: "It's the cornerstone which the builders rejected."

SYLVA *(Barks):* "I don't understand what you mean."

I looked at the dark pools made by Sr. Sarah's brown habit.

SYLVA *(Sniffs):* " . . . ?"

SISTER VERCORS: "You have a Deaf body. It is a gift for others."

SYLVA *(Whines):* "I don't understand."

SISTER VERCORS: "Go find someone who signs."

She stood up. I realized: *It's time to leave.*

I rode home on the bus, looking out at the grey spring slush through the dirt-streaked windows watching the trees bend toward the bus as it careened around tight corners. *Their branches are thin, frail bones waiting for the flesh of summer.*

☙

I wondered: *Can they see that I'm deaf. I hope not.* I gingerly sat on the edge of a black vinyl couch in one of the meeting rooms in St. Thomas More College. Sr. Doreen Smith, who was hired by the Diocese of Saskatoon to work with the Deaf, had gathered a few university students to teach them sign language so that they might assist her in this ministry. There was a Deaf woman there, Diane, who smiled constantly while Sr. Doreen signed and spoke at the same time. I gathered that Diane was her assistant.

I told myself: *I am only here to learn a few signs, to satisfy my curiosity about the world of the Deaf, no more. I might even incorporate this experience into a research thesis, expanding on the significance of the visual in literature about Deaf people and its application to the mass media. After all, my English professor liked my last essay about Marshall McLuhan. Furthermore, I have done my research. I've come to this class armed with the history of sign language, the linguistic discoveries of Stokoe affirming sign language as a true language. And, of course, the Deaf culture.*

The sign language class was most boring. Lists of signs, grouped according to function, sat on transparent sheets humming atop an overhead projector. Diane was patient, sometimes reaching to mold another person's hand into a shape that might be the letter *K*. I sat at the back of the room, thumbing through my textbook. I saw that American Sign Language sentences were odd: "You Deaf You?"

I thought: *Why repeat "you" twice?*

I looked at the word lists in my lap. *They want me to start at the beginning like everyone else.*

More classes transpired, the long list of signs was exhausted, and we were to make sentences for the first time. Diane had everyone make a sentence from a list of beginning phrases. *Boy blue. Girl fast. Nice meet you.*

It was my turn. I wanted to say: "Happen today boy fell."

Instead, I sat back with arms crossed. I had read ahead in this ridiculously slow class, watching others fumble with their signs. But Sr. Doreen and Diane's sternness increased with every minute. The students were not to talk, ever. We had to forfeit small change in a cup if we bleated out any kind of a noise. Diane no longer mouthed the signs, no longer flashed the transparencies up on the overhead. Her signs swam by like iridescent minnows, while the Hearing students were stone still, sitting in a circle watching Diane attempt conversation: "You Deaf you?"

All the Hearing students shook their heads. I couldn't, and I suspected: *They can't figure out these strange inversions,* "boy tall, girl sad," *the beginning of a story with the word* "happen". I thought: *What's wrong with last week, or yesterday, or once upon a time?*

Three hours later, I snapped my textbook shut. I didn't want to start all over again with another language. I didn't want to think in baby phrases anymore. I joined the file of students leaving the classroom.

A voice: "Wait." Sister Doreen touched me on the arm. Her signing was slow and she mouthed: "You should meet Patti, one of the Deaf teachers at the School for the Deaf. How about I take you to see her next week?"

෨ඁ

I nosed into the parking lot at the back of the School for the Deaf on Cumberland Avenue, near the University of Saskatchewan.

The school was a dream of the twenties, a sprawling mansion on an expanse of sloping green lawn lined with poplar and oak trees. I stood in the cool spring air on the football field. The still leafless trees at the other side of the field scratched at the grey sky. I paused. *This is a building that contains a culture and a language few are privy to. I'm about to step into a foreign country.*

I hurried around to the front of the building, tripping on the uneven concrete slabs in the sidewalk, the steps to the Tyndall stone arch, the heavy oak doors of the building. It clanged behind me, the fusty smell of chalk, sweat, and old carpet assaulting me as I stood in the large stairwell leading up to the main floor.

Patti spied me before I saw her. Her hand shot out of a crowd of students who'd gathered around her. She continued her signing so I had to wait outside the circle until she finished. Her tight golden curls, pushed back at the sides with small combs, bounced as she wove her hands in and out of a story. Finally, she looked over their heads at me and nodded, quickly dismissing them. Her Texas drawl was evident in her speech: flat, nasal, and weak on the endings.

I realized: *She talks like me.*

Her hands were strong as she coordinated them to sign in unison with her words. I realized: *It's not a natural way for her to sign. She is doing this so I'll understand.*

I began to attend Deaf socials with Patti, who did not help me comprehend any of the signing. Instead, I sat in a steady stream of signs, catching a phrase here, puzzling over a swoop or a long flight to the right or left, observing how the tongue clicked as the hands travelled across the chest. I sat in a shallow riverbed of signs, watching the streams form rivulets around my legs and arms. There was no intervention from anyone, no practice, no exaggerated attempts to explain the meaning of signs I hadn't seen in class.

After a few months, I realized that everything about sign language was about circles. They sat in circles, their hands moved from the chest up to the left side of the head, up to the forehead and down to the chin, and then down to the chest again, or the signing was in figure eights, horizontal, vertical, against the chest, away from the head, down to the waist even: a flight of bees and hummingbirds touching down flower to flower.

The meanings began to slide together like a nearly-completed jigsaw puzzle. The syntax of sign knitted itself into my brain, to the point where I could sign without difficulty: "Want coffee you?"

I eventually understood that the circles were shapes and paths made by classifiers, a series of handshapes that can represent various actions and motions. The Deaf used the visual space in front of their bodies to made three dimensional models, representations of complex actions with even an index finger. Timidly, I entered into the frenzy of hands slapping, swooping, twisting, sliding, lifting my head in agreement, nodding my understanding, and smiling when a joke was finished. It was as though a sheer curtain lifted before my eyes, the Deaf, who were once shadowy figures behind the curtain, began to take on colour, shape, and form, I'd seen them before in coffee shops, waiting at a bus stop, butting out cigarettes in front of the Social Services building, their bare hands reaching out of the sleeves of their dirty, down-filled jackets. But there was now Allard, whose full moustache rested on his top lip, whose clunky ring seemed to control his dominant hand like a marionette on strings, the president of the Saskatchewan Deaf Association, a lobbying organization that had never made much headway with the government officials, and Mr. Foster, a teacher at the school for the Deaf, who signed with hands bounding in large clear crisp loops, and the Deaf were curious about me, they wanted to know why I'd joined them. One day over a coffee downtown at the little café across from the bus stop, they nodded in sympathy when I told them of my loneliness, frustration, and isolation in school, and were eager to show me new signs, to include me in every Deaf social, tell me that few oral deaf from the Hearing world had come to them, and they were patient with me while I fumbled in their language.

They signed: "We've been watching you."

I signed: "Watching?"

They signed: "Yeah, you were born in Wilkie, right? You were supposed to come to the School for the Deaf. But your parents wanted to mainstream you."

I signed: "They did the very best for me." My wrists felt suddenly stiff. The Deaf nodded as I dropped my hands back into my lap.

Patti asked: "When are you going to Gallaudet?"

I signed: "Gallaudet?"

Patti signed: "The only university for the Deaf in the world. In Washington, D.C."

I signed: "They have graduate programs there?"

The Deaf nodded vigorously.

Graduate programs in sign language? I'd finally earned a master's degree in library science after that tortured stay at the University of Alberta. After a brief stint in St. Thomas More College library, with an archival collection, I knew I'd never become a fully-fledged librarian. But graduate programs where the course contents were delivered in sign language? There, the only thing that would prohibit me from understanding the content would be lack of fluency, something I could overcome if I studied ASL. What would my parents think?

What would my mother say, after all these years she'd devoted to me, to my speech, to my life in the Hearing world? Would she think all her hard work was a waste, that she should've taught me in sign language first? How should I answer to all those years of home speech therapy, where my mother whipped out her pad and corrected my pronunciation? How would I express my gratitude to my father's tender love for me, his guiding me through difficult moments in communicating with others, his generosity in studying deaf education classes at Minot State College so that he could be a better father to me?

How should I explain to my parents that I wanted to be Deaf? That I actually wanted to be Deaf, that I must go into a foreign land to become Deaf? That I must travel for many days, months, and perhaps even years, and I might not even come back as the one they knew. Should I say to my mother and father: *Look, you've made the wrong decision, you should have let me be Deaf, should have let me learn sign language, should have sent me to the school for the Deaf in Saskatoon?* Should I tell them: *You've been wrong all along? I should be Deaf, not Hearing. I must go now to the Deaf world and you can't come with me?*

Armed with books on Deaf education, sign language, and Deaf culture, I arrived in Wilkie for a visit. After doing supper dishes, I spread the books out on the table, and opened one for my mother to read.

I said: "See, Mom? See this passage about American Sign Language being a real language? It's just a different modality. It's got all the linguistic requirements to be called a bona fide language."

My mother nodded her head slowly. Her face was strong. Her lips were firm. Her small eyes staring through her large, rimmed glasses, she read the passage again. She replied: "Yes, that makes sense."

Heartened, I led her to another passage, this time about speech discrimination, the lack of which divides the signing Deaf and the speaking deaf. I asked: "Mom, why do I only wear one hearing aid?"

"You would never accept another aid. You kept tearing it out of your right ear."

I asked: "Could I hear with it?"

"You could hear sound, but you couldn't make sense of it. Our audiologist recommended that we leave you alone and let you just use a hearing aid on your left ear."

I sat back at the table, looking at my mother, whose eyes were brimming with tears. I asked: "You mean, that the only thing that divides me from the signing Deaf is that I can hear with one ear?"

She said: "You have very good ability to discriminate speech in that one ear. Your right ear has no speech discrimination ability whatsoever. This means that no matter how much we tried with speech therapy, we couldn't teach you to make use of the residual hearing in that ear."

I thought: *The Deaf have told me how they hated to wear hearing aids, how it caused them headaches, how the noise they heard through hearing aids was meaningless. They told me how they threw them away, hid them, fed them to dogs, placed them under wheels of cars.*

"What if my left ear was like my bad right ear?"

"Well, then you'd have to sign."

"Would you have let me do that?"

"Of course. We knew we had to give you language. That was more important that being able to hear and to speak." Mom's gaze was steady as she stood up. She left the kitchen. I heard the low hum of the television set in the living room where my father sat. I knew he was listening to our conversation. I suddenly remembered his words to me during high school, when we walked uptown to get the school mail, how he touched me on the arm, suddenly turning to me, his words carefully chosen: *I wonder if we should have let you be Deaf, instead of pushing you so hard.*

JOHANNA

I am writing a community literacy plan for Deaf and hard of hearing learners of all ages in Saskatchewan. It's a government-funded report and I slog through weekends, evenings, summer holidays, Christmas, and Easter. It includes a lengthy literature review which constitutes about seventy five percent of the report. My motivation for writing this report dries up about half way through the year which is: shame. I'll shame the government, educational administrators, teachers, and parents over their deliberate ignorance of the needs of Deaf learners from the cradle to the grave. I want to believe that this report will stop the suffering of many Deaf people.

JOANNE RESEARCHER: "But who is going to read this thing?"

RETIRED TEACHER OF THE DEAF MURRAY: "Don't worry, some schmuck in the government will get paid to read it."

This doesn't help. I am floundering in the rubble of words, losing heart, losing energy.

WEARY RESEARCHER: "I'm exhausted."

DEFINITELY RETIRED TEACHER: "We'll go out to Sylvan Lake. A change is as good as a rest. You can work in the car."

DISILLUSIONED RESEARCHER: "But who is going to read this and be impressed enough to develop programs based on fact instead of emotion and prejudice?"

HAPPY WANDERER: " . . . " *(Shrugs)*

FRUSTRATED WANDERER: "Even the federal government is closing down research divisions, laying off scientists. Who is going to . . . "

IRRITATED WANDERER: "Don't give away your joy."

So I don't. Now, the new research becomes even more fascinating. I pore over academic journals, books, government reports, unpublished PhD theses in the car while Murray drives with his dark glasses on. I sneak looks at him from time to time. He might as well be wearing a uniform and a cap.

Just over the Saskatchewan border, I realize I'm the one being paid to read, to learn, to plan better lessons for my students. Now I understand that even words of truth can make me bitter. These words in a government report won't shame anyone into action. Why would I even want anyone to be propelled by shame? Love, which is freely chosen, is freely given. Better to be reading and writing in silence, in contemplation. Indeed, the silence in joy is a kind of mortar, building a house for me, for my students.

Nineteen

My father hugged me as I stood with my large suitcase, waiting to board the plane to Toronto: "This is like a finishing school, Joanne."

From Toronto, I would fly to Washington, D.C. to attend a graduate program in the education of the Deaf at Gallaudet University. Last night, my sisters Ruth and Carol made me a cake decorated with brown hands spanned on a bed of white icing. I clutched the wooden Jerusalem cross, Sister Sarah's farewell gift, which hung from a leather thong around my neck, as I looked down at the cake, at the hands that were to convey my new language instead of my mouth and voice.

Mom said, smiling: "You'll finally have the personal power you never had."

I thought: *What an odd thing for my mother to say. She's been thinking about my journey toward the Deaf community although she and I have been working on my pack list, running downtown for last minute items. And: I'd never have known. Mom usually shrouds herself and her thoughts in hard work.*

My sisters and brother stood in awkward silence as I cut the cake.

I thought: *Do they know I'm about to leave their world for one they cannot enter?*

My stomach lurched as the plane sped on the runway, its roar over-tasking my hearing aid and running down the battery quickly. I sat in silence as the plane climbed into the clouds. I fussed: *What will this newfound power look like? Will I be able to do things I've never been able to do?*

I nibbled on the peanuts and remembered Sister Sarah's words: "Hold your questions with reverence, Joanne."

I was grateful for the tall sister in brown, her sleeves pooling on the table, the lady of situations, pregnant with possibilities, insights, and bodies waiting to be accepted, and looked down wonderingly at my hands resting in my lap, and heard Sister Sarah, again: "You have a Deaf body."

By the time I walked through the airport in Washington to the sliding doors where the taxis were waiting, my ears were humming. As I stepped out onto the greasy grey asphalt and hailed a taxi, the August heat assaulted me. Through the windows of the cab, I saw the Black ghetto — a long street of stores barricaded with wrought iron bars with garbage licking the curbstones, that leads up to the gates of Chapel Hall — whose porticos open out onto Kendall Green in the centre of the Gallaudet University campus. Chapel Hall was glowing in the evening, its red bricks and porticos softened in the heat. The clock tower nestled against low grey clouds — the oldest building on the campus, built in 1870, an ancient watch over the hordes of Deaf students who had traversed its gates for over a century. I hoisted my backpack and walked to the dorms at the back of the campus, edged my way past students signing in clusters, and heard an occasional whoop rocket out of the groups, tried not to look at a student describing a girl he had seen the night before at the Deaf bar, making shapes with his hands, describing her voluptuous breasts.

I told myself: *It's eyedropping, don't be so rude.*

I shielded my eyes in the lowering sun. I was to live on the twelfth floor in Carlin Hall. During the elevator ride, I imagined: *I will step out into a long hallway like Thornfield Hall, punctuated with ten doors on either side.*

To my surprise, I found few doors. My own door opened into a suite with a foyer looking into three rooms.

The front foyer of Thornfield Hall flashed into my mind, the long forgotten delight of being able to see inside many windows and rooms at once, the lights, the opening and closing of doors, the solitary figure at a window, the tête-à-tête in a gaily-decorated room, a shout or perhaps a gesture laden with meaning.

Then I remembered: *Everyone signs here.*

My roommates, all graduate students, and I, were to live in the three rooms. I sat on the bed and looked at the white walls, and knew: *I won't put up any pictures. Not even a family photo on my desk.* I closed my eyes. Silence moved into my body. *In the silence, I was swimming in an ocean, along with other creatures of the sea: flipping, floating, bubbles running alongside my body as if I were a mermaid, with room for me to do backflips as everyone moved away politely, every creature in the silent waters making room for me, the sudden spaciousness, amazed, I was an amphibious creature, at home in both land and water.*

Nancy came in first. Blond curls framed a square face. Her smile was easy as she flashed a quick hello with her short, strong fingers. I instantly liked her, and I liked her more when she bounced on her bed and announced that she was from Arkansas.

She was a Hearing teacher in training. She said: "The Hearing actually want to be a part of this Deaf world."

I thought: *I've never heard of such a thing.*

After a few days, the absence of voices felt natural. The flutter of hands erupted in every corner of every building and out in the sparkling green bowl in the middle of the campus. The vowels found in the English language left me. I didn't hear the long "aaaa" in my head anymore. Instead, hand shapes were imprinted on my brain. The handshape A was now useful for a number of signs, like: *try, establish, help, sorry*. The A was more important now than in the sign class in Saskatoon, where the Hearing either mouthed it, or spoke forgetfully as they tightened their fists, leaving the thumb out on top, into As. I realized: *The Hearing think that* A *is a vowel.*

In small classes, we sat in a circle. In large classes, inquisitive students formed a line at the side of the room, ready to stand before the professor in full view of all the other students. It was all too easy now. I wondered: *Do I deserve this life of ease, where communication is this accessible?* At night, I wrote in my journal: *Love is building a house according to an unknown design for a mysterious purpose. Nobody knows about this secret house. I have privacy for the first time, away from being tested, evaluated, rehabilitated, assessed as to how closely I can approximate a "Hearing person."* I ended each journal entry at night with a quickly drawn picture of myself sleeping in a house that love was building.

But a month later, I was still not sure about this newfound privacy. I came to Gally with an aching right hand, which had been diagnosed as tendonitis. Six months after I began learning sign language, my right wrist became pinched and my fingers swollen. I couldn't hold a pen and had begun to scrawl childishly with my left hand. Every word I finger spelled brought about excruciating pain.

People warned me: "That sort of thing doesn't go away, especially if you're signing all the time."

I wondered at this cruel irony.

The Deaf told me: "It's the result of learning to sign later in life. Twenty-five years of unused muscles resulting in pain just when you need sign language more than ever. There is nothing that can be done." My entire arm ached as if a small and narrow silver plate was trying to work its way up the surface of my inner wrist in order to insert a stiletto knife into my index finger.

In the evenings, with my right hand encased in ice packs, I began to do my assignments with my left hand, in an uneven, loopy script that looked like the effort of a five-year-old child. One evening I couldn't sleep. To forget the insistent dull ache in my thumb, index finger and wrist, I reached for my journal, and began to write with my left hand. The childish scrawl, the nearly inch high letters opened something inside of me.

On impulse, I addressed my left hand: "Who are you?"

I didn't expect anything but a flippant remark, but this tumbled out in poorly formed letters, slanted to the left.

How do you think I felt, forever locked up here while you excelled in school and received all the praise? Your love affair with words, you and your poetry and philosophy. Did you ever ask me what I really thought and felt? No. You just fabricated feelings out of thin air. If you wanted feelings, I could've given you my anger and my resentment, even my hatred.

She was a child in a little red coat, her voice raw and animal-like, but this shadow child, her small white hands flashing in the dark wasn't finished yet. My left hand continued its rough scrawl: *No one has ever known me. All they see is you. You got all the attention, the praise, the applause, and the awards, while I got nothing. Who gives me an award for being Deaf? Come and see me. I'm just asking you to see me for as long as you want at 9:30 sharp every evening. You can stay for two minutes or for two hours but you must meet me at 9:30 sharp or else I will die.*

I thought: *She's holding me hostage.*

I told her: "You complain a lot."

Little Red Deaf Coat said: *I will give you a picture of myself so that you'll know what I'll look like when you see me. Then you won't be so scared.*

She scribbled over the entire page. I was shaking when she finished. It was a large ear over which an image of a deformed fetus was superimposed. The fetus was hooked up to a box with a long cord. In the corner of the page, she had scribbled: "Malformed fetus with an artificial mother."

I looked down in horror, uncertain as to what I'd drawn and what I'd done. I thought: *Multiple personality disorder? A creature climbing out of my mind, locked up for so many years? Impossible. Moreover, she wants me to visit her every day.*

I visited her for a week. I pulled out the paper and scrawled with my left hand: *Okay, I'm listening. What do you want me to do?*

Then there was an outpouring of rage, anger, bitterness, loneliness, and neediness: *You always abandon me. Don't ever do that again.*

I tried to reason with Little Red Deaf Coat: *Not every day. I'm too busy. Papers, classes, you see?*

But she didn't see and I gave up in disgust — in relief even. I thought: *If I let her carry on like this any longer, she'll destroy me.*

❧

At Gallaudet University, I was homesick for the first time in all the years I'd lived away from Wilkie. I wanted to see my mother's face and hear my father's voice, but all I had were weekly letters, and Washington might as well have been on the other side of the world, and I'd never felt so lost in the sea of people, but at least at the University of Saskatchewan I was bound to run into people who lived in familiar towns, or in towns where my relatives had settled, there was always something to connect us: a shared ethnicity, religion, familial or geographical ties, networks of friends and professionals whose circles lapped out wider and wider, even at the University of Alberta, I met many people who were from Saskatoon or Regina, and now I went to mass on the Gallaudet campus and Father Larry, a tall rangy man with black, fuzzy hair and fierce eyebrows, signed and voiced the mass, a Hearing man fluent enough in his signs in an Englishy sort of way, and his seventy-five-year-old assistant insisted on squawking out the hymns in her best Deaf voice, and I tried to follow along with my voice, but quickly abandoned it, and I signed instead, but there was a guitar player, a young woman, who was watching the older woman carefully, managing to finish at the end of the old Deaf woman's songs, and I realized: *She is Deaf too.*

She extended her right hand forward, her eyes kind, her hair bobbing in a page boy cut, in a wool sweater and Birkenstocks, and said: "Hello, I'm Deb."

I looked down at my own feet: socks and Birkenstocks.

Deb was in grad studies too, counselling, after trying the graduate program in Deaf education in Minnesota. We were quickly dubbed the Bobbsey twins, but I had difficulty trusting her, not because she was a granola type but because she knew too much, she understood too much, she had progressively lost her hearing after the age of five, her sign was Englishy, a rhythm not quite fluent, although her fingers were strong and quick.

Soon we were racing in her battered car into Virginia to join a reel dancing club, where I was spun around regardless of rhythm up and down a long row of quartets, men breathing upon me while Deb's eyes laughed as she passed me, and we attended the National Theatre of the Deaf performance of *Dybbuk, Between Two Worlds*, and dined with the Deaf actors afterwards, who'd performed the anachronistic play in ASL, without pause or hesitation, and on Fridays she put on Irish harp music in her dorm room, lit a candle and massaged my aching arm, and Kurt, another student in the grad studies department, came to join us afterwards, and we took her guitar to the open common area, to sing and sign. Badly.

Kurt was in counselling too, and struggled to make his signs. I saw him on the first day at Gally, looking rather shell-shocked, a head taller than the signing clusters of students in the Ely Centre, conspicuous in that he was the only one in the room who continued to wear hearing aids flat against his closely shorn head, bewildered, befuddled by the signs whirring about him. He caught my eye. Soon, we were a trio, taking subways to the Catholic University, George Washington University, and Georgetown, to study. We attended a golden evening at the Ole Jim, a red brick antebellum house, where we watched Clayton Valli perform sign poetry, wondering how the rhythm of hands could guide the body in its many sways, then Chinatown, the Smithsonian, cherry tree blossoms in the spring, the White House, Library of Congress, Georgetown, the Catholic University of America, on subways and buses, and we signed to bus drivers because the city had a special affection for the Deaf.

Despite my inauguration into the Deaf world, there was still a nagging sense that somehow I'd descended to a level lower than myself, that in the eyes of deaf education professionals, particularly in Saskatchewan, Gallaudet was not a "real" university, because it churned out undergraduates who were still not wholly fluent in English, although they'd developed a sophisticated fluency in ASL. Most of the students in our graduate programs were Hearing, and there were only five Deaf students including myself in the entire graduate studies department; our signing, our new found culture was still worth little to Hearing people who couldn't sign.

Kurt was determined to do something about this. He grabbed my hand. We ducked into a classroom at George Washington

University, Deb having gone off with another friend to Virginia.
He printed carefully on the blackboard: "How often do you clean
your ear mold?"

He turned to me sitting at a desk in the empty classroom.

I giggled and scrawled my answer close to the question: "Once
a year."

He wrote: "Eeew." He wrote, with solemnity, the names of
hearing aid companies. Danavox is in. Oticon is out.

I joined him: "Who needs a Phonic Ear?"

He answered: "My ears are carrying enough hardware
already."

Through fits of guffaws, giggles, and snorts, we quickly filled
up the blackboard with slogans from hearing aid companies,
cochlear implant companies, speech and language pathologists,
audiologists, and the last one: "What is so great about hearing
birds sing if you can't even understand a conversation?"

Kurt and I were nearly in hysterics when we finished. We sat
in desks across from each other, surveying what we had done.

"I say, we leave it." I began to insert my books in my backpack.

Kurt said: "For the others."

I said, remembering Saskatchewan: "For ourselves."

On the subway home we were quiet, letting the train rock us
through the tunnels and open ramps above the city. I thought of
the economy of deafness: *the hearing aid dispensers, the cochlear
implant companies, surgeons, ENT specialists, the teachers of the
Deaf, interpreters, all make their livelihood off the Deaf. They will
save us from our deafness and make lots of money doing it. But, I
should not bite the hands that feed me.*

Yet I was now in the Deaf world.

In May, near the end of the second semester, after an afternoon at the Catholic university, Deb and I were stopped at the gates of Gallaudet, before we pushed our way past knotted crowds of students, whose hands were striking sparks. There was anger flying everywhere. The university was under siege. Every entry gate was guarded.

We discovered: the Gallaudet Board of Governors had appointed a Hearing woman, Elizabeth Ann Zinser, who had a Ph.D. in nursing and who couldn't even sign, as the new president of our university. The board had explained to the student body that Ms. Zinser would take sign language classes and promised to immerse herself in the Deaf community.

We walked through the eerie quiet settling over the campus bowl. The Deaf students had closed the cafeteria. Garbage overflowed in disposal areas. Clouds of flies hung over the bags. Mice skittered on the grey cement pad behind the dorm buildings. Students streamed in and out of the dormitories to bring in food off campus for themselves and their friends.

DEB: "This is a great moment of history."

MS. HEARING WEBER: " . . . " *I'm not sure if I can support this protest movement. Beneath all that is Deaf in me is the persistent, nagging feeling that being Deaf is not the answer. Somehow, it's not good enough. When we leave Gally, we will all have to make our way in the Hearing world somehow.* I realized: *Saskatchewan. It's never far from my mind.*

Suddenly, I had too much work to do. The psychology paper was due next week, and I had to read the text for my speech therapy class, prepare for the Signed English exam and finish the language development assignment. Through the dormitory window, the red eyes of the tall Washington monument blinked, one off, one on, impervious to the marches, meetings, sudden groupings of signing students, and empty buildings. The early mornings were grey with a late spring overcast, although the cabbage roses along the footpaths were in full bloom.

On the third morning of the "Deaf President Now" week, Deb smoothed the fraying quilt on my bed.

DEB: "You've been holed up here for the last three days. Why don't you come out with me and find out what's going on with the protest?"

MS. HEARING WEBER: "I have work to do."

DEB: "But this is history in the making. You should be out there."

MS. HEARING WEBER: "Look, I know what's going on, okay? Gally students want a Deaf president to replace the new Hearing president who can't even sign."

DEB: "But there's more. I found out at the Abbey bar last night that the students want a board that has fifty percent Deaf and fifty percent Hearing representatives."

I sent a page flapping across my desk. "Uh uh."

She explained: "They want Jane Spilman to resign as chairperson of the board. She's Hearing and is the real problem. She's controlling the entire board."

I straightened my legs over the edge of the bed and arched my back, then asked: "Why are you telling me all this?" Today, the roar in my ears sounded like water rushing toward my tangled feelings, trying to break its way into the knots, the coils, the beginning of the snarled mess. I began again: "Deb, it's a special interest group. We're behaving like victims. I don't want to be anybody's victim."

DEB: "We've not been able to communicate in American Sign Language at educational institutions for nearly a couple hundred years."

MS. HEARING WEBER: "Yes, but this is *not* the way to go about it. It's against my conscience. I shouldn't have to argue from the view point of having a special language and a culture in order to be treated with respect. I am not a victim."

DEB (Sputters): "Joanne, this is USA in the twenty first century for God's sake. Nobody will understand that."

My eyes narrowed. I was surveying Deb with the precision of an x-ray machine. Maybe there was a flaw that would explain her obtuseness. I tried to isolate that flaw from everything else that rang true about her. I said: "Look, the whole premise is wrong. I arrive at Gallaudet, only to find myself on the lowest rung of the social ladder because I can speak and because I went to school with Hearing kids. Now, because I'm not fluent in American Sign Language, didn't have Deaf parents and didn't go to a Deaf school, I should start up a protest for the hard of hearing, oral Deaf, mainstreamed people who are being treated like shit by Deaf people? This is just one group vying for power against another group. It's all backwards."

DEB: (Coldly) "What do you suggest then?"

MS. HEARING WEBER: "Argue from the basis of needs as opposed to rights, I . . . "

DEB: "No one will listen to your needs."

MS. HEARING WEBER: "It's just an ideology."

Deb picked up her jacket and left the room.

❧

That night, I dreamed of visiting a leper colony. The lepers showed me their stumps and patches of rotting flesh and I saw how infectious the disease was, I could even catch it from the ground by walking over the graves of deceased lepers, then I stooped into a low doorway of a thatched hut, a tall, gaunt priest was curled up in a fetal position in a very large shallow bowl filled with stagnant water, stirred, and the midges fluttered around him as he woke.

He said: "Please hold me."

He said: "Kiss me."

I woke up chilled, and realized that I'd kicked off my covers in the middle of the night.

I asked myself: "Who is this man in my dream and what does it all mean?"

The answer came easily, too easily as I squirmed into my jeans: *Fr. Damien, the priest who lived with lepers on Molokai, an island in the chain of Hawaiian slands, who eventually contracted the disease and died a leper.*

But I'd read enough Jungian psychology to know that dream figures represent a dimension of myself, that the little girl in the red coat has morphed into Fr. Damien, who wants to be held despite the hideousness of leprosy, uh, deafness, and the Deaf, who've absorbed the shame of being deaf by being told that the Hearing world is the only world they can possibly fit into with their defective hearing and speech, they are my leper friends who show me their wounds, but the Deaf who are barricading the gates of Gallaudet University are triumphant, because they've shown the world that they are capable of deep thought and action.

❧

The next night, Deb came into my room to tell me that the protesters were going to carry the banner from Martin Luther King's historic protest on Capitol Hill thirty some years ago, "WE STILL HAVE A DREAM." The next morning, I left my dormitory room to march in the protest up to Capitol Hill. It wasn't only the promise of carrying the historic banner that propelled me out the door but my own dream that carried me to the front gate, where I took my place in the crowd behind the banner, Deb falling into step with me under the balmy May sky, Kurt catching my eye and grinning, then hands slapping against chests, wrists, palms, and arms, signs punctuated by hoots toward individuals caught up in other signing clusters, while the march inched up Capitol Hill with the long canvas sign as the masthead, the black slum community lining up along Florida Avenue and cheering as the Deaf students walked down the middle of the road with their hands flying, cars honking their horns, and many business people carrying briefcases waving as we approached Capitol Hill.

The day was sunny and the mood was jovial. A week without services, classes, or cafeteria food had catapulted the student body into a holiday mood. When we arrived at Capitol Hill, the student leader, Greg Hlibok with fiery eyes bulging from a pale face and blond hair, punctuated the air with "Deaf President Now!" Then the news came: *Elizabeth Zinzer, the president elect, has resigned.* Now the signs went up with the number 3½ scrawled all over. The Deaf students now wanted three and a half demands to be met. They demanded that Jane Spilman, the chairman of the board resign, the new board to be comprised of fifty percent Deaf and fifty percent Hearing, and no reprisal for the student activists. After a few days of tense negotiations, the Deaf students were excused from any sort of discipline and returned peacefully to classes.

The night before I was to fly back to Canada, Deb gave me her Derek Bell tape of Carolan's harp music. We sat and listened to the entire tape, watching a candle flicker in her room, casting shadows against the wall.

She finally said: "You don't really trust me, Joanne."

I felt Little Red Deaf Coat rustling around inside of me. She rattled her bars: *The whole Deaf thing is just wonderful, don't be silly.*

But I thought: *If I can't manage more than a trite or facetious remark, then I better keep silent, because I don't know how I am going to explain to her this crazy desire to go back to Saskatchewan. Even if it means entering hostile territory, it's still home.*

Twenty

Mrs. Woodward, the Director of Speech and Communication Disorders at the Saskatoon School Board office wore a jacket with beaded outlines of giraffes craning their necks over tall sequined grasses, a tribute, no doubt, to the richness of multiculturalism. I sat across from her, tucking my legs under the chair. I'd just returned from my year at Gallaudet hoping to land a job with this school board. She leaned forward to shake my hand. We played our story out:

MRS. WOODWARD: "Your resume is very impressive, Joanne. All that work at Canadian universities. You did graduate work at the University of Alberta?"

JOANNE, MAYBE HEARING, IT DEPENDS: "Yes, I earned a master's in library science, but I'm now a qualified teacher of the deaf, since I went to Gallaudet."

Mrs. Woodward refocused her eyes on me. She drew in her mouth as if to keep herself from blurting out something. She composed herself before continuing.

MRS. WOODWARD: "We are concerned with how neutral you can be as a teacher of the deaf. After all, you have excellent speech skills. But you sign too. We are very committed to oralism."

I tried to swallow, but a small plate seemed to lodge itself sideways in my esophagus.

JOANNE NOW HEARING: (*With difficulty*) "Mrs. Woodward, I assure you that I value my speech skills. I have no difficulty with oralism."

MRS. WOODWARD: (*Smiling and nodding*) "You're wise not to give into the Deaf community and their demands for ASL. The Deaf here became so emotional over that Gallaudet University protest and picketed outside of the Provincial School for the Deaf here in Saskatoon. Even the local television station reported on their protest."

JOANNE CERTAINLY NOW HEARING (*Stammering*): "You don't need to worry. I'm committed to oralism as much as anybody else." (*Praying, silently: God, I need this job*).

MRS. WOODWARD: (*Laying Joanne's resume down on her desk top*) "What do you think of the Deaf Pride movement?"

JOANNE STILL HEARING: (*To herself*) Did something happen in Saskatchewan while I was away? (*Carefully*) "I don't know of any organization called Deaf Pride." (*She shakes her head*)

MRS. WOODWARD: (*With a knowing look, as if to say: you don't fool me*) "I remember you when you were about ten. You gave a presentation to a group of parents in Regina. You gave those parents a lot of hope. (*Extends her hand across her desk*) Remarkable, just remarkable. I'm sorry to say, however, that we have no work for you."

I remembered: *She thought I'd been involved with Deaf Pride, because I was interviewed by the CBC during the Gallaudet protest and that footage appeared on national television stations across Canada.*

∽ତ∽

I was naïve to think that genuine dialogue could happen between government officials, educators, and the Deaf community, and naïve enough to attempt it during the Task Force for Deaf Education underway in my first year of teaching at the school for the Deaf. Although the interview with the principal took all of five minutes, and essentially was a job offer, it didn't occur to me that engaging in the meetings, consultations with stakeholder groups, full frontal attacks on the "enemy," a.k.a. oralists, were forms of professional suicide. The Deaf school was threatened with imminent closure because of its swollen budget and the small ratio of staff to students. But I was resolved to defend the school because of the new language and culture that now fed my bones. It was an ironic homecoming indeed from Gallaudet.

Patti and I travelled to Regina. I was excused from my teaching duties to attend a meeting with her and Bill Lockert, the school's principal, and the rest of the newly-struck Task Force Committee on Deaf Education. At the hotel room we shared for the night, Patti threw the draft copy of the Task Force Report onto the bed.

She said: "The other Hearing members of the Task Force say that if Lorne Hepworth, the Minister of Education, accepts these recommendations, the future of deaf education is very bright. More programs, more services throughout the province and more trained teachers and interpreters."

Detecting irony in her hands, in the tightness of her mouth, I said: "But you don't believe that."

Patti's mouth drew downward. Her lips tightened to show her disgust.

I asked: "Why not? Think about it: the money from the school for the Deaf, over a million dollars a year, will fund all of that."

She said: "I don't trust their forked tongues. They don't want sign language, and they are not going to carry out all those recommendations, there's over seventy of them. They will only implement one: close the school for the Deaf and shove the responsibility onto the school boards. Look, Bill and I wrote a dissenting report. We recommend that the school for the Deaf remain open for the sake of the kids that can't be oral, with changes, of course. We'll give the report to them next week."

I walked to the window. The afternoon was already wearing away, a grey pallor was falling over the street below the hotel room, and the faces of the people scurrying by were pinched with cold. I turned suddenly and signed: "Gee, I hope they don't think I'm crazy, wanting to be part of the Deaf community."

Patti signed: "You're Deaf. You're one of us."

I signed: "No, not really. I never grew up in a residential school for the Deaf."

She signed: "That doesn't matter. You're still one of us."

I signed: "Yes, it does matter. I was mainstreamed in a small rural school."

She signed: "But it didn't work for you."

I signed: "Not entirely, no. I had to read my way through school and the teachers were no more helpful than mannequins in a store. But there were some good things about it."

She asked: "Like what?"

I answered: "I learned to survive. At least, I learned to read."

She signed: "Reading isn't everything."

I answered: "It is to me, and it bothers me that many profoundly deaf students are semi-literate. They can't read past grade four or five reading levels. There's something really wrong about that. I don't understand why."

But she signed: "Joanne, your ability to read and write as you do is the result of many years of practice."

I answered: "I just happen to have this innate ability to read and write."

She signed: "That's nonsense, Joanne."

So I asked: "How else do you account for the median reading level of deaf people being at grade four?"

She answered: "Practice, damn it, bloody practice. Not everyone has the motivation and work ethic that you have."

I signed: "But written English derives from spoken English. It's hard to learn it any other way."

She answered: "There are other ways to educate a Deaf person. There are many Deaf who can't speak a word yet have doctoral degrees from Hearing universities. Take Dave Mason for instance. He's a professor at York University in Toronto."

The hotel room was pitch-black. I descended quickly to a deep sleep, but woke three hours later. I needed to go the bathroom but I didn't want to turn on the light to see my way because that would wake up Patti. I tapped along the wall into the dark bathroom, searched with my foot, sliding it over the cold ceramic tile, feeling for the toilet. I felt the air move. I stopped. Then a hand brushed past my wrist. Frantic, I tried to snatch the hand. My only thought was to protect Patti sleeping in the bed, but the bathroom light ambled to a full glare. Patti stood before me, shaking in laughter. Finally, I began to giggle too.

A few minutes later, I curled myself around a pillow. The afterimage of Patti's face wreathed in laughter reminded me of a cool, refreshing rain, in which the patter of our hands beckoned me into a forest whose thick leafed boughs shielded me from an applauding crowd. The noise of their hands melted into sleep. Then I jerked suddenly awake, my throat constricted, my chest tight. I realized: *I have no choice but to stand with Patti if I want to be Deaf. I know that my reputation as a Deaf professional will be forever marred in this province, but I've found the other half of my being in my Deaf body. If this costs me a living in Saskatchewan, so be it.* And a voice urges me: *Get out of the province. Find a job in a Deaf school in another province. Just be Hearing or be Deaf. It's impossible to be both.*

ᴏ

Murray and I talked over coffee in preparation for a meeting with Department of Education officials, to work out a strategy to prevent the Government of Saskatchewan from making poorly informed decisions about the future of Deaf education. We had formed a coalition on Deaf education: me, Patti, and Peter Sicoli, another Deaf teacher, a parent, and Murray as the SGEU Shop Steward. I was impressed by Murray's union savvy, how he had been able to advocate on the behalf of workers in workplaces for years. He won every grievance; the staff had dubbed him "Defender of the Universe." He had no difficulty discerning the purpose of the Task Force — to close the school, under the guise of consulting with stakeholders.

ᴊᴡ: "What if the government gets really ticked off with you? Are you worried about losing your job? You were suspended for three days last week."

ᴅᴇғᴇɴᴅᴇʀ ᴏғ ᴛʜᴇ ᴜɴɪᴠᴇʀsᴇ (*Chuckles*): "Well, I am still here."

I sipped my coffee again, not sure what to make of his sacrifice for us Deaf, then said: "What really bothers me about the Task Force is that no one really knows what really works for all deaf children. There are all these recommendations without any real research."

Murray nodded thoughtfully, and said: "And the Task Force is hiring a research company to hold meetings with people."

"But that's all opinion, not facts. Just a bunch of meetings with stakeholder groups who all have vested interests. We need unbiased information, something we can draw upon when making recommendations."

Murray suddenly grinned, leaning back in his chair until his feet touched mine.

"Did I ever tell you about Stephen Quigley?"

"The language development guru?"

"Yeah, we got him up here from the States for a conference. Anyway, he asked us an interesting question. He wanted to know if we thought that deaf people could read up to Grade Four. Of course, all of us put up our hands. Then he asked, 'Grade Five?' Some hands went down. 'Grade Six?' More hands went down. By the time he asked, 'Grade Twelve?' I was the only one whose hand was still up."

His thick index finger was the size of a cigar and the hairs on top of his hand bristled in the weak sunlight from the window. The hand looked large enough to cradle a newborn infant, cup an entire breast, and span the space across my belly. My face grew warm. Yet his hands would never sign well. He wasn't able to cross his thick fingers, or manipulate them easily into a complex handshape. His brilliant ideas on Deaf education would show up in a book written by someone else, who'd beat him to the punch. Soon he'd tire of Deaf issues.

I told myself: *He's only another disinterested amateur researcher, a book away from the truth about deafness, American Sign Language and the value of Deaf Culture. As an educator, he'll go on to something else at the end of the day, because he'll never achieve fluency in sign.* I reminded myself sternly: *He's just another book, his body flattened on a page.*

Murray had already drained his coffee cup, and was searching his pockets for change. He had such a keen, intelligent face. *Two households, both alike in dignity.* The introduction to *Romeo and*

Juliet came into my mind unbidden. But the lovers were star-crossed. I thought: *I wish he were Deaf.*

Murray's warm smile disarmed me, and a bar of music, notes on a piano, began to play in my head. The tinnitus. I had never heard the music before. The music was slow, soft — a fugue. I tried to hear Murray over the notes in my head. I was thankful for his signing. I realized: *He wants me.* I cast my eyes away from him, although I knew it's rude to break eye contact in Deaf culture.

Piano notes slowed to a few dying bass notes in my head as I stood up, preparing to leave. Behind Murray's head, I saw the new rain skitter down the panes of the window. A weak yellow light had begun in the sky, lighting the tips of the curls atop his head. *I must go now before this evolved into something we'll both regret. He's married. Has two sons.* Although he'd assured me that his marriage was finished, and that it was only the matter of paperwork, I dared not entertain any ideas of meeting with him in the future. Even if it was over the Task Force.

He called: "Wait, Joanne."

In the split second before he spoke again, I told myself: *This is futile. Not only is he married but he is Hearing.*

He asked: "What's wrong, Joanne?"

I said: "This is not right. We must not meet like this again. We'll only work on Deaf education issues with the others."

Murray inspected his butter knife closely. The knife was a heavy dull pewter. He placed the knife on the table, lengthwise between us. He asked: "Why don't you reach beyond the knife and see what happens?"

I asked: "Is this a game?"

He said: "Maybe."

The knife lay on the tablecloth: a sword between us. My head began to spin. *Rochester did this to Jane, when he wanted to flush out her real feelings about him, dressing up as a gypsy, pretended to tell her fortune, probing, prying, trapping Jane into admitting her love for him.*

I pulled back, startled by my new and immediate greed for knowledge beyond books, beyond the warnings from my parents, and beyond the teachings of the Church. I told myself: *I've been ripened for this moment.* Words rattled in my head, searching for the trapdoor of my mouth where I might innocently agree to do whatever Murray wanted of me.

On impulse, I put my hand over the knife and Murray immediately encased my hand in his. These words rammed themselves against the door of my mouth: *This is wrong, wrong, wrong.*

Murray pulled my hand and said: "Why don't you come with me?" He held my hands. I'd become mute.

I rose from the table, my hand in his. I became sure that there was another language I'd never heard, seen or felt. Language was a function of the brain. Its complexity separated humans from most animals. It came from agreed upon sets of rules: grammar, syntax, semantics, units of sound called phonemes, and signs. The language I now glimpsed was a language of the body: the house of bones, sinews, and blood.

Greedy for more knowledge, I went toward it, thinking it a new country.

◈

Last night, I'd come to the bed as if I'd been Murray's lover for years. I thought: *He'll never know that I was a virgin until our long and languorous night.* Now guilt and doubt assailed me: *This is wrong. He hasn't finished his business with his wife. Why should I believe him?*

I rose from the bed, disgusted with myself. I thought: *I know better than to do something like this. After all, there was no language or country, only the sweat of our bodies. This is where my greed had led me.* My curiosity sated, I became my own Inquisitor: *Did I come to his bed because he can squeeze out handshapes in the half light of the lamp over the bed?*

I watched the early light steal through the slats of the hotel room's closed blinds and rest upon my discarded jeans draped over the worn easy chair and my socks on the floor. A frenzy began in me, stirring like sludge at the bottom of a muddy slough. Finally, furious with myself, I pulled my clothes on. I snapped the waistband of my jeans in self-loathing. I told myself: *I've forsaken the Deaf who welcome me with jokes, hugs, and a whirlwind social life for a Hearing man. Worse yet, I've compromised my own values and religious beliefs.* I thought: *I know better than to get involved with a married man. Why am I not satisfied with my new life in the Deaf community? The school might be about to close, but there is still a history, drama, poetry, art, dance, and a solid intellectual tradition associated with sign language and a life I could never hope to have with the Hearing.* I told myself: *We'll fight to keep it alive. I don't need to run into the arms of a Hearing man, especially now.*

❧

Between meetings, where Murray and I continued to work on lobbying strategies, I kept badgering myself: *Why have I put myself in such a dangerous position? How can I be so stupid? How could I sleep with Murray? He's already married! His wife is devastated and rightly so. How could I be so selfish? What propelled me toward such madness?*

But there were too many places for us to be alone. My apartment, his apartment, hotel rooms, classrooms, cars, the winding paths along the riverbanks, meeting rooms. I began to feel displaced. Soon I became literally homeless. I carried a backpack of clothes, since I never knew where I'd stay for the night. I left my backpack stuffed with my clothes, toothpaste, deaf education briefs, the dissenting report by Patti Trofimenkoff and Bill Lockert, and the newly released Task Force report, propped in corners of rooms like an uncertain and weary traveller.

∽

I couldn't concentrate on the interpreter's signing. It was not his fault. I just didn't trust this speech I was listening to. A decision had been made today by Hearing people for me and for all the Deaf in this province of Saskatchewan, embedded in the language of government that rolled off the interpreter's hands, a meaningless repetition of signs, while the interpreter was trying to find the nugget of meaning. *The political agenda*, I thought, *never spoken so how can it be interpreted into another language?*

Irritation bubbled up in my throat as I shifted wearily in my chair, until the interpreter relayed a succinct message: " . . . the Minister of Education, Lorne Hepworth, has accepted the Task Force on Deaf Education report and intends to implement the recommendations this coming spring."

I slid my hands under my thighs, and sat up to concentrate. The other Deaf Community members were sitting still, hands folded in their laps.

Paulette signed furiously beside me: "What of the dissenting report?" The interpreter's voice shot over the table like a wayward hockey puck for Merv Houghton, the chairman of the Task Force.

"Many of the recommendations from the dissenting report have been incorporated. We assure you that we seriously considered Mr. Lockert's and Ms. Trofimenkoff's desire to maintain the school for the Deaf albeit on a smaller or changed scale, but —"

Paulette asked: "The school for the Deaf will not close then?"

"The Minister intends to implement all recommendations we've made. Closure of the school for the Deaf is only one of the recommendations we've made."

Paulette asked again: "What about the students who are presently enrolled in the school for the Deaf?"

"They will be given the option of returning to the schools in their home community or attending the Alberta School for the Deaf in Edmonton at taxpayer cost."

Paulette asked, her face white: "And what will happen to this school?"

"The building will be given to the University of Saskatchewan. They'll likely use it for ESL programs for foreign students. Of course, we're reserving two rooms for the Deaf community. We'll call it the R.J.D. Williams Deaf Cultural Centre."

Paulette protested: "But the school is where we learn our language. How are the Deaf children going to learn their language during the day? We can't wait until evenings and weekends in the Cultural Centre to learn language. It isn't an option for them. They need the language to learn in school."

JOHANNA

We Deaf are still plagued by low expectations. I think. I scratch my head, my scalp is so irritated from fatigue, the report writing, the long hours in the night thinking about why my students are not achieving, why they are growing into stunted human beings. They do not identify with the Deaf community despite my encouragement. They cannot sustain long and meaningful conversations with most persons in the Hearing world. They remind me of the twisted trees northwest of Hafford, Saskatchewan, whose trunks twist and turn in weird configurations. People say the trees twist because of some paranormal reality; others say the malformed trunks and branches are a result of genetic mutation. My students have become warped as Myklebust suggests in his research. No wonder the Deaf academic community detests his conclusions. Participating in the life of a large and vibrant Deaf community would allow them to develop in similar ways to Hearing. How do I straighten them, when they are marooned between two worlds, when the Hearing are doggedly cheering them on with undulating praise and the Deaf community in Regina is dying?

Then it comes. My mother and her brutal corrections: *"Don't read those Harlequin romances, you can read better stuff than that."* Or: *"You've done a snow job on her, you need to be more responsible."* Or: *"You must learn the difference between lay and lie."* Or even as an elderly woman, poised with paper and pencil, making her diacritical markings: *"Say this word properly."* Each correction has jolted me out of my isolation, my inability to see what other people see in me, and the tendency to live inside my head. And to this day, I know that every one of those corrections were done out of love. And I've done it even with my own students, and it does work in very limited and small dosages. There is recognition in their faces when I do it. I shouldn't glance at the shocked looks on the interpreters' faces when I do it. And: my mother's way echoes (although for different reasons) the Deaf Way. Blunt signs. No beating around the bush. Just the facts, ma'am. Point out the obvious.

Later that morning, I look at the small half circle of students facing me. It's time for the talk, usually given after a month of watching, listening, and settling in. The leaves are already dirty against my classroom window, and the mornings are frosty. I sigh. It's going to be the same damn speech. The same as last year.

"Look", I say. "You've got to stop being such dumb deaf people. There is nothing wrong with your intelligence. But teachers are giving you pity passes because they think you can't do the work and they just want to shove you on. Or they give you high marks because they think that will make you feel better about being deaf. You know you are not doing the work. And you are manipulating the interpreters into giving you answers to questions in homework and on exams. In this room, you will earn your marks. If you don't work, you will fail my classes." I pause. "I've failed plenty of kids in here before. Right, Jonathan?" He nods knowingly, a tall gangly young man, who is growing sideburns now that he has turfed the Alfalfa cowlick at the back of his head.

"And what's this flopping your hands around like half dead fish? And your arms are like windmills, way too much to the top, the bottom, left and right sides. You were obviously taught sign language by hearing people who learned it from a book. They were too afraid to hang out with Deaf people. They thought sign language was easy, that knowing a few signs made them experts. But now, you will develop respect for our sign language. Sign has to be done in a certain way, your handshapes have to be correct, you will sign in the space that is mostly in the centre of your chest, you will learn to use classifiers. You will learn the grammar of ASL, you will . . . " I pause: "You will learn to sign like real Deaf people."

A student says: "But I'm not deaf, I can hear."

"You're deaf. You may hear, you may talk, you may sign but not having a full language either in English or ASL has affected your learning. That's why you are here. You're deaf. So what?" I flip the back of my hand out from under my chin. "You will learn to grieve over your hearing loss. You will see your Deafhood as a gift for others."

I turn my back to these students, to hide my grin as I plug in my laptop into the projector, readying myself for class. I turn again to see their stricken faces.

"It's not your fault," I remind them. "You were never taught these things. And you will learn now."

"Jonathan," I sign to him: "You want to add anything to what I've said? You were here last year. You might want to share some of your wisdom."

Jonathan's smile is wide on his face as he signs: "JW, we make you crazy but you love us."

Chapter Twenty-One

IN EARLY OCTOBER, I WAS DETERMINED to see a doctor. I'd put off the inevitable. Murray and I were together all the time, day and night. He had moved into an apartment. I still maintained mine. But it was for appearances only. I couldn't think beyond this, couldn't think of the pain this was causing my parents, Murray's ex-wife, his children. I was too busy arguing for the validity of Deaf experience, knowledge, and wisdom.

The waiting room in the doctor's office wasn't inviting: chairs littered with magazines, people melting in their fall coats as the day started with a stern frost and ended up with an Indian summer afternoon.

I said to the doctor: "I am spotting."

The doctor's voice boomed over his clipboard pinned against his chest. He asked: "How about a pregnancy test?"

I asked: "Pregnancy test?"

I began a frantic search in my mind for the date of my last period. I thought: *But I know, but I don't want to know, but I know.*

I said: "This arm." I began to rub my right arm. "It's causing me a lot of pain."

He said: "Sometimes pregnancy will cause a condition like carpel tunnel. It goes away after the pregnancy."

I said: "But I have had this problem for at least two years. It comes and goes but recently it has gotten worse."

He said: "Well, that can be a repetitive motion injury, especially if you started signing late in your life. The only way you can heal is to stop signing. You're about thirty now?"

I asked: "I have to stop signing?"

He answered: "Well, let's take a pregnancy test first."

An hour later, I asked the secretary in the medical clinic to phone Murray who was at school. I didn't want to try to hear on the phone and the clinic didn't have a teletypewriter, which would enable me to make the call myself, by typing to an operator who would then relay to Murray via voice.

I rehearsed explanations in my head while the secretary finished the call to Murray: *I was trying to follow the natural family planning method, but I guess I misunderstood it.* I thought: *Murray will respond with silence. I have three university degrees, am a voracious reader, and have actually taught sex education to Deaf students. How it is possible that I've misunderstood some pamphlet or manual?*

I was huddled in the corner of the examining room when Murray walked in, his overcoat fanning out behind him. The doctor was sitting on a stool, scribbling in the file opened on the examining table. The fluorescent light was flickering and humming overhead. Sterile gloves were already tossed in the open garbage. I had the curious sensation of floating up near the ceiling and seeing my arms wrapped around my waist, my eyes smudged like a trapped raccoon's.

Murray moved his chair in front of me, sheathing my knees with his large hands.

He said: "What's wrong, Joanne?"

I said: "I'm pregnant."

His mouth opened in shock: "Well, Joanne, how would you know? We really don't know yet, right? It's possible that you may not be pregnant."

Murray took my cold hand and covered it with both of his hands.

Dr. Williams had his say: "Because Joanne has some spotting, we're not sure whether the pregnancy is viable. But her uterus does feel bulky." He closed his file and stood with his arms crossed.

Murray said: "Why didn't you use the pill or something?"

I stumbled out: "Uh, I don't want to put chemicals in my body."

Murray responded with: "Well, you'd have to do something if you didn't want a baby."

My voice broke into: "There's the natural family planning method."

Murray's answer was: "That just doesn't work. You'd have to abstain for at least a week out of every month."

The doctor rolled his eyes and tapped his folder, while Murray eyed the floor, his mouth set in a line.

I explained: "It's against my religion. Artificial birth control, I mean."

Murray said: "Joanne, I thought you were a thinking sort of person. Karl Marx —"

I snapped: "I don't know, Murray, okay?" I pronounced these words as if I were proclaiming a final judgment on the state of things.

But I did know. I thought: *It's hard to live with so much nothingness, the dullness that seeps into my brain, leaving me to wander among fantasies and half-formed thoughts. I know that being Hearing, in my family, at school, and with Murray, is an opiate, mollifying me with the promise of togetherness, homogeneity, and ties of blood and kin. A deep passivity has seeped into my bones, tempting me to not to think about difficult topics, to assume that someone else will take care of me. Being Hearing is like being drugged, dragged down into the quagmire of half understood sentences, words, and phrases; it's easy to say yes or no to stupid actions, half-baked plans, and idiotic schemes, because I don't have enough hearing to participate in anything with anyone.*

Murray was conferring with the doctor.

About the child in my womb, I suppose. I thought: *I have come to the limit of my moral development. And I really don't have a clue what will happen next. Only the vague sense that someone else will figure it out for me and tell me later.*

Murray's face clouded in confusion as I laid my head against the tissue on the examining table and sank into heaviness. I knew what Murray was thinking, I thought: *If my faith, my beliefs are that important to me, why am I sleeping with a married man? Why am I living a life separate from my beliefs and values? Why don't I live according to what I know to be true? Has deafness so set me apart from the world that it no longer matters what I believe or value? It doesn't matter that I'm physically present at every Mass. Am I to be satisfied only with a life of reading? Shall I be satisfied only with those summer nights alone in my satin nightgown, rolling atop the nylon sleeping bag in the heavy canvas tent in my parents' backyard?*

In that cold examining room with Murray sitting at my knees, those questions were rhetorical, because I was pregnant.

Outside the clinic, the sky seemed like a sheet of steel coming down to press us flat. It was October, so the leaves in the parking lot lay in scraped piles against the clinic. As Murray opened the car for me, something caught his eye. He asked me to wait. I saw him disappear behind the clinic and come back carrying a box. He walked to a gutter between the parking lot and the clinic and picked something up. I couldn't see it closely, until he walked up to my window and tilted the box toward me. It was a pigeon with a torn wing.

Murray took the pigeon to his classroom and the Deaf students helped him to care for it during the week until he set it free.

I began to wake up in the middle of the night and drain tall glasses of milk before going back to sleep. I wrote letters to my unborn child in my journal, explaining the situation: *It isn't that your father doesn't love you, or me, it's because he's struggling with having made a horrendous mistake, of not finishing up his marriage in an appropriate way. Now he's not sure if he wants to be with you and me, or with his wife and two sons.* And I fiercely scribbled across the page: *I'm waiting, and I hate it.*

I still couldn't believe that I'd betrayed my own religious values and beliefs. My mother was more tolerant. She explained: "It's your biological clock. You're almost thirty, for heaven's sake." Other women on staff at the school for the Deaf reminded me: "You're not a teenager. You've got your education at least."

But they said nothing of Murray, who was teaching in his classroom in the far corner of the school.

Finally, the day arrived when I had to tell the whole school. Patti had called all the students into the library. I stumbled in, wearing a loose blue jumper and blouse. They'd known me as a lover of granola clothes, loose fitting dresses, and bulky sweaters, so they were surprised when I signed to them, my signs tumbling out in guilt and shame: "I'm pregnant, and I've acted inappropriately and don't do what I've done."

Daily, Murray and I sat in restaurants, contemplating our lot in glum silence. Murray wanted to explore reconciliation with his wife. I wanted to clean up this mess in the best way. I thought it meant doing the hardest thing ever.

JOANNE FIX IT FAST: "Murray, I want you to be free to choose whatever you want to do."

MUDDLED MURRAY: "But I'm emotionally committed to you."

LOGICAL AND HEROIC JOANNE: "That doesn't mean anything, Murray. You know it. I'm going to give the baby up for adoption. You don't want to make a commitment to me, and I don't want to raise this baby alone. Every child needs a mother and a father."

BETWEEN ROCK AND HARD PLACE MURRAY: "It's much more complicated than that."

JOANNE QUICK QUESTIONS: "But then, what do you want?"

Murray shrugged. A look of bewilderment spread across his face. My fingers flew over the dirty dishes on the table, bringing my signs close to my enlarged breasts and distended belly, signing: "Look, if you don't make any decisions, then I'll have to."

UNFOCUSSED MURRAY: "Let's just focus here. Life is very messy. You want to clean it all up by leaving me, giving up the baby, and moving to another province to get a job."

JOANNE ON HIGH HORSE: "I have to live according to my values and my faith."

DESPERATE TO SLOW IT DOWN MURRAY: "The only reason you can believe what you believe is because your parents support you, send you money, and tell you to come home and live with them. You know they don't think much of me."

The tips of my fingers hit the lip of my coffee cup, sending black hot liquid over the table. My signs were tight, while my speech had become slurred. I couldn't think anymore, I couldn't sign and talk and think all at the same time. I finally said: "We have to do what's right, Murray."

"But what is right?"

Weeks went by and my face felt like a heavy stone mask. On the weekends, I either slept with Murray in a narrow single bed in his sparsely furnished apartment, or at Dorene's. During the week, I stayed with David and Marion Gorrie, who'd taken me into their home. David taught in the Deaf Blind program at the school and he must have seen my stricken face, because he invited me to live with their family during the rest of my pregnancy. Meanwhile, I still had an apartment downtown. I thought: *I have too many homes and nowhere to lay my head to sleep in peace.*

Christmas came. I was five months pregnant. My family and I were seated around the dining room table. Bubbles clung to the underside of the glass lid over the holopsti, a delicacy reserved for Christmas. My father had painstakingly wrapped the gelatinous mixture of rice, pork, beef, garlic, ground potatoes, onions into rolls with sour cabbage leaves. The moist mixture lay steaming in tight rolls, stacked side by side in the warming dish like Cuban cigars. I was able to eat again after vomiting steadily for the past five months.

My father gave me a kitchen knife and a high-necked flannel nightgown for Christmas. I thought: *What's with the knife? And the flannel nightgown?* My mother had baked Scotch oat cakes, which to my surprise I could eat too without vomiting. She told me: "Your grandmother used to eat dried oatmeal by the handful when she was pregnant."

Back in Saskatoon after Christmas, Murray slid behind me in the single bed, pushing me toward the wall. Only the narrow space between my extended belly and the wall gave me enough room to bring my knees up some. Murray began to move his hands over my belly and breasts, while my mind turned over and over again, a tangled rope of images. Then there it was, the language between us that lured me into this mess.

But Murray was sending new messages that I didn't understand. I was no closer to the meaning of this language. I sprang up, round bellied and naked, frantic in my search for my clothes, Murray leaned on his elbow, his eyes blinking in the lamplight, I ran naked into the bathroom and crouched close to the toilet, retching most violently, as if giant pincers were digging into my belly. I rested on the cool floor, waiting for the spinning in my head to stop.

Murray sat beside me, his arm on my shoulder, his face crestfallen. He said: "Joanne, this has been going on, night after night. I think you're allergic to me." His face was sad, his eyes shining with tears.

Finally, we went back to bed. Murray sank back into his pillow, his arm across his eyes. I waited, but he didn't lift his arm. I slid out of bed and donned my clothes. It was now two AM. I put on my coat and quietly closed the door to his apartment. I shivered in the idling car in the subzero winter night. I wanted to return, open the door, and back my body into Murray's chest, sleep between his head and knees, and become a part of his dream, but I drove over the University Bridge to my downtown apartment.

After I let myself in, I sorted through my mail and breathed a sigh of relief. This was my home after all. I needed to be here, not sleeping at other people's houses. I ran the hot water for a bath and later fell into a deep sleep.

The next morning, I called Christian Family Services to arrange to give up my baby for adoption.

Between months five and six of my pregnancy, Murray and I rushed time and time again to the emergency ward, only to be told that I had false labour pains. Then my doctor began to investigate more, and announced that I must have an operation.

He said: "You have an incompetent cervix. You'll have to be sewn up to keep the baby from coming out too early. If you have another baby, you'll have to have this operation again."

This was the simple explanation, I knew, but I didn't tell anyone of how I'd dreamed the night before about lying on two single beds pushed together, giving birth to the baby, and seeing her fall between the two beds. I realized: *I'd fall too, if she falls.*

Anneliese was born blue and bloody on May 18, 1990. Murray had been at my side during the entire labour, massaging me during contractions and spraying me with hot water in the shower when I was too tired with the pain. He even interpreted for me in my meeting with the doctor preparing an epidural, and laid his head and arms over my head as the doctor inserted the long needle. I realized: *He is with me in this pain.*

A nurse inserted a plastic tube into Anna's mouth to help her breathe and wiped down her mucous, and blood-marbled body. Murray came over to my side, holding our daughter swaddled in a pink blanket, and cooing to her in a low voice. His heavy brow lifted high over his blue eyes, while I strained to hear the first words between father and daughter. I couldn't hear Murray as he searched through the blanket for Anneliese's body, checking for any imperfections.

I sank back into the pillow, eyes closed, escaping into the red hot desert under my eyelids. A few moments later, I opened my eyes, still slumped on the hospital bed, sucking ice water. I closed my eyes again, until I felt a presence in the room. Someone had walked in. I opened my eyes to Patti, holding Anneliese in her arms. By now, my baby was only an hour old.

Patti signed to me: "What are you going to do? Keep her?"

Murray's back was turned to us, a rare moment of privacy.

I signed back: "I don't know anymore. Murray wants her to be given to those parents we selected."

Patti inserted her finger between the blankets to stroke Anna's chin and looked into my eyes.

She said: "Her name sign will be *A* on the chin and will land as *A* on her heart. That's because she started in your head and now has landed in your heart."

Green Journal

I thought, well, with her being nearly thirty, I'm hardly surprised she's pregnant. It's as if those two planted a crop and hoped for failure. The worst thing is that Joanne is so impulsive and highly suggestible. This is not the sort of thing she'd do on her own. Clearly, Murray was able to persuade her to compromise on her values and to abandon her faith. I know how much Joanne values being Catholic. He obviously persuaded her to fling away her morals and beliefs.

I don't think that Joanne realized that she wouldn't have a job after this Task Force business was done. We did our best, even wrote a brief and attended a few meetings. The school for the Deaf needs to remain an option for deaf kids who can't function in a mainstream environment. Not everyone can do what Joanne can do and that's okay. But not everyone involved in the stakeholder groups has teaching experience and understands this. Ed and I have no problem understanding where, when, and how mainstreaming might not work for many deaf children, but now the school will be closed at the end of June and Joanne will be out of work.

It's so hard to believe the path she's taken. She was always a good girl. We never had to worry about her, and Ed always gave her the car anytime she asked for it. When she talked about how bored she was cruising up and down the main drag with her friends, I knew she'd be okay. She was too much into her books and all her activities — figure skating, swimming, drama, volunteering at the developmental centre, piano — to be a worry of any kind. But she really balked when we wouldn't allow her to attend the bush party on her graduation night. She stomped up to her bedroom during supper when we remained adamant, but I knew that she'd be bored there. She'd been bored at the last one. That party seemed to lodge itself in Joanne's mind as some significant ritual, some rite of passage. She'd even found an escort, one of Ed and Fay Keller's boys, and I'd bought her a pink dress. Her Aunt Joanne and Uncle Paul were invited out along with my mother and I thought that'd be plenty of excitement right there. Ed and I didn't want her to go out to Coldspring and drink in the bush with all those kids. I had a keen feeling that something bad was going to happen. We made sure that Joanne was delivered to our doorstep at midnight. It turned out that one of her classmates did die that night. He was drunk when he rolled his car on his way back from Coldspring.

Now I'm beginning to wonder if Joanne skipped her teenage years. Perhaps this is the payback for not allowing her to go to that bush party, and now she's pregnant by a married man who can't make up his mind whether he should go back to his wife or be with her. I often tell Joanne: "If he's worth anything, he'll go back to his wife and look after his two young boys."

I'm not sleeping well these nights and have moved into one of the small bedrooms so I don't disturb Ed. Too many dreams. Too many thoughts about Joanne. Perhaps something went terribly wrong in the way we raised her. Last night, though, I dreamed of her baby being born. The sky outside the hospital room was very dark when the child was brought in. I watched the sky become emblazoned with different colours, first a dark purple, then a lighter green, then a warm orange, and then it turned into the normal flush of early morning: a light grey blue. It reminded me of Julian of Norwich: *All will be well.*

Twenty-Two

Green Journal

Joanne's been unemployed since the school closed in June. She turned down offers of deaf education jobs in Manitoba. She thought there was hope that the school for the Deaf wouldn't be closed. Anyway, she's right not to move with a small baby on her hands. How ironic. Joanne has put all this effort into becoming Deaf, and is now allowing some Hearing man to keep her trapped in Saskatchewan. She tells us there's going to be an exodus of her Deaf colleagues. She'll be the only Deaf teacher left behind. Simply because she got pregnant.

At the end of summer, on the first day of the term for the last year at the Deaf school, Murray came to see me. Anna played at our feet, clutching her yellow quilt with the white swans while he showed me a letter he'd just received. He was shaking his head.

"They've fired me. Damn." He folded up the paper in his hand. "And to make it look like an innocent layoff, the Ministry sacrificed Angela too. She's been in her classroom all last week getting it ready for the new school year. She got this letter just now. I was talking to her a few minutes ago. They did this to shut me up."

Green Journal

Well, Joanne's foolishness is not likely to end anytime soon. She's pregnant again, and it is six months since Anna was born. And Murray is now in Regina, living with his boys and working at his new government job. Joanne just got a short term job at SIAST in Saskatoon, replacing a teacher in the deaf adult program there. She'll have her hands full, being pregnant, looking after a toddler and teaching full-time. And I don't think she wants to move to Regina to join Murray.

I told myself: *It's a scorched landscape*, as I held Anna and Paula's hands to prevent them from running pell-mell down the quiet, abandoned hallways of the former school for the Deaf —open during the day because an English as a Second Language program administered by the University of Saskatchewan had encroached upon the former classrooms. Meeting with other Deaf in the cultural centre felt like huddling in a bombed-out shelter. I didn't know this Deaf life as a child, but I had no difficulty understanding how Deaf culture depended on the school for its survival. Everyone in the Deaf community attended every graduation, play, concert, performance, tea, barbecue, and picnic and every softball, volleyball, and darts game hosted here. The older Deaf women were surrogate grandmothers to the students. The boys slammed each other into lockers along the halls, swearing vociferously, but remaining brothers even in their adult years, after growing up to be barbers, printers, house painters, postal workers, and farmers. They had cousins, aunts, and uncles scattered in a radius around Saskatoon. They didn't visit them much. Those weren't their families.

We were a straggling bunch now, bolstered occasionally by Deaf leaders from Ontario and British Columbia, who flew out to exhort us to keep up the fight and not lose hope. Murray urged me not to give up, but I could barely think of Deaf education anymore, now that I woke up in the middle of the night to breastfeed Paula, and change diapers on both daughters.

I thought: *Murray and I can't get it together.*

I couldn't bring myself to move to Regina though I wished I could. I even put a deposit on an apartment near Murray's home, then panicked. Meanwhile I was on social assistance, living in a tiny apartment in Saskatoon, completing small contracts for the Catholic School Board. Murray continued to coax me to move, but he was too unsure of what he really wanted. I liked my tiny Saskatoon apartment. It was the only life that made sense, to be far away from a Hearing man who was in too much grief over his collapsed marriage, yet I couldn't stay in Saskatoon longer than three or four days. I packed diapers, toys, and blankets for a short trip to Regina every weekend to visit Murray in his house. After a few days in Regina, I was anxious to get back to Saskatoon, to my Deaf women friends, to the playgrounds, parks, and paths along the riverbank. Anna was nearly three. I was spooked when I thought of myself at three, in a red coat. The tiny apartment seemed haunted when I woke up in the middle of the night, sure that a hand had passed over my face. *Jane Eyre wakes up too*, I reminded myself, *to the screams of the mad wife*. I felt chest pains and choking sensations in my throat, but I told myself: *I am being overly dramatic.* But somewhere, someone was crying in me. All the time.

With Anna and Paula firmly strapped in their car seats behind me, and the roar of the wind, and a few hours of the exhilaration of being on the road with no one to disturb me, and the smell of canola in August taking me back to when I was a child riding in the car with my father, I arrived in Regina, but the next morning I wanted to pack up and go back to Saskatoon again. I could see the Wascana Freeway through the trees as Anna and Paula played in the backyard. Murray worked throughout the day. I looked after his sons when they came home from school, and cooked meals, but during the day I listlessly wandered through his house, singing to my daughters like a distracted Ophelia.

I thought: *There are too many things wrong with this life. I don't see enough Deaf people in Regina to feel all the ways I am Deaf in my body, other than not being able to hear very well. In Saskatoon, I'm a single parent without a job.* And: *There's no place for me. I don't belong anywhere, least of all with Murray. He's still grieving. He's kind to me and clearly loves Anna and Paula, but he keeps mementos of his wife in his house and garage.*

Meanwhile, in my backpack, I carried pictures of my childhood: the red coat, the yellow dress, the doll I'd forgotten, and the red playhouse by the sandbox, and thought: *There are too many things that are wrong. Everything is lost, gone, or destroyed.*

In all this restless shuffling from place to place, I was too lonely and too isolated. Something was devouring me from the inside.

৵৹

Traffic was already thundering along the Ring Road in Regina when I awoke and breastfed Paula, who fell asleep again with a droplet of milk snaking its way down her chin. Anna was playing at my feet, looking into a hand mirror that Murray had bought for her birthday. She tried to fit her round three-year-old face into it by holding it at different distances. After breakfast, Murray bent down to kiss Anna, then stood before me, where I was cradling Paula on the couch.

He said: "You look tired, Joanne."

I said: "I'm fine." I bit my lip. I wanted to make it a proper goodbye, but my tongue seemed locked inside my mouth. I was uncertain about leaving him. I wanted to say one more time: *Let me have a room here in this house.* I thought: *This solution is more reasonable than taking children away from their father.*

But he still didn't know what he wanted, his wife or me. He just said: "Stay indoors today, Joanne. This heat wave is very dangerous."

I nodded. My mind was racing. *This is all wrong. He cares for me, I've got it all wrong.*

He said: "Joanne, did you hear me? Make sure you put sunblock on the girls and a hat if you have to go out. And always take a water bottle with you."

Then he held out his arms. Surprised, I put Paula down on the couch and walked into his chest, interlocking my cold hands around his neck, but during the short embrace, I thought: *How condescending he is. Always telling me what to do. As if I don't know my own mind about things. He is the Hearing man who is only with me because he wants to feel powerful.*

He called out: "Goodbye."

I said: " . . . "

I was waiting for the faint click of the doorknob.

I was not going back to Saskatoon that day. This was the journey I had to take, to find out where I must go from here. Dorene was waiting for me in Calgary. She knew how tormented I was. The week before, she'd phoned me: "Come to Calgary, Jo, and stay with us. David and I miss you, we love you, and James and Desiree will be happy to play with Anna and Paula. Come so you can make your mind up about things."

My small car wasn't air conditioned. The drive from Regina to Calgary would take all day. I hadn't done much long distance driving, except back and forth between Regina and Saskatoon. I picked up the keys by the phone and gently pushed Anna toward the door. She was clutching her swan quilt. I backed the car out the garage slowly, like pulling a sticky popsicle from its thin paper bag. I wanted to leave, but I didn't want to leave. I stopped for groceries, and at least five pounds of chocolate. The air rushing through the open windows didn't bother me. I'd tucked my hearing aid in the glove compartment. The sky was cloudless and defiant. The heat wave that Murray warned me about was following us across the prairie, Anna and Paula sucked on ice water in their bottles, I popped a chocolate into my mouth every few minutes, soon the car was on the Yellowhead. I clutched my written directions at the wheel, glanced at Paula and Anna strapped in their car seats behind me, they'd gone to sleep again under the steady hum of the car, with its windows wide open to the sweet pungent smell of yellow canola. In Swift Current, I was desperate for a paddling pool. After a few moments of dipping our ankles in the cool water, a thunderstorm chased us back into the car. Out on the highway, swathed in damp towels, feet streaked with long blades of grass, we sang until our reedy voices became drowned by the roar of the air coming through the rolled down windows.

The clouds on the horizon continued to fulminate in angry colonnades as I pulled over to a little town huddled around a gas station and an adjoining restaurant. A fall of multi-coloured beads separated the restaurant from the gas station. Short runs of red, blue, green, pink, and orange glass beads clacked against each other as Anna and Paula ran back and forth through the doorway. I clenched my jaw as the beads separated over their heads and crashed against the door frame. I called: "Anna and Paula, stop running through the beads." But they ran to the end of the restaurant past me. I could feel the stare of the farmers pausing over their coffee cups. I clapped my hands smartly, "Paula, Anna, come to Mom, come."

Paula charged from the far end of the restaurant, whipping past my outstretched hands. Anna was a close second. The restaurant cook, an energetic woman in her sixties with a badly stained white apron, came out of the kitchen to watch. She stood with her hands on her hips. She ordered: "Come here."

She beckoned us past the soup simmering on the stove to a back entry padded with large black garbage bags. Finally, we were standing at the back of the building, in the tall grasses, watching the cook fumble with the latch on a plain wooden door silvered with age. The door flattened the grass as the cook stepped inside, feeling the inner wall for a light.

She talked over her shoulder before preparing to lead us down the wooden steps into the basement: "Ooo ay in eer."

My daughters and I sat on chairs around a dirty card table in the cool, dark room, staring up at the shaft of light through the open door, where tall blades of grass bent in the cool wind. The cook hurried down the creaking steps, and I caught her face as she came near.

She said: "Here's nice cold water." She set glasses down on the dirty table between Anna and Paula. I let the cool water roll over my tongue, taking my breathing slow. The cook was standing on the first stair up. Light surrounded the back of her head, casting her face into shadow. She was talking and I couldn't see her face well enough to lipread her. I wondered: *Is she an angel?*

Then I was back on the highway to Calgary, and realized: *I'm more than halfway on this journey. I've outrun the angry clouds. My children are thriving. The goodwill of the angel cook and the chocolates have kept my fear at bay.*

In Medicine Hat, in the approaching evening and persisting heat, I found a park with a swimming pool, and made sandwiches on top of the cooler, watching the girls play in the playground. Later, when the lid of the black sky was about to close on the horizon, they were suddenly quiet in the car. The car windows framed the snapshots of lightning as I hunched over the steering wheel. Wind buffeted the car toward the shoulder. I could see my white knuckle bones as I gripped the wheel to force the car back onto the highway. I reached into the cooler beside me and felt melting ice and floating bits of lettuce, soggy bread crusts, and torn cheese slices. No more chocolate. A thousand spears of rain rushed towards the window. It was now a mask of swollen rivulets. I slowed the car again and made out a roadside gas station. I stepped out of the car. The wind was at my back.

A gas attendant in saggy grey overalls stood behind a dirt encrusted cash register and pulled his cap further down on his head as I approached him.

I asked: "Is there a tornado warning?"

He said: "Oonan oooo leeen aaadeeoo?"

I lied, pushing in my ear mold for a snugger fit as I didn't want a squeal to betray me: "The car radio is not working. It is okay to go on? Yes or no?"

He said: "Yeah." He nodded.

I came into Calgary at midnight. A wasteland of lights sprawled before me, a city sleeping in the wake of storm. I cruised down ghostlike freeways, calm and mysterious in the dark. The girls were sleeping in the back, Paula's fine black hair awry in wisps across her forehead and Anna's blond curls sticky with heat. I clutched my written directions and slowed the car at each street corner so that I could decipher the house numbers. Finally, I eased onto an empty street, turning off the motor as lights sprang on in a house.

Dorene greeted me wide-eyed at the door, with: "Jo, I've been so worried. A child died in a car today because of the heat."

I said: "We're all right." I laid my sleeping daughters on the foldout couch in the living room. In the kitchen, lit only by the back porch light, I sipped tea and explained the delays.

I awoke with the sun already high in the window, and I could see Anna running back and forth on the deck through the sliding doors in the kitchen, playing with James and Desiree, Dorene's preschool children. I found a clean coffee mug and strolled out onto the deck with a book of haiku I'd stuffed into my backpack. The morning sun poked through the large apple tree in the backyard, onto the carpet of yellow and red crab-apples. Already some leaves had turned yellow — the first flames of autumn. I opened my book on my lap. The words were petals: cherry tree blossoms in the spring, tea ceremonies on low-lying tables, clean-swept houses with sliding bamboo doors, a delicacy, a measured way of life, no visual noise, no busy lines, shapes, forms, dots, circles, rectangles, or bold colors, no confusion, none of Murray's anguish about whether he will have me or his wife, no more waiting for him to make up his mind. I thought: *My house is a Japanese house. Sliding doors to large open rooms. Low furniture, sparse and simple. A house that contains an intelligent and thoughtful life.*

I bit into my thumb, pulling skin from near my nail, causing it to bleed.

Now my thoughts were: *I've ripped the fat from the meat, have torn the girls away from their father. I have run away, to keep myself, a Deaf woman, intact.*

I wiped my bleeding thumb against my jeans and looked away to the apple tree, whose spent blossoms had spit hard, gleaming yellow red fruit onto the lawn, thinking: *Soon I'll have a home of my own in Saskatoon, where my daughters' hands will move like mine, mimicking my own swoops and falls. Their finger spelling will be loose and quick but carefully formed. There'll be a time when life between us will bear a sweet lightness, a delicacy like the song of the Japanese, a domestic happiness between small birds fluffing their nest for the winter.*

I moved my children to a larger apartment on the east side of Saskatoon, and later to a townhouse. I became part of a community of single parents who'd all found their way into this low rental housing complex. I now owned a consulting business: Lang Tree. Initially, I hoped to serve the deaf students placed in schools scattered throughout the province. After a few contracts, I saw that I couldn't provide support to anyone in the mainstreamed setting. I was called by principals desperate for a solution for a deaf student unable to speak intelligibly or comprehend what was happening in class, students were already outfitted with cochlear implants and additional technological equipment, I couldn't recommend using sign language because there was no one for miles around who could sign, and I couldn't recommend sending the child to a neighbouring provincial school for the Deaf, because school boards were obligated to provide services to all children with special needs within their home communities. I ended up recommending very little other than a gentle admonition: *Keep trying.*

I began contract work with Saskatchewan Deaf and Hard of Hearing Services to a burgeoning clientele of Deaf and hard of hearing clients in Saskatoon. I became a jack of all trades, even counselling under the supervision of a licensed therapist. I became increasingly frantic. I wrote proposals in the hope of securing funding from the government to meet the need for residential housing, provided educational seminars on drug and alcohol abuse, entrepreneurial training, rural outreach workshops, and mental health workshops, and also substitute taught at Bishop Murray Tutorial High School, which had a resource program for high school deaf and hard of hearing students.

My mother warned me: "Stop working so hard." She came up to Saskatoon to stay with me and the girls, trying to keep us all from crashing.

One day, I woke up with my entire left side numb. I held on to the walls of the hallway, fully dressed, ready for work.

My mother said: "Stop. You must stop doing all this work."

I arranged for a two week leave of absence and visited Tam Jim, the traditional Chinese medicine practitioner.

He felt my pulse, then paused. "Tell me about your dreams."

I told him: "I'm always dreaming about escaping from a group of people to the mountains, where I must go to look after Anna and Paula."

He wrote notes on his papers in the file folder. Then he said: "Maybe you don't want to help Deaf people anymore."

I nodded in agreement and walked out of his office, feeling lighter and happier than I had been for the past five years. I'd always fought to keep some kind of a foothold in a deafness-related field, only to have the work evaporate: the first two years at the school for the Deaf before it closed, then SIAST for a six month temporary position, then the consulting business, where I become a community service worker at an agency, along with short term contracts with the Catholic School Board, because there wasn't any work with the Deaf anywhere else, because I was so sure that my life passion was to work with the Deaf, because, after all, I borrowed a large sum of money to attend Gallaudet

University and now, with my arm in intense pain, and the lack of steady work, I knew: *I don't want to do this anymore.*

~❧~

I prowled the halls of the empty North West Regional College in North Battleford at night, peering into semi-lit offices with darkened computer screens and empty chairs, with stacks of papers and notes tidied on desks, and the frames of family portraits catching the light from the hall. My office remained lit, its floor littered with piles of papers containing data on the literacy levels in the northwest region of the province. It was 1998. A year since we'd moved here. I thought I'd enjoy the benefit of steady work in a small community. Instead, I spent several nights at the college, trying to finish up reports and projects left unfinished by people I'd hired. At seven in the morning, I nodded at the night janitors as I entered the bathroom — freshly bleached and deodorized. I stood at a large window in the hall and watched the pink fingers of morning across the low horizon. On the frost-crusted asphalt of the parking lot, I shivered and fumbled with my car keys, then went to have breakfast at my sister's, where my children were sleeping, and wondered: *Perhaps I'll see them before they trip off to school. I haven't seen them for three days now.*

After I picked up the girls from school that day, I scanned the dusty bookshelves in my home, estimating the number of books on the shelves. A sense of loss flooded over me: *I no longer read. Too busy, too tired these days. These books warmed my childhood, creating a vividness that I couldn't have experienced if I hadn't been forewarned by a similar incident in a story. Hearing comes by knowing what sounds exist around you. I can't hear any sound until I first read about it in a book.* Memories flitted through my mind as I gently brushed the spines of the books with my fingertips: *Little Women, Little House on the Prairie, Anne of Green Gables,*

Rosemary Sutcliffe's *Dawn Wind;* then the Russians: Tolstoy's *Anna Karenina* in a red leather binding and gold leaf, Turgenev's *Fathers and Sons*, Solzhenitsyn's *One Day in the Life of Ivan Denisovitch;* on to the French, Balzac, Cocteau, Baudelaire; *David Copperfield*, I'd read five times; the Bronte group; I lifted my finger over *Jane Eyre* before moving on to *Vanity Fair*, then Oliver Goldsmith's *She Stoops to Conquer*, stopped at Christopher Fry's *This Lady's Not for Burning*, a play I also read in that summer tent long ago, rolling in my cream silk nightgown.

The emptiness stretched out in my mind for miles in every direction. I realized: *If I'm to live with my daughters in this small city, I have to live without the Deaf community. I have to live in a desert. But it's hard to live with so much nothingness. The real desert, the rubble of stone, broken rock, barren mountains, and hills of sand, gives way to the world of broken vowels and suddenly torn words and phrases.* I tortured myself with: *At least, the desert fathers and mothers renounced the world, fled to the desert to live a life of prayer and sacrifice. But where can I go when trapped in a desert of broken sound? What is there to renounce?* I whispered: *Anyway, I'm not made for a life of renunciation and prayer.*

I picked up *The Brothers Karamazov* to read again. The next week, I rented *Anna Karenina* from the video store. The young man, Aaron, behind the till startled me as he exclaimed, "Oh that is such a wonderful movie, and the book is even better." The week after that, I began *Kristin Lavransdatter* by Sigrid Undset. I now read to know that I was not alone.

Green Journal

Joanne's move to North Battleford is a relief. We won't have to run up to Saskatoon to bail her out. But she's not working any less. She says she loves her job, and I imagine it brings her plenty of recognition and admiration in her workplace and from those

Indian people she's working with, but Anna and Paula don't get enough time with her. Ed fixed the back porch on her house and found a secondhand garage door which he installed at the back of her garage. I've been organizing her food and wiping down shelves. She's having trouble with those ants, so I mixed up some borax and icing sugar for her to put between the cracks in the walls and floors. I guess she's all right, although Ed thinks it was a mistake for her to leave Saskatoon and the Deaf community. She had the sign language, he says, and no real difficulty with communication, now she's back to square one. I guess you could look at it like that. I just wish she'd stop working so hard. She's very creative, coming up with these proposals for more literacy programs at the college, but she has that same wan, tense face she had before she left for Gallaudet nearly ten years ago. The difficulty with her working so hard is that it keeps her from realizing that she's deaf. I suspect that she thinks her hearing has improved because she's pulling off all these amazing projects single-handedly. She doesn't seem to want to stay home. She spends hours on the road, driving to meetings in Regina, Saskatoon, and all over the North West region, and out on the reserves. She's such a wanderer, dragging Anna and Paula with her everywhere. Her sisters, Ruth and Carol, have roped me into praying a novena for her. Apparently Ruth has heard from her sisters-in-law about receiving hothouse roses from Thérèse of Lisieux as a favour in exchange for their prayers. I don't put much store in these things, but we all prayed for a husband for Joanne, for someone to father those poor little girls. Nothing came of it, except on the last day of the novena, Rebecca, Ruth's three-year-old daughter, came toddling over to her with three wild roses in her hand, picked from the field beside St. George School where we were taking a walk. We figured we got our roses, as Joanne is such a wild thing.

Johanna

In the spa, my body is slowed to a few delicate flutterings as I push against the amniotic like fluid. Here, silence is an additional molecule to all the mineral components lying in wait to penetrate my swollen joints in my hands. As I sink deeply into the steaming waters, outside in the weak winter sun, then I see it. Why King Lear doesn't have a wife. The story bothers me since I've been considering it as an alternative to teaching *Hamlet*. Maybe my students will understand the story of a father with many regrets. They have father issues. Very few fathers are willing to learn sign language while mothers consult sign language dictionaries while going to the bathroom. And *King Lear* is the key to Anna and Paula that comes wafting over the waters in winter mists. His daughters have sided with their father in hopes of gaining his approval. Although Anna and Paula are hardly Goneril and Regan currying favor with their father for his kingdom. But there is something of it — in their turning their backs to me when I am in the room. They are still angry. And they will not know it until they meet some wise CODA woman in their futures.

I wave my hand weakly in the water as if it were a wand to dispel the mists of what I don't want to remember. Anna at age three, sobbing at the bottom of the long flight of stairs up to my office in Saskatoon: "*I want my daddy, I want my daddy.*" Blonde in a sky-blue knitted sweater, her large azure eyes rimmed red with tears, and I am helpless to explain why the waters have closed over us, why we are drowning without Murray in our lives. Instead, I am too bright, too cheerful with Anna though I know that I will pay the price for this decision someday. I will be made out to be a hysterical mother, easily dismissed. God forbid, no one will ignore a Deaf wife (not entirely), but a demented mother? Of course. We are everywhere.

Now I am in Regina with the girls, having moved back from North Battleford several years ago and Demeter is still not very generous. Even though my daughters, the two little birds have flown away, left home, I am still going crazy with grief, keeping seeds in my tight fists, refusing to nurture plants, flowers and trees. Demeters all lose their daughters, especially to men they don't approve of. We sniff, noses high in the air, of course we know better now, will always know better, until we find a way to nurture gardens going on without them, until we become more generous in our grief.

Where's the story for that? I ask myself. An answer comes too quickly. *What, you are still relying on stories to explain your life to yourself?* Why not? I retort. I can't hear anything else, and it's all I've got.

Twenty-Three

JOHANNA

Sometimes I make the mistake of fishing for compliments from Murray. "Do you think I'm generous?" I ask him, early one Saturday morning in bed. He shrugs. Every time I ask these impossible questions, I feel I've thrust myself into some nebulous space, hurtling toward galaxies, dodging meteorites, my eyes blinded by some crazy warped speed. *I'm nowhere with this, suspended between two points, and I want to be somewhere solid, fast.*

"Well?" I persist. "Sometimes," he finally says. And he pulls our white quilt over his head and drops back to sleep. But not until I feel his arm around my waist.

ﾟﾟ

Another school year and it was the first day. I shook hands with one of the new teachers and explained that I worked in the Deaf and Hard of Hearing Program and that I was profoundly deaf.

He exclaimed: "Isn't it wonderful how the deaf are being integrated into our schools?"

I continued, with caution: "Yes, but there are still many issues."

He expanded with: "But technology is taking down so many barriers for the deaf, isn't it? The internet, text messaging, Facebook. It has opened up new worlds for them, hasn't it?"

I snapped out: "I'd prefer a warm body to a computer screen." I turned away hastily and walked away.

In my newly-dusted classroom, disconsolate, I shook my head, thinking: *Nothing has changed. I've healed no one. Many students leave just as wounded as they arrived four or five years ago. Despite Sophie's calm ministrations, our listening, and my attempts to comfort, to guide, to challenge, and to teach, many students haven't been able to make a healthy transition into adult life. Some leave with an idea that they are Deaf, but haven't been able to integrate the knowledge into their bodies. Many leave, dispirited, unmotivated, fearful, and perpetually dependent on their parents for their future.*

My hands were cold. I picked up my stainless steel tea cup to warm my fingers. As I sipped, warmth spread throughout my body. One of Nolan's paintings was on the wall: an aboriginal elder, a woman clutching a bundle of eagle feathers.

I remembered, when he showed it to me, I asked: "Is the woman Deaf? Her back is turned to us. All we can see is her grey streaked braids. She isn't connected to anything else in the picture."

Nolan nodded his head slowly, and we stood there, looking at the brilliant cobalt-blue background and the corresponding blue in her fancy dress, beaded with intricate silver and white designs.

With the autumn sun floating into the one window by my desk, I reminded myself: *Nolan's painting is a sign that he has begun to cherish his Deafhood as a gift for others.*

I took a deep breath to go on with the rest of the first day, resolved to welcome the new signing deaf student who will arrive soon.

≫

Gina couldn't understand my signing, although she'd been signing all her life. She sat beside her father. Her interpreter sat beside me. Sophie and Catherine had arranged themselves further back, watching Gina's interpreter very closely. The room was warm this late in the afternoon. The other students had long gone home for the day.

Gina signed to me: "You don't sign like my interpreter." Her sign was English-like but with many misshapen handshapes, incorrect endings and prepositions.

I resisted the urge to show her how her signs should be correctly formed in American Sign Language. Instead, I asked: "How many Deaf people have you known?"

She shrugged.

I asked again.

She signed: "No one." The sign for "no" and then held up her index finger to indicate the number "one."

That sign looked strange, even though it was technically correct in signed English. But the Deaf wouldn't respond that way. They'd make the sign for "zero," which looked entirely different: two 0s moving apart.

My supervisor motioned to a middle-aged, heavy-set woman with strong mannish hands, and said: "Monica works with her."

I asked Monica: "Are you the only one who has worked with Gina?"

Monica said: "I'm the only one in her home town that can sign. I've been with her since she entered kindergarten."

I asked: "So, you two have been together for . . . "

Monica answered: "Fifteen years. Gina's nineteen. I'm the only interpreter she's had."

I nodded slowly. I could now easily predict the answer to my next question.

I asked: "What about you, Mr. Ellis? Do you sign with your daughter?"

Mr. Ellis lifted his hands to demonstrate. He talked and signed: "Yes, uh, a little. Slow . . . It's . . . How do you make the sign for the word 'hard'?"

I asked: "She has no mother?"

He said: "Her mom abandoned her in the hospital when she was born."

I glanced at Gina. There was no expression on her face. Perhaps she'd had nineteen years to get used to the idea. Only, something told me that she wasn't used to it at all.

I signed: "Well, you'll just have to learn new signs if you are to be with us."

Monica signed, pointing at Sophie, Catherine, and me: "But everyone here signs so different."

I answered: "That happens when you get into a community. People have different styles of signing, different vocabularies, different hand shapes and movements. We call them 'dialects' depending upon which Deaf community they are from." Gina warned us: "It's going to be hard for me."

I nodded my head absently. The room had become suddenly too warm and I couldn't wait to leave and go home for the day.

Later that fall, I realized: *It's harder for us. She wants constant attention. I can't turn my back without her putting down her pencil and watching me work with another student. Her reading is at a grade two level. She can't read most books that I give her.*

I decided that we'd start with *The Miracle Worker*, a play about Helen Keller, because Melissa had to complete her English credit. At first I'm delighted with all the questions Gina had, like: "Why is Helen Keller deaf? Why is she blind too? Where is United States?"

I paused at that one. Then I got out the atlas and showed her. Melissa sat tapping her pencil restlessly.

At lunch time, Gina had a barrage of questions for Catherine, who was eating a savoury soup she'd brought from home. The smell of onion, rosemary, garlic, and basil dominated the air.

Gina asked: "What's in your soup?"

Catherine: "Garlic."

Gina: "What's that?"

Catherine hunted for a picture in one of our picture dictionaries. By the time she finished explaining "garlic" to Gina, her soup was cold.

In a meeting afterwards, I proclaimed my delight with Gina's inquisitiveness. Catherine politely agreed. Sophie said nothing. I insisted: "She wants to learn."

Two days later Melissa tapped her pencil with boredom as I laboured to explain the word, "disease." Later that day, I told my staff: "I have to put Gina on a separate program as Melissa is getting too frustrated." They nodded their support.

We tried the *Heartland* books, because Gina said she loved horses, and even rode one at her uncle's farm. She clasped her hands in pleasure when I began reading the first novel to her, using ASL. She interrupted: "What's a bridle?"

I explained, then pick up the book to resume again.

She interrupted again: "Reins?" Then: "Saddle?" Then: "Ranch?"

I was beginning to notice a pattern. We didn't have conversations. Instead, Gina asked questions all day, every day. All of them in rapid fire succession. The minute I finished explaining one word, she lobbed another question at me. Question, answer, question, answer. I was becoming more and more exhausted. The other students sat quietly, watching me gyrate my arms, labouring intensively to convey meanings of words. I slumped at our meeting table after school.

I said: "How come she can't remember anything?"

Catherine offered: "She's not very smart."

I responded: "We don't know that yet because of the language delay, but I can't quite put my finger on it, this incessant need for information and not being able to remember any of it."

Sophie had it: "She doesn't need to. The interpreter does all her remembering."

I said: "I don't think that Gina understands what an interpreter is supposed to do."

Catherine: "She doesn't watch me for very long. She wants to interrupt me with questions every time I'm interpreting in the other classes for her and Melissa."

Me: "Well, she doesn't know how to use an interpreter properly. She needs to understand that the interpreter is for Melissa too. She'll have to learn to save her questions for later."

Sophie, suddenly: "Gina is not at all curious. She just wants attention."

We all sat quietly at the table. The heavy curtain that was drawn partway across our window to shut out the afternoon sun, fluttered in the breeze. I placed my hands on the badly scratched table and announced: "It's about the mom, then. Gina told me that her dad told her that when she was born, the mom went screaming down the hallway out of the hospital."

Catherine, indignantly: "Why on earth would anyone tell a deaf child that story?"

I mused: "By asking people all those questions, Gina is trying to make sure that no one ever leaves her. It's a way of trapping you into the same space with her."

Catherine, with a sigh: "We're going to hate her in the end."

Me, resolutely: "No, we're not. We'll do something about this problem. We'll *teach* her how to have relationships."

Sophie's eyes remained hooded and cautious.

And I concluded: "She is so alone. And terrified of being abandoned."

The interpreters nodded politely.

꩜

I began going to bed earlier each night in the hope of catching up on my sleep. It was darker and chillier in the evenings anyway. I was waking up at four o' clock in the morning, among shreds of dreams and waking images, picking at the twisted ropes of sheets and quilts, with Murray's back beside me, the curtain lifting slightly in the current from the warm air register under the window.

Too early one morning I couldn't sleep and thought: *Winter is coming soon and I won't have enough.* Then: *Enough of what?* I tried to remember, without thinking too hard on it. Then it came: *There won't be enough light. Hold on until St. Lucy's Day, the winter solstice, and then the light will begin to come back.*

I scurried into my classroom at seven thirty each morning, clutching my winter coat, cursing the coldness that settled in my feet, sipped my steaming coffee, sensing something tightening inside me, I was becoming trapped by the darkness in the morning and the evening, and I thought of Gina who was due in an hour, and shuddered at how she brought out the very worst in me.

An accusing voice interrupted my thoughts again and again: *You still don't get it. I don't have a voice, Gina doesn't have a voice.* I saw a dark face come before me in the night where I twisted the sheets on my bed, unable to sleep. The voice accused: *You don't spend enough time with me. You slammed the door in my face at Gally. Must I wait another twenty years before you'll even look at me again? You think you can save the deaf kids in your classroom. You'll show them the way. Indeed.* I couldn't get this taunting voice out of my head. The voice of the malformed fetus. Hooked up to the hearing aid. As her life support. I thought: *She'll never leave me. Never.* And: *How can I get away from her?* I awakened weeping and Murray took me into his arms. Under the weak light over our bed, I knew I had to tell him something, so I signed:

"When my mother and father left me in that crib, I had no idea how long they were going to go away. My mother felt terrible afterwards about leaving me in the hospital and she didn't like the way the nurse handled me, she was too rough, but I thought my parents would never come back. Two weeks was like eternity, especially when I had to endure those rough hands."

I relaxed in Murray's arms, and pondered: *Maybe recalling childhood memories is enough. Relive the trauma and let it go. Isn't that what all therapists say? It's a calm, reasonable move toward wholeness, the certainty of being healed from the past. We North Americans are very good at poking into our pasts to shape our futures. Maybe it's all we really need to do.*

I rose from the bed and grabbed my housecoat, tottering on feet that had swelled during the night. A few minutes later, standing in the shower, feeling the hot water pound on my neck, I was not convinced. Now I thought: *All the optimism and the technology in the world will never make me into a Hearing person. Nothing will ever take this deafness away from me.*

Later that morning, I drew a picture of an interpreter and a Deaf person on the blackboard. Gina sat at the table, waiting. Other students lifted their heads from their work.

I began slowly: "The interpreter is not a friend."
Gina demanded: "Why not?"
I signed: "Because that's not the role of an interpreter."
Immediately I saw my mistake but it was too late.
Gina cut in with: "What's 'role' mean?"

I signed: "Never mind." I was shocked at my brusqueness, but I repeated: "It's not the interpreter's job to be your friend."

Gina demanded, again: "Why not?"

I signed, again: "They are not supposed to help you." I explained to myself: *Well, yes and no.* Trying to find a way to convey this without bringing forth a tidal wave of questions. Then I stopped myself and signed: "Gina, what is a friend?"

Gina answered: "Someone who helps me."

I signed: "Do you help a friend?"

Gina shook her head: No.

I stood beside my hastily drawn sketch on the blackboard and tried again, with: "Gina, the purpose of an interpreter is to translate English into sign language."

Gina's face was blank.

I stumbled on, like this: "You're supposed to watch the interpreter and then communicate with the Hearing person through your own signing."

Gina's face remained impassive.

I shouted with my hands, making large signs, and pushing my brows together until they hurt: "The interpreter is *not* your friend."

The other students quickly returned their gaze to the books opened before them.

Every day, Gina's need was a giant maw, opening every time I dropped my hands to rest, to think of what to do next, but once I was inside her great need, the most I could do was to feel alongside the walls, looking for ways to escape her. I began with her voice, that high pitched squeal that had my other students clasping their hands to their ears in pain, even if they were wearing hearing aids and cochlear implants. Sophie and Catherine shuddered when they heard it and I tried not to wince when she squealed in front of me, and wondered: *Has no one has taught her the importance of decorum or manners?* I could hear her squeal in the hallway when she tried to talk to teachers using a combination of her hands and voice. Teachers nodded politely, ignoring the offensive sound, until one day, I came up to her in the hallway, and said: "Stop making that noise, Gina. You've got your aids on, you know that Hearing people don't make those noises."

She answered: "I thought I was supposed to use my voice. Hearing people want that."

I signed: "It makes you look dumb, Gina. Don't use your voice in this school. Use an interpreter."

I walked away. I knew that my savage signs would hurt her, but I thought: *It seems there is no other way to tame a beast.*

From that day in my classroom, when I heard the squeal again, I waved at Gina, and signed "voice shut off."

Sophie and Catherine began to remind her too, and we now had some quiet in class.

Catherine ventured one day: "A Hearing teacher would never say that sort of thing to Gina. They'd want her to use her voice. Thank God you can say that to her. You know, Deaf to Deaf." There was relief in her face.

I said: "Anyone should be able to tell her that she squeals like a stuck pig. Otherwise it's just plain patronizing."

I tried in vain to feel more compassion for Gina. Instead, I woke up in the mornings even more angry. Determined, I walked into the classroom, feeling Gina's eyes on me while I removed my jacket and opened my briefcase.

Gina said, immediately: "JW, I want to know . . . " She ran up to me and grabbed a book off my desk.

I signed: "Don't you ever touch anything on my desk." My signs were angry, hard, and my wrists were fiery with pain. I signed: "You don't need to know anything about what I have on my desk. It's personal."

She recoiled. Shock registered on her face. She brought her hand to her face, as if I'd slapped her. Then she sat on a chair by the table and began to cry.

I rushed over to her, placed my hand on her shoulder. I thought: *How could I be so heartless, cruel, and angry toward her? Her questions are the desperate replacement for undivided attention from the mother she's never had.*

I told my staff later that day: "She needs therapy. Years of it."

Catherine asked: "Yes, but who is going to do it? With her language delay? Who has the training? The sign language skills?"

We all looked at each other helplessly. There was no mental health professional with an in-depth knowledge of deafness and sign language in this province.

Sophie said: "They're just going to medicate her."

In desperation, I began photocopying workbooks, something I once vowed never to use in my teaching. Anything, just anything to keep her away from me.

I explained: "Here, Gina, fill in the blanks here."

She demanded: "What does this mean?"

I explained: "Here's the first example, now fill in the rest."

She demanded: "Is this going to help me get my Grade 12?"

I sat down in the chair opposite her. I asked: "Why do you want your Grade 12?"

She said: "So I can be like you. Have a good job, make good friends."

I said: "You can have a good job right now, without your Grade 12. I know of a place where you can work."

She signed: "But I want to be educated. I want to be like you."

I tried to draw her out with: "Gina, why is it so important to be like me?"

She said: "You can speak. You can talk. I want that." Gina mouthed her words as she signed.

My shoulders sagged with sadness and I felt my eyes soften. I said: "Gina, you're okay the way you are."

She signed: "No, I'm not."

I sighed again. I thought: *In two minutes, I'll be shouting at her with my hands,* but I said, calmly: "Maybe you need to think about how you feel about your deafness."

Gina signed, quickly: "I can't accept it." Gina was so ready with her hands, bringing them close to her chest, *accept.* There wasn't even a moment's hesitation.

We went through the rest of the day quietly. Gina asked her incessant questions, and I tried to oblige, because I didn't know what else to do.

Catherine suggested: "Make her do some work on the computer. Find a math manipulative website that she can do for a half hour every day."

I found a website. I directed Gina to do some simple addition and subtraction, using her mouse to drag brightly coloured shapes back and forth over the screen. I was elated at her apparent attention to the screen and walked over to my other students who are waiting for me.

Within five minutes, Gina twisted around in her chair to sign: "JW, what does this mean?"

She had clicked on a link which has opened a fractions page. Suddenly she turned away. She had seen the anger in my face.

Sophie walked over. She asked: "Joanne, are you all right? Your face is so red."

❧

Then one day, Gina didn't show up for school. We found out from her father that she had run away. He reassured us: "Wait until she comes back. She has done this before. Every so often, she wants to get away from my protection, you see, she resents it, that I have to tell her what to do all the time. But she has no sense about anything. She's like a wild animal."

Three weeks later, she returned, nervously swallowing as she walked up to my desk. She looked different somehow, her hair had been streaked, and she was wearing jeans and a navy sweater, an improvement over sweat pants and bunny festooned sweatshirts. She said: "JW, I know I've missed a lot of school. Please may I come back?"

I answered: "Of course." I looked closely at her face. She looked rounder, fuller. I asked: "How have you been?"

She said: "I'm living with my boyfriend now. He took me to his doctor and he gave me these pills. I'm on anti . . . something." She tried to spell it but gave up. "The pills make me calm."

A much more subdued Gina refrained from asking questions, but watched me incessantly from the corner of her eye. If I walked over to an interpreter's desk, she would find a pretext to use the pencil sharpener fastened on a nearby wall. If I sat with another student, she walked by, pretending to look for papers and books.

Catherine finally went over to her and scolded her: "Focus, Gina. Focus on your work."

At our meeting after school, Catherine announced in a loud, emphatic voice: "I've never seen anyone like this in the thirty years I have worked with deaf kids."

I watched Catherine steadily, observed the bird-like tilt of her head, her greying hair, her hands roped with veins. I thought: *She looks fatigued.*

I replied at last: "If you think there's no help for her, what would you recommend?"

She said: "Work. She needs to go to work, to earn a living. That way, she can grow up. She'll never get over the mom thing, she'll always be on meds, but at least she can earn a living and support herself. That will give her some pride."

Sophie nodded.

I rose from the table, snapping my daybook shut. I said: "I've been thinking the same thing but I didn't want to come to this. All right, then. I'll release her from the program. There is nothing I can do for her."

Sophie warned: "She'll be very upset. She doesn't want to work, because she thinks she is going to finish her Grade 12."

I said: "There is nothing I can do for her. The intervention that she needs is too little, too late."

As I snapped off the reading lamp before going to bed, I reminded myself grimly: *I should be able to sleep now.*

Instead I tossed and turned with guilt, as though I'd given into the darkness all around me. I reminded myself that St. Lucy's Day was coming soon, but the darkness grew, then I heard Sister Sarah say to me as she gave me a leafy philodendron: *Joanne, you need to learn to care for living things, to have something depend on you for its sustenance, even if it is wild, even if it has neither language nor words to share with you,* and how, after a few months of religiously watering it, I became so busy with my six university classes, my part-time jobs, and correcting papers for a professor, that the philodendron withered on my night table.

I woke at four o'clock, pulling the quilt over my shoulders, wondering: *How am I going to tell Gina that I cannot care for her and that she must go away from me?*

Gina wept when I told her that she must leave the program after Christmas. She wailed: "But JW, there is no one to communicate all day with. Who will I talk to?"

I said: "You can go to the Deaf community in the evening. Take ASL classes so that you can sign better. Go play darts on Wednesday nights with the Deaf. During the day, you can work at the grocery store."

She said: "I want to get my grade twelve. Why can't I get my grade twelve?"

I said: "I don't think this is the right place for you."

She asked: "Why? JW, why? This is the only place I can go to learn."

I explained, quickly: "Because you are not ready to learn. You are too hurt inside."

I rose and left her weeping in the wake of my fierce, abrupt, and clipped signs. I felt sick. Thoughts flooded my body: *Who am I to deny her an education, an opportunity for her to learn? How could I refuse her opportunity to sign with me and my staff after being stuck with one interpreter all those years? How can I be sure when she hasn't had adequate language development for most of her life except from an uneducated and untrained interpreter? When she has had only one person to interact with up until now.* Everything seems too late, too final.

Catherine, Sophie, and I sat around the table after school that day.

We say: " . . . "

Two weeks before Christmas, Gina rushed into the classroom with a book clasped to her chest: a small slim volume.

I eyed her suspiciously.

She explained: "Mrs. Sernich gave this to me. It's so beautiful." She thrust the book at me.

It was a book of poetry, *Amazing Peace*, by Maya Angelou.

I flipped through the pages, bewildered. I thought: *There is no way she can read this. Too abstract. The vocabulary would kill her.*

Gina touched me on my arm. She signed: "I want to make a sign video of this poem. Do it in ASL. You can teach me." Her face was glowing, her eyes bright with excitement.

She said: "I want to make copies for my father, my boyfriend and his family. The video will help me learn to become an actress."

I asked: "Do you know what this is about?"

She said: "Christmas!" Her eyes were shining.

I told Gina that we couldn't do the whole book, only a section of Maya Angelou's poetic work about the spirit of Christmas.

Soon I was translating lines about snow-covered villages, the coming of peace, the erasure of division between religions, the spirit that descended upon us all, reminding us that we are human, capable of great things. I prepared a gloss for each line, carefully writing them out underneath the neatly printed words of Maya Angelou on large sheets of newsprint, practised the lines to myself, taking care to incorporate features of ASL poetry, and I thought on these lines, the advent of hope, the charge Angelou made, that we were imbibed with the spirit of creation and need not resort to war, darkness, and deprivation.

Gina giggled in excitement as I shook out the large sheets of newsprint with the ASL gloss I had prepared for the poem.

She began: "It will help me get a job as an actress."

I nodded hesitantly. I wondered: *Do I scold her for her impossible dreams? Or let her remain in her fantasy?* I said: "Gina, you'll need to memorize this."

Gina sat with the large sheets for a few minutes while I attended to a math question posed by Melissa, who was watching this whole scene with immense curiosity. Soon I felt Gina at my side.

Gina pointed to a word: "JW, how do you make this sign, and what does it mean?"

I struggled to be gentle, to be kind, thinking: *She is leaving after all.* I said: "Gina, it's okay. I'll stand out of the range of the videocamera and you'll copy me. That way you don't have to memorize anything."

Gina copied my signing exactly as if she and I were mimes in a mirror. For the first time, I saw exactly what was on my own face. At first, I was startled. *She is too exaggerated,* I thought, as she shook out her hands for the signs *"lose friends, family, people."* The grief, the loss, the devastation of war, the spreading of hatred marred her face like an ugly crack. I thought: *Dear God, is this is what I look like when I sign? Like some feral being?* As she signed of hope, and of the peace to come, living in harmony, her face had the excitement of a child kneeling before the crèche on Christmas Eve, opening up her presents.

Every time we rehearsed these lines, I saw these faces appearing before me.

Twenty-Four

JOHANNA

I've realized I don't like Demeter. Her lack of generosity still bothers me. I've decided to discard that story. Demeter doesn't tell me about what I can be. With her, I can only be in one place at one time, either in the dark, or in the light, either above or below, in spring or in winter. Very Greek or Roman, very Western. A stingy woman, she won't let me be in two places at once. Stories like that aren't worth bothering with unless you want to nurse yourself through teenage rebellion or tell a third grader how spring comes about in an interesting way.

At night in early spring, I lay awake, thinking: *How can I survive five weeks in the United Kingdom?* We were to book our flights the next day. I tossed and turned in bed, I thought: *What am I supposed to do on this trip? Other than sightseeing?* I worried: *Murray and our daughters are going to make quick, off-the-cuff decisions and I'll have to follow behind them on strange streets, through unnamed alleys, and through throngs of crowds, an additional child, while Murray makes all the calls, navigates the road with Anna's help, she'll comprehend*

his mumbling questions regarding the need for directions as he turns another tight, tense corner in London; I'll have to listen over loud traffic to hear anything they say. I can't use a sign language interpreter for any performances. Or museum tours. I don't know British Sign Language. We'll huddle over maps in subway and train stations and I'll miss the conversation while I watch fingers travel over various points on the map. I'll be a child in strange cities and towns. I'll have no means of escape.

In the coffee shop the next day, I thought: *This is not a pilgrimage. We are not going to any holy shrines, not even to Celtic shrines, because Murray is not religious and has no interest in such things.* Yet I couldn't shake the feeling I was supposed to do something on this trip, learn something other than historical facts, and I felt my eyes harden in an effort to concentrate on the idea of a pilgrimage, that is not a pilgrimage, only the jostling crowds, the grey skies, the museums, the sudden bursts of rain, the Tower of London, and I thought: *Perhaps this pilgrimage is my consent to imprisonment, it will be the equivalent of being buried alive, for a reason I cannot yet fathom, there is simply nothing, nothing but years of being plugged in and out of sound, being at the mercy of some malevolent being delighting at yanking the cord that binds me to sound, speech, language, and communication at random intervals for the entirety of my life.* I wanted to protest: *But it is hard to live with so much nothingness.* I wanted to shout it out to everyone in that coffee house.

Crucible Journal

En route to London: My black pen burst due to the cabin air pressure. It's been a long day. Started at 6:30 AM. Checked in at Saskatoon airport. Meandered around Walmart in the Confederation Mall. Boarded at 11:35 AM. The flight to Toronto was uneventful. I'm so cramped and bloated. I think it's anxiety. Couldn't really eat dinner

278

after the big breakfast at the hotel. How will Murray and I get along? He's really trying, so I need not get my defences up so high. We've only been together for three years, the girls are now firmly ensconced in their early teens. We no longer have any romantic intentions toward each other, we really have had no time to get close to each other because we had to first pull together as parents to our daughters. Now there's a weariness in this pulling and yanking at each other. And it's about to get worse, now that we're at close quarters and I can't easily run away from him for a few hours. The crucible in which our foibles will become heated. The beauty of the husband shall emerge. I hope so. I want it to. I watch Murray lay his head back against his seat. He's anxious too.

Halfway to England: Hearing and Deaf. The opposites that don't mix, like oil and water. Everyone wants me to be Hearing. It's what my parents wanted for me as a baby, what teachers wanted for me and what young men wanted for me then too, and my daughters want for me as their mother. Everyone wants me to be integrated seamlessly into the Hearing world, with no, or little, effort on their part, but I want to be Deaf too. The two must mix somehow, so that I can remain intact. Perhaps when I come back, I can stay home, live in the Langley Hall in peace. If I come home. The London bombings happened five days ago. We aren't finished with terrorism in London yet.

ॐ

Six-thirty AM London. A dreadfully long, crowded, and hot subway ride to Victoria Station, twenty minutes of crowds, noise, heat, and jet lag, the twisting backpack that I'd balanced on top of my suitcase heavier with the 26 ounce bottle of whiskey Murray bought on the plane, over curbs, down flights of stairs, into the subways, and I screamed: "I hate London!"

Murray, Anna, and Paula turned around to look at me, their faces registering shock and embarrassment.

I thought: *Already, the crucible is heating up.*

We took a break in Garfunkel's, in the mezzanine floor overlooking Victoria Station, paying eleven pounds for two meals of eggs and toast, divided between the four of us, it was that expensive, then the train out to Croydon, a district in South London, calmed us with its gentle rocking as we peered out at slate rooftops, ivy covered gates and walls, and red-brick row houses. We picked up the keys to our flat and to our surprise it was a much more spacious apartment than we saw on the internet: very English, chintz, peach tones, flowers, beautiful dishes, clean ceramic tiles, washer and dryer in the kitchen, a tiny balcony with chairs, clean, well kept, and upscale.

Deaf Joanne said: "But the TV is not closed captioned."

She consoled herself with a book.

The girls and I walked a long way trying to find Whitgift Centre, where we struggled to find the groceries (that elusive jar of peanut butter, where is it?) and joined a long line to the till, with baskets of groceries weighting the crooks of our elbows. Then the power went out.

At first, I thought: *It's another terrorist attack, so soon after the subway bombs.*

In the dark, a click, and then nothing.

I started to flick the switches frantically on my hearing aid, until I realized that the battery was dead.

I thought: *Now I'm really deaf.*

I began to sweat, I looked about me in extreme agitation, my heart began to pound: *What if it is a terrorist attack? How can we get out of here unharmed? How can I escape? And keep the girls safe too?*

And I couldn't hear a thing.

I searched my purse for batteries.

I thought: *Damn, I left them in my suitcase at the flat.*

Sweat ran down my spine and settled in the hollow of my back. I looked up at the ceiling and there were windows allowing some natural light into the store and I signed to the girls: "Don't move."

I began to make out the shapes of people all around us. They were all standing still. As if time had stopped. We were about to be whisked to an unknown destination. I could see a bus waiting outside in my imagination, and gunmen in black masks. We waited in the lineup for nearly ten minutes. Then Anna nudged me. In the dark, I tried to lipread her, I made out her basic signs: "The till is closed. We are to leave our groceries on the floor and vacate the building."

Out in the late afternoon light we blinked, and merged with the subway travellers walking from the nearby station toward their homes.

Back at the flat, my knees shook with relief as I inserted the new battery into my hearing aid. As a flux of noise entered into my head, the comforting sounds of Murray and the girls' voices, the drone of the television, the low hum and tumble of the washer/dryer in the kitchen, I reminded myself, *London is hardly a desert landscape*, but there were too many images, sounds, and unfamiliar sights clamouring for my attention, as if everything was vibrating inside my head, molecules jumping around, perhaps heating up to an unbearable temperature.

❧

On the train to Victoria station to begin our day. I read several analyses on terrorism in British newspapers which had been discarded on train seats. Some articles were thoughtful, some callous, and many were impassioned. After reading, I thought:

One of the roots of Islamic terrorism is poverty, the grinding humiliation of not being able to obtain the basic needs for food, health care, employment, water, and shelter, the repeated inability to control one's destiny, to be always at the mercy of forces beyond one's control, the Iraqis resent being exploited by the rich Americans, who aren't satisfied until they've obtained it all, the dragon of terror only sleeps for so long until awakened by hunger, it will snatch all those arrogant American bastards who can never get enough oil for their vehicles, according to Al Qaeda, the powerful will crumble soon, fall to their knees, and beg for mercy for having not listened sooner to the cries of the deaf, uh . . . the poor.

Armed policemen stopped us at Piccadilly Station. The tube line was closed due to four small explosions on a train, one from an abandoned knapsack. Stunned, we walked on, looking for a bus stop. The air was muggy. The grass was even browner today. Sweat rolled down my back. I trailed behind Murray and the girls. We finally found a bus stop. The sidewalk was overflowing with people unable to use the subways to get home. We hopped on the double decker even though we had no idea where we're going. The bus lurched forward. Murray paused to ask a man standing near us where the bus was headed. The man was friendly, even though his white shirt was soaked with the heat. He wiped his brow with his hand.

He said: "I'll ask the driver for you."

The driver unleashed a stream of orders and abuse. He yelled: "Siddown! Don't ask me any questions about anything. I don't know what's going on."

Our new friend came to stand beside us. His face was apologetic. He promised: "I'll call my friend on my cell phone and get some information for you."

Outside, thronging crowds. Walking in different directions. London pressed itself down on me. Piccadilly, Drury Lane, and Hyde Park streamed past the windows. But I only saw the terror imprinted in the faces of thousands of Londoners milling about in the streets.

We were grateful to get on a train three hours later at Victoria Station. But we were on the wrong train. It took us out into the country, where we stared at open fields darkening in the summer night. We stood at a lonely station in the dark, waiting for a train back into London. The eeriness of the abandoned station, with its shops closed, and bars drawn down on windows, had me eying the other lone man carrying a briefcase.

I signed to Murray: "Watch him. We don't know what's in that briefcase."

Murray nodded and then signed back to me: "I know why so many people live in London. They think they can't leave for fields, and an open sky. They can't handle the nothingness of a field."

Two days later, a male suspect was shot dead on the tube.

Murray said: "What if that was you, Joanne? If the police called at your back and you kept walking because you couldn't hear, you would've been killed."

A madness had descended upon London. We'd flown right into a crucible heating up with fear.

We woke up late, and after about two hours of switching trains and buses, during rush hour, we arrived at the Tower of London at 10 AM and Murray rented satellite-linked recording devices for himself and the girls, so they could hear the history of the haunted fortress while they walked about, and I followed, clutching a guidebook, looking as hard as I could so I could remember the fleeting visual, emotional, and spiritual traces of memories locked into every stone, even if I didn't know what they were, and the upper rooms of the Bloody Tower were full of the spirits of prisoners who carved their desperation and lines of encouragement into the stone walls, the most heart-wrenching was a simple "Jane" carved into the limestone by the window, the Nine Days' Queen, Lady Jane Grey, who was executed at the age of sixteen, and, look, King Henry the Eighth's last armour, made for him at fifty-eight years of age, huge and could've fitted two men inside (okay, one and a half), a breastplate and below it was a huge round protruding ball for his penis, a testament to the overwhelming preoccupation with defence: stone walls, arrow windows, heavy arms, prison, torture, the traitor's gate where St. Thomas More entered.

I realized: *This is the territory of men. They make confining spaces, castles, halls, turrets, even torture chambers. Dark, dark places. Hades.* And: *The most feminine aspect of the tower was the chapel in the White Tower whose ceiling vaults rise high above our heads.*

After five hours of wandering about the tower, I became irritated by the traffic, heat, and the constant prodding by Murray and the girls to keep up with their long-legged strides. *I've no good reason to be rude and uncooperative,* I chastised myself, *at least, I'm not a prisoner in the bloody Tower of London, slowly chipping my name into the wall, marking my hours, waiting for death. Five out of seven men who have sworn with their lives to put Lady Jane on the throne, for their own purposes, have abandoned her, except for her father and her husband. While Queen Mary I is proclaimed Queen of England at the Cross in Cheapside, Jane's father enters the throne room to find Jane waiting there alone in the shadows. She steps down wearily from her throne, and asks her father: "Can I go home?"*

She blinks as she steps into the spring air. And later, as the axe severs her spinal column.

ॐ

The train out of central London jolted me against the cotton sleeve of a passenger, who shifted closer to the wall of the train compartment and stared out the window. I thought: *These Londoners are polite and cold, each locked into their silence. There's a tacit agreement between us: "I'll not bother you if you don't bother me." I've consented to this non-involvement too, and have turned away from people, burrowing into the den within myself.*

I sank into the lulling rhythm of the train and remembered: a closed custody facility brought a twelve-year-old male prostitute to my classroom, picked up for drugs by the Regina City Police: a First Nations child, deaf, and nearly languageless, since he couldn't comprehend my signs. I asked him how old he was. He merely shrugged, until his worker informed me that he was nearly thirteen. He had no speech, although he had a cochlear implant. But the processor, the external component of the implant, had been lost in a snowbank somewhere on the reserve. I watched the worker sign to him, making shapes obviously gleaned from a book and winced when the signs were made incorrectly. I inwardly shuddered as I watched this young man make the same incorrect signs back to the coordinator. He'd never make himself understood in a Deaf community.

After our meeting, I contacted an ASL instructor from our Regina Deaf community and facilitated his hiring by the school board.

Sophie said: "We're going to sweat blood for this kid."

I snatched up books from our school library. I rifled through the pages of picture books, wondering: *What does a deaf prostitute, who's nearly languageless, know? How to give a good blow job?*

Sophie's eyes were large and sad.

I told her: "We'll start by naming things in our classroom. We'll check to see what signs he knows: table, chair, student, teacher, pencil, paper, and book. We need a baseline."

Sophie's answer: "And if he's making those signs properly? The people who work on those northern reserves have no access to the Deaf community. They'll be learning signs from a book. If anyone claimed to be fluent in French after learning from tapes and books, he would be laughed out of town."

I wondered: *What world am I about to give him? Do the people and things in my world have any meaning for him? Developing language at the age of thirteen is a daunting task. The window for maximum receptivity to language learning closes around age seven.*

Then I learned that he wasn't coming after all, that his First Nations band had decided that the best placement for him was back on the reserve with his family, that it didn't matter that he'd escaped the reserve and was found five hundred miles south, prostituting himself. His deafness and lack of language was of little consequence. He was neither Hearing nor Deaf. He was dead. He was merely a possession to be retrieved again.

Sophie asked: "How are his people going to prevent him from escaping from the reserve again? Are they going to do anything different, like learning sign language?"

I answered with a shrug: "When he has a cochlear implant? I don't think so. They'll just replace the processor and probably confine him somehow."

Deaf dead Deaf dead, the train rattled on, lurching around corners and screeching to stops at stations. *Hearing Deaf, Deaf Dead*. I couldn't be both at the same time. There was no crucible that would forge the two halves in me.

Twenty-Five

I LOOKED DOWN FROM THE UPPER deck of the bus at the stone-faced Londoners rushing through traffic and wondered at the general happiness of the Britons, thinking about divorce. I remembered how the Deaf women in my small circle of Deaf friends used to cluck over Agnes, a Deaf woman married to a Hearing man. They'd sighed and signed, *"Husband Hearing,"* barely concealing the pity in their eyes. For them, the word *Hearing* had little to do with the ability to hear sound but everything to do with domination. They added: "He controls her because he can't sign her language."

Paulette's signs floated up in my face, her usual friendly smile was troubled: "And it's always worse if you're almost Hearing. If you marry a Hearing man, then your life will be on his terms. He'll expect you to use your voice all the time and lipread. He won't sign well enough for you to understand him easily. You'll have to do all the work."

Murray pulled at my sleeve: "We get off here."

Anna and Paula were already disappearing down the stairs to the lower floor of the double decker bus.

◦<

In the heat, burnt by hours of walking in the sun between Westminster Abbey and the London Aquarium, we strolled among the willow trees of the promenade along the South Bank. On the burnt brown grass, we listened to the buskers and finally paused at a caravan parked in front of the National Theatre and shaded by a large awning. Two men were playing a trumpet and a saxophone on the quickly fading patch of grass. The saxophonist was wearing a multi-coloured patchwork vest. The other man, who was black, continued, utterly engrossed with his music. The man in the vest beckoned to us.

"Are you a family?" He motioned with his finger.

Not prone to giving away much information, Murray nodded cautiously.

The man looked over his shoulder at the trumpet player. He said: "That's my cousin. He plays all the time. Can't quit." He looked around nervously, his face reddened by the sun. He asked: "How would you like to come inside our trailer and hear a story about a bear?"

We hesitated. We didn't come to London to be gullible tourists. Al Qaeda was still high in the air, and the smell of those failed London bombs still filled our nostrils.

He pleaded: "It doesn't cost you anything. Come, have a little food, a drink perhaps."

He beckoned us toward a trailer parked on the lawn backing the theatre. To my horror, Murray nodded, and our daughters followed him in single file. I trailed behind.

Soon we were sitting on an L-shaped bench that ran along the length and width of his cramped and smelly trailer. Another man sat at the long end of this seat, his face visibly trembling. The saxophone player stood in front of us, his back to a short, narrow workbench holding a bottle of vodka and a plate of crackers smeared with some sort of red sauce and topped with green peppers. A curtained partition made from a green paisley fabric ran across the ends of the L-shaped seat and workbench. Small black and white photographs festooned with sprigs of dried herbs hung above the seat, in the sweltering van, while the black trumpet man continued to play softly outside. A woman swathed from head-to-toe in dark blue broadcloth with a scarf around her head crawled out from underneath the curtain and beckoned a timid young man in his thirties to come out of the small opening behind her. The green curtain quickly settled into place.

She spoke in a heavy accent: "It eeez too hot." She made fanning motions with her hands and flapped her apron. She encouraged the nervous man to sit with us, at the end of the bench nearest the curtained wall and made our host open the windows, then she smiled and left us.

I looked through glazed eyes. Our host was gesticulating wildly, running rapidly through an assortment of accents. The first was Spanish.

Murray was quite good-natured, and murmured: "Sí, sí."

Alarmed, the man switched into another accent. He boasted that he could speak several languages, including "Canadian."

The stricken-looking man dressed in khaki shorts and T-shirt suddenly bolted from the trailer. Our host nodded briefly at his disappearing back and clapped his hands, then rubbed them together. Now for the story he promised us. He began by offering us the stale crackers topped with a tomato sauce and jalapeño peppers. The smell of tomato that had sat out in the heat, for hours, I suspected, filled me with nausea.

Our host flashed a bottle of vodka at our teenage daughters. They vigorously shook their heads in the negative. I wondered what Murray would do, but he shook his head too.

Our host seemed quite disappointed. Nevertheless he switched on a tape recorder. I heard the indistinct sounds of a man talking.

Our host said: "That's my grandfather talking. He was a bear trainer."

He whipped out a jar in which suspicious looking stones rattled. He rang a bell by each of our ears, rattled the stones again, and instructed us to sniff the jar.

He said: "It's bear cheese. My grandfather used this to train the bears."

Dutifully we sniffed. Or pretended to. I held my breath while the smells of dust, sweat, and stale crackers threatened to overtake my queasy stomach. Murray and I looked at each other, eyebrows raised in warning. He closed his hand over his wallet in his pocket.

Undaunted our host went on: "See these photographs. These are people who have the heart of a bear." He looked at me sitting almost beneath him. "And women's hearts are like teabags."

I nodded gravely, hoping not to overly arouse him, lest he move on to less desirable topics. He rapidly flipped through the pages of a laminated homemade book, ignoring much of the text. I squinted to look at the text and then watched his face carefully, until I realized that he wasn't following the story at all. He paused at intervals to point to some of the pictures which looked suspiciously like poor black and white photocopies of illustrations from *Winnie the Pooh*.

He said: "There was a boy who had a bad heart. He was often sick and wasn't strong enough to participate in sports. And he had a good friend, a bear. One day, they took a walk in the woods and fell asleep. The boy woke up to find the bear dead, with his heart removed, and found a curious long scar running the length of his chest. He felt stronger and braver than before, until he realized the bear had given him his heart."

Our host flipped the pages even faster. He said: "Reluctant to tell anyone, he now had the heart of the bear and wanting to protect the rest of the bears in the forest, he sewed his lips shut. And that's why there are still bears in the forest."

I thought: *Well, then he'd have to sign.* I was about to make the flippant remark when he snapped the book shut and looked at us with a great intensity.

He said: "Now you can see the bear."

He smacked the curtained partition. He smacked it again as if to alert the bear of our coming. Then he pulled aside the curtain for our youngest daughter to enter. My husband motioned to me to go in after her. I was about to protest, wanting to kick Murray for making the women go first, but my petite daughter had already disappeared through the small hole. I scrambled after her.

The back wall of the van was covered in green fabric. A tree stump stood in front of us. A light was placed in the corner on a floor littered with wood chips. The beam shone upon the stump, where a wooden carving of a bear was placed precariously. The bear was upright. A large heart was superimposed against his chest.

The man's voice came in from the other side of the curtain.

Paula whispered to me: "He said, 'Go on, pet him.'"

I wondered: *Go on, pet him?*

Anyway, the voice commanded us. My daughter gingerly touched the bear's head. Incense began to rise all around us, while we stood, politely wondering what to do next, waiting for a signal of some sort. An onslaught of self-recrimination fell upon me. I signed to Paula: "Do you realize that we've given this man so much power over us? We've eaten his food, we are standing in this tiny trap hole, this is so dangerous and stupid."

Neither of us moved, wondering, submitting, and absorbing the incense, the heat, and the growing silence in the green bower. Finally a call from the other side of the curtain reached us. Gratefully we swooped down to crawl out of the space. My husband raised his eyebrows at me as he followed Anna into the bear sanctuary. Our host glanced at my husband's behind as he squeezed through the small hole.

"Whoa, big man. A big bear. How do you like being married to a bear?" By now, he sounded American. I decided to play along.

I said: "I have to have a very strong heart."

He said: "You have a woman's heart, like a teabag." He jabbed the air with his finger, his eyes strangely triumphant. "You have to absorb everything and then release it. You can't hold anything back."

Our host paced back and forth before Paula and me, who were sitting obediently on the bench. He finally said: "You must have found it quite peaceful. You stayed so long."

Murray and Anna quickly emerged from the cavity, with vague nods of appreciation.

Mute, we shook hands with our host, stood still long enough for a picture with him, and hastily retreated to the long promenade along the South Bank. Blinking in the bright sun, we found a bench and roared with laughter and relief, although we had simply no way to make any sense of it. Uppermost in our minds was gratitude for having escaped the van without being robbed or harmed.

Paula asked: "What was that all about? You are our parents, you're supposed to protect us."

I protested: "I saw a bobby nearby. It must've been okay."

Otherwise, my lips were sewn shut. I couldn't explain what happened, how we stumbled into a story that is strangely mine and Murray's. I reminded myself: *We are risk takers, and have* committed many acts of colossal stupidity. But things have a mysterious way of working out despite our foolishness. And, in that hot, cramped crucible, I realized I have a Deaf teabag heart. It absorbs the murmur of voices, and then releases whatever I've been able to make sense of. I thought: *I have to share my heart of Deafhood which makes Murray and our daughters stronger, more patient, slower, more willing to listen.*

But I was cautious not to repeat the teabag heart business. Murray was removing the disk from the video camera. The willow trees tittered in the gentle breeze.

He said: "Bear-baiting was a popular pastime in Elizabethan England. I guess the story is about having compassion for a bear who sacrificed his heart for a human."

In the softening light of the late afternoon sun, the waters that lapped the South Bank move quietly among the sailboats and the odd dark trawler, following the Thames out into the sea. We walked along the Strand in this way, ignoring the cries of the buskers and the laughter of the crowds. I thought: *The beauty of my Hearing husband, what he will risk for me, taking on Deafhood as if it were his too. How generous he is. And our Hearing children are just as shaped by my Deafhood as I am by their Hearing ways. Does it matter that we are Hearing and Deaf, all of us?*

Soon the sun lowered and sat on the brown London waters, turning it into blood that pulses in and out of the heart of the city.

❧

I was grateful that I'd thought to purchase a copy of *The Tempest* two days before to follow along in addition to listening carefully. We sat in the second balcony, on hard wooden seats in the Globe theatre, the replica of Shakespeare's own theatre.

Murray signed: "I can't follow this play." He read along with me in my playbook.

Anna and Paula wore looks of exasperation, because four characters were playing multiple parts.

I signed to them the clues: "When he puts his head inside the noose for a few seconds, then that tells you that Prospero is now Alonzo."

They shrugged. They didn't understand enough sign language to comprehend what I was trying to tell them.

Now I poked Murray: "Sebastian is Miranda, see, he puts that lace collar on. Tell the girls."

Each character merged into the other with amazing ease. Prospero freed both Ariel and Miranda, who were being played by one male actor. Prospero forgave Alonzo, who was the usurper of his kingdom. I became increasingly excited. I thought: *Do we not have a dark side, the shadow that usurps our own inner kingdom? Do we not have parts of ourselves that need to merge, to work together?* I leaned over the balcony in eagerness, almost dropping my playbook.

A single actor played Gonzalo, whose intentions toward Miranda were noble (and most wordy), and Caliban, who acted ignobly toward her. But Ferdinand, played by another actor, got the girl. I sat back dazed. I thought: *Are we not a mixture of ignoble and noble intentions, of darkness and light?*

Then Prospero slowly relinquished control over the people, his magical powers, and his own destiny, entering his human existence, the crucible of his own limitations.

We ambled along Southwark under the plane trees after the play while the girls grumbled in disappointment.

Paula pronounced: "I had no idea what was going on. That was the worst Shakespeare performance ever."

The conversation swirled about me. It dawned on me that Prospero is all of these characters. I thought: *These people are facets of his personality, all heating up within his own crucible, as his life on his island draws close to an end. Moreover, Prospero really doesn't make choices, whether to be this or that. He lets the collection of characters, which all represent a facet of him, simply play out their parts. His only role is to keep his eyes on the end result, like a runner focused on the finish line. He can do this because he relinquishes control. And: I don't have to decide upon any identity, whether to be Deaf or Hearing. I am Deaf when I need to be Deaf and Hearing when I need to be Hearing. It doesn't matter anymore how often decisions are made for me or how often I make my own. I no longer need to keep a score of how many power imbalances I must endure, trusting, like Prospero, that things will come out all right in the end.*

I ambled behind the girls and Murray, letting the breeze from the Thames play in my hair, a new confidence beginning in me, that all was well.

Just outside the small village of Chepstow, Wales, we stayed in a fourteenth century tower that formed part of a stone manor house with an inner courtyard flanked by a wide- stepped stone veranda decorated with carved columns. The grounds were manicured, with mown grass, trimmed hedges, and clipped bushes. To the left of the manor was a small church, with a graveyard: a heavy grey stone set against pastoral green hedges and full, leafy trees. That night, I felt the smooth and cool white cotton sheets against my legs, and realized: *The days of the crucible are leaving.*

The next night, after touring Dylan Thomas' Swansea, I made love with Murray while Thomas' poem, "Do not go gentle into that good night" pounded into my brain without ceasing. I felt too disturbed by Dylan Thomas, frightened by the darkness in him, which ironically made his poetry sing. There had been nothing delicate or gentle even about this reunion with Murray after nine years of living apart. Instead I'd reached the elemental things darkly hinted at by Thomas: God, sex, my body, my faith, and the power of language. I'd travelled this far, even though I'd been a fractious Arabian horse, rearing up at the slightest indication of neglect, demanding attention, remonstrating against my children's and their father's lack of acceptance of me as a Deaf woman. I'd been demanding and difficult. They often recoiled in hurt and surprise when I roared like a dragon who is always asleep with one eye open.

My eyes both flew open in the dark. Murray's sleeping body was heaving under the cool white sheets in the ivy-papered bedroom high up in the fourteenth century tower. There were dragons in Wales. Fiery red, upright dragons, emblazoned on shields, crests, and roadside signs that dotted the landscape. I thought: *St. Michael is preparing to do battle with a dragon. The battle of man and beast.* I turned away from Murray, pulling the white lace coverlet over my shoulder, shuddering. A thought came to me, unbidden: *I am still in the crucible and now a dragon is flying towards me.* I buried my face in the pillow, now tense, waiting. My mind raced. *I will come face to face with a dragon. Soon.*

Twenty-Six

JOHANNA

Sometimes I get stuck in the wrong stories. I got tied up with a dragon once. Thought that the dragon would explain me, my angst, and heat things up so much for me and then spit me out of his mouth. Couldn't quite see where I was going with that one. I forced something out of the story to leap toward me and explain what was wrong with me. Dragons have a way of doing that. They are shadow creatures and not to be ignored even when their jewelled chests blink in my eyes. They demand that two twigs be bent into one branch, dammit.

I almost explained myself with the wrong story, but it was still the wrong story. But it was not a waste of my time. The story led me to a partially torn away wall in the old broken-down house where we live. I have yet to turn into another room, knowing that in the centre, there is a bed with fresh sheets, where I can lie down with my love, nestled in stories about what is right in me. Indeed, love is building a house.

ॐ

Driving up to Selkirk in the border country of Scotland was one long drink of beauty. I had no inkling how this strange and terrible beauty would soon nearly destroy me. The terrain changed from flat moors with sparse clumps of trees to a land dotted with sheep grazing on low, mountainous hills. I gazed through forests as we drove over low streams trickling over the stones in their beds. Further north, wide mountain valleys were parcelled by stone wall fences. The houses were far apart. Some were large stone manors. I tried to imagine my mother's ancestors in the Scottish Borders, but I only felt a sense of melancholy and displacement. Then I recognized it: it was a dour Scotsman, eternally pining for the hills and heather, the wide green valleys, the sudden darkness of the forests and languid waters smoothing the stones in the streams. It was *The Lord is my Shepherd* scene that my mother inherited from her mother, Grandma Mary Carson — an old-fashioned print from the Scottish Borders.

Murray drove quickly on the long winding roads and up and down the hillsides. My stomach lurched after each plunge. There were so many. The roads were narrow, and even though one could see a car approaching, passing could be dicey. I tried to concentrate on the lonely, dark valleys instead.

Anna woke me during the night and asked to move in with Murray and me on the sagging foldout bed in the cottage we'd rented. Of course, I was squished in the middle, and Anna pulled all of the blankets toward her, leaving Murray and me cold, Murray moved onto the couch, but Anna sprawled over the narrow hide-a-bed, her arms and legs jerking me awake, so I got up and crawled into Anna's bunk, and now I saw why she complained that her hips hurt. The bunk was a mere slab of foam and I couldn't stretch out to full length, and Anna was taller than me, no wonder she couldn't sleep there. In the morning, I awoke weeping, although I told myself: You're merely sleep deprived and the bed is impossible. We'll set up better sleeping arrangements.

But I knew better. *The dragon was coming closer and I had to flee.*

જ્જ

I bolted from the cottage for the twisting streets of Selkirk. The wind was bitter. None of my family realized that I hadn't had a real conversation in days, because we'd been together constantly since we'd arrived in the United Kingdom. I didn't catch anything at meals, in the car, on the street, or in museums, travelling with them had become solitary confinement. I couldn't hear well enough to talk on the phone, to talk to my friends, I couldn't go anywhere without feeling so left out of their laughter and silliness - it was like layers of varnish, dirt, and gunk on a hardwood floor. I thought: *The build-up is making you crazy. You've reached your saturation point.*

The wind pushed harder in my face and I zipped up my light summer jacket, and walked past a small stone house whose front door was a mere foot back from the sidewalk. I thought: *There are people living in this house, so close to the street. They can see it all.*

I glanced at the flowers in the window boxes and turned away, guiltily, as I could see right into the house. I felt like an intruder who had easily unbolted the front door, and as I hurried on, I wondered: *How do people live so close to busy traffic?*

At the river, lamentations began in my head: *By the rivers of Babylon, there we sat down, yea, we wept, when we remembered Zion. We hanged our harps upon the willows in the midst thereof. For there they that carried us away captive required of us a song . . .* I thought: *Indeed, the Hearing are my captors. Demanding that I speak, that I hear, that I sing their songs. I am captive. No matter where I go. Langley Hall, coffee shops, my classroom, England, and now the Borders.*

I took longer and faster strides along the narrow streets. I was so close to the danger. The dragon now held me in its gaze. I felt the flames all about my head, the flames in the winds coming off the Highlands. I told myself: *Be strong. You have to hold this mystery, to contain this Deafhood, somehow, in your own body. You're the only one in this family that can carry the Deafhood.* I told myself again and again: *I carry the Deafhood for them. I do it for them. Because they can't carry it themselves. This is not the time to run away. Not again. Go back to the cottage. Talk to Murray. Tell him how you really feel.*

The dragon's fiery breath cooled on my face, and I only felt the Scottish wind rolling down from the hills. I told myself: *The dragon will return again and I must be prepared to stay with my family and fight.*

I went back to fight.

But there was no time to talk to Murray, because we had to leave for Stirling immediately, Murray was *not* pleased about my bolting from the cottage, he and the girls were forced to wait, patiently, until I came back.

Sheepish, apologetic, I climbed into the car.

A couple of hours later, we were wandering about Stirling Castle, where I consoled myself like this: *This is the closest we can get to my ancestors of Dumbarton Castle, because its artefacts were moved to Stirling, including an axe, my family's axe, I never saw that axe, but my great, great, great uncle Charlie was born in the bedroom used by Mary, Queen of Scots when she was imprisoned at Dumbarton. Legends, mostly.*

I'd read that the baptismal ceremony for Mary's son, here at Stirling, included an elaborate ceremony in which a "fantasy castle" was built to enact a siege. People linked hands around the edifice and danced. Then the effigy was burned and a magnificent fireworks display ended the ceremony. I tried to imagine: *I'm at the ceremony, in the middle of the night, with dragon flames hot against my face, people cheering in the night, dancing in rings, because the siege is over, the castle is in ruins, and a royal child is baptized.*

My mind balked. I didn't understand the need for fire at a baptism. Unless it was the dipping of a burning candle into the waters of baptism, as in the Catholic Easter liturgy. I thought: *Perhaps, burning the castle at the end of the siege is a symbol of old life giving way to new freedom. Fire has its usefulness. It razes forests to the ground in order to make way for new growth.*

In the cottage at Selkirk, I woke up at 4:00 AM again in tears. I heard voices in my head, all of its meaningless chatter, and I knew it was merely tinnitus, but there was a plaintive voice that came through. I breathed slowly, trying to listen. I heard: *"You are still not paying any attention to me. I won't let you ignore me any longer."* I cast about in my head, trying to remember where I'd heard this before. I heard her again: *"I warned you. Now I will destroy you, because I will not be ignored or dismissed any longer. All your reading, all your Hearing ways, your English will not save you."* Her ominous words had a familiar ring. I quickly pushed it away and let the bubbling Hearing voices in my head crowd her out, the only time I was grateful for the tinnitus. I finally fell asleep again at 6:45 AM. Murray woke me only minutes later. When I opened my eyes, a terrible sadness fell over me. I heard: *"I long to go away."* I closed my eyes, to fight the tears. Under my eyelids, I saw the dragon's flames.

Later that morning, Murray tried to hold my hand and sheltered me with his large chest from the bitter wind while we waited for the bus to take us to Edinburgh. I looked at him, and wondered. There it was again, how the beauty of my husband with his tall and wide girth, his large hands that stumbled in his signs, his kind eyes, his ready laughter slipped inside of me. I saw: *Murray's kindness is a shield from the dragon who is spreading his wings all about me, his flames licking at my hair.* Suddenly I seized the shield and apologized to him, looking up into his face, shivering in my shorts and sandals. I looked about me, at the gust of wind that tore at us, I no longer saw any flames. I knew that the flames would come back, but for now, I rested in the warmth of Murray's body.

On our way out of Scotland, we drove through the purple heather and rounded, swollen hills (they seemed to be with child), and valleys dotted with sheep. I thought: *I want to remember these stone fences that plait the valleys, and the bluffs of trees, and the worn pebbles in the streams, how they let the streams trickle softly over them as if they are saying, let it be done to me. I want to always remember the homes built into the hillsides, their heavy stone walls softened by brave flower gardens. It is enough for me.*

Liverpool. Sunday morning. We'd been looking for a Catholic church but had stumbled on an Anglican one instead, St. Margaret's of Antioch, with two men waiting outside in the churchyard, who gave us directions to the Catholic church and mentioned that they too had the Eucharist that morning, and since the Catholic mass was at midday and we'd have to wait for an hour and a half, we accepted their invitation.

The church was dimly lit and poorly maintained. We sat in a pew, two down from the only other occupied bench — apart from a solitary man sitting across the aisle. Halfway through the Gloria, a family with four children noisily entered the pew in front of us. The mother was commandeering, the children huddling around her. A rustle in the back and a quick look over my shoulder confirmed the presence of another newly-entered family. The sermon was on racism. The families, in front of us and behind us, were black. Murray signed: *The priest announced that a black teenager was killed a week ago. The community is still in shock.* The sermon was long. I couldn't hear a word. Instead, I gazed at the newly made banners standing near the altar. All of them depicted dragons. I sat dazed. Despite the sparse attendance at this service, there were enough dragons to make up for the lack of parishioners.

After the service, there were tender hugs, firm handshakes, and friendly chatter. The priest invited us into a small kitchen for coffee. I asked him about the dragon banners.

He said, excitedly: "We made them!" He began to retell the tale of Margaret of Antioch and the Dragon. Apparently she was the patron saint of childbirth, since she was ejected from the innards of a dragon. In the Middle Ages, people venerated her so much that copies of her story, written on long strips of parchment, were wrapped around the abdomens of women in labour. I bent my head forward to listen more carefully to this strange tale. The priest said: "Margaret was incredibly strong-willed but her heart was like a songbird in the morning." He waved his hands in a majestic motion as if he were conducting an orchestra. "She lived at Antioch with her father who was a magician during the reign of Diocletian; as a young woman, she became a Christian."

I said: "I bet her father didn't like that."

The priest shook his head, his eyes full of mirth: "She laughed when the grand governor at Antioch, Olybrius proposed to her. He tried to torture her to get her to consent but she continued to laugh and sing. Then he became angry and his cries of fury woke a sleeping dragon. The dragon rushed out and swallowed Margaret whole."

I tried to imagine: *Margaret, trapped in the belly of the dragon, trembling in fear, swooning with the fiery heat of the dragon's innards, her gorge rising at the sulphurous fumes from the dragon's liver, certain that she won't survive the ordeal, the heat is unbearable, she is trapped, she only knows that the dragon is carrying her somewhere, perhaps to digest her bones.*

The priest's voice went on and suddenly I was not able to hear him anymore. I could only see his animated face. I had become too tired with all the lipreading.

Soon we were standing on the church lawn, blinking in the sunlight, apologizing for having to leave so soon. As I waved goodbye to the priest and his wife, he thrust a copy of the story into my hands and I held it flat to my stomach in order to keep it from flapping in the strong sea breeze, and the sun was warm on our backs as we walked over the grey stones toward the harbour, and again, I sensed flames about my own head.

I felt something dark spread over me, like wings blocking out the rays of the sun. *The dragon will shift shapes, will come in a form that will be too ordinary, that I won't even recognize it before it can blast me into pieces.*

Twenty-Seven

BELOW THE BROADWAY BRIDGE, THE RIVER was already filmy with translucent patches of ice. Even though this December was mild, I wished the Deaf could have their year-end banquets in the spring. Murray was struggling with a cold, and I'd been distracted with preparation for my classroom, pounding away on my laptop in our hotel room. We pushed through the revolving door into the Ramada, where I combed my hair with my fingers before taking the elevator to the banquet floor. The warm, steamy room admitted only the Deaf, along with the Hearing interpreters and the few Hearing people who had some ability to communicate in ASL. For a few precious hours, the order of the world was reversed. The Hearing, mostly professionals, became shadows in the room, while the Deaf commanded. They were the new aristocracy, sitting under the crystal chandeliers at snow-white tables set with gleaming cutlery, reflecting the night outside the long, tall windows. The Deaf men were dressed in their best suits, and their wives in their evening dress fluttered their signs like courtly fans. Black-and-white-uniformed waiters threaded their way among the tables. Choppy waves of signs rose above steaming plates of food. A black-skirted waitress bent over my shoulder and gestured with her coffee pot. Murray sat at my side, bewildered, as a sea of hands pushed against him like waves. He remained unfocused, until Tommy tapped him on the shoulder. Murray's eyes lit up in recognition of his former student, who was already telling the others how angry he used to be at Murray, how he hated Murray for forcing him to read: "He wouldn't answer any of my questions about the paragraph I was supposed to read. I hated him. I thought he was an awful teacher."

Murray winced, though a smile played about his lips.

Tommy extended his hands from his mouth toward Murray. He signed: "Thank you, V." He formed the handshape for *V*, Murray's name sign, against his left shoulder. "You are the greatest teacher in the world. You taught me to read."

The other Deaf nodded appreciatively, while Murray signed: "You did the work, Tommy. You went through the struggle."

The light from the chandeliers dimmed and brightened. The guest speaker stood beside the podium so everyone could see his hands. He was Gary Malkowski, the first Deaf Canadian to become a M.P.P., a Member of the Provincial Parliament in the province of Ontario. He was from Toronto. He had come to galvanize the Deaf community into action. He unfastened the buttons to his grey suit and removed his navy tie, hanging it over the podium. He was balding, his sharp black eyes darted restlessly over the tables, ice floes in a restless sea of signs. His signs were large and emphatic, he hitched back the sleeves of his shirt as if preparing for a great fight, and signed: "The school for the Deaf was closed down fifteen years ago by the Saskatchewan government. Do you realize that this closure came the year after the great protest at Gallaudet in 1988? We now have a Deaf president at the only university for the Deaf in the world. Do you understand? Fifteen years ago, in Washington, D.C, we were finally heard. We fought hard for our rights and we won. But one year later, in Saskatchewan, the Deaf school was closed. What

is wrong with your province? Your government?" He gazed over
the sea of greying seniors, whose eyes were trained on him like
obedient children. A fury began to travel down his arms into his
fingers: "No young Deaf people are entering your community.
They are now scattered throughout Saskatchewan, doomed to
live in isolation in their home communities. You must stop this!"

The senior Deaf nodded in polite agreement, but I knew:
*They can't step out of their twilight years and reverse this form of
linguistic genocide. Some are struggling with ill health or with caring
for grandchildren.* I pleaded silently with Gary, *they need their
retirement*, but he was gyrating his arms in fury up on the stage.
I coughed politely, careful to drop my hands into my lap, in case
people were thinking I was signing something.

Murray raised his eyes quizzically. He wasn't able to fully
grasp Gary's signs. I leaned over to explain. I voiced: "Gary wants
us to fight for Deaf children who are in need of sign language."

Gary continued: "Yes, you lost the school for the Deaf, but
the fight is not over. We must save our Deaf children from a
paternalistic and oppressive system of education. We've been
through the educational system, we've suffered the impact
of thoughtless oralism, we are told that we are not valuable or
important unless we can speak fluent English, that we are to
study English for many years in the hope we'll hear and speak
just like Hearing people."

Again, more vigorous nods. A man shouted and waved at the
back. More hands went up, in unison, to cheer Gary on.

I searched faces, the Deaf seniors who merely wanted to play
cards, dote on their grandchildren, and travel, and thought: *They
can't take up another cause again. They can't do anything to save the
Deaf community or return it to its former glory. Everyone is too old
and tired, and the most politically savvy leaders have left the province.*

Gary Malkowski continued despite the growing islands of fluttering signs: "We know what will work for our Deaf children. There's no one who will understand them. Not even their parents. They are all being mainstreamed. They will be lonely, frustrated, and without friends. They will feel strange, isolated, and misbegotten. Worse than that, they'll be handicapped because of their inability to read and write well. Deaf schools across Canada prepared us for life, gave each of us a trade: barbers, printers, painters, bakers, and jewellers. At the Deaf school, we washed our own dishes, scrubbed our own floors, and cooked our own food. We cared for each other. And now, we're looked upon as the unfortunate ones. We, who raised families, paid taxes, and held our jobs for more than thirty years."

The audience shifted in its chairs. The woman sitting next to me was fingerspelling under the table.

Gary pounded out: "Look at Ontario. We stayed strong. We organized and fought the government, and we still have our Deaf schools, our language, and our culture. You must do the same. Stay strong, work together for the sake of our Deaf children." Gary ended by throwing his fist in a punch at an invisible foe.

The Deaf waved their hands with vigour, applauding his address. At that moment, the double doors of the dining room burst open and a stream of Deaf welfare recipients swarmed among the tables. Dressed in finery, mostly gleaned from second-hand clothing stores, they came for the cards, gossip, and impromptu storytelling. They couldn't afford a ticket to the banquet, but they would not miss a rare opportunity to see all those who once attended the Deaf school in Saskatoon. Gina ran over to me, pulling her Hearing boyfriend by the hand. They were both beaming at me, and Gina was excitedly pumping Murray's hand and saying: "Thank you for editing that DVD! When will I get it?"

The boyfriend signed to me: "Isn't she beautiful?"

Gina blushed and held her hand to her mouth.

Murray nodded, and I smiled.

Gina and her boyfriend turned away to visit at a nearby table.

Already, many tables were abandoned. People were crowding to catch a story by Art Hillcox, known for his clever way with signs. The conversation around my table turned to D brushed over the heart, who founded the school for the Deaf and died several years ago who entertained the school's children with stories while he worked his shift as a supervisor on the dorms. Many former students said they saw the ghostly figure of Williams patrolling the halls in the grand old school. Someone fingerspelled the name of another teacher, and giggles began to erupt, as every mistake and mishap was dissected and acted out to the tittering and hooting audience, red-faced in tears and laughter. Only a few teachers escaped this pitiless retelling of faults and foibles. The Deaf have long memories.

I glanced at Murray to see his reaction as many of his old teaching colleagues were being mercilessly roasted, but he still looked rather bewildered and nodded politely.

I felt a tap on my shoulder and turned around. It was Roger Carver and his wife, Shelly, their faces wreathed in large grins. I hadn't seen them since Paula was born. Now they stood before me, older, eyes more sunken, but with the same energy and passion travelling through their fingers. Roger earned his master's degree in deaf education at the University of Alberta. Shelly earned a degree in social work at Gallaudet University. They'd just moved back to Saskatchewan.

I asked: "What brought you back to this godforsaken province?"

Roger answered with a shrug: "Shelly's family is here."

I cocked my head and said: "But you've been in the best places in Canada. You've lived in the most active, and advanced Deaf communities. Vancouver, Edmonton."

Roger nodded and said: "Yes, well, there's lots to do here."

After each story, all hands rested in laps, or languished carelessly on the table. I sat with my hands under the long table, my eyes feasting on the richness of the bodies, how they swayed. I'd never seen the Deaf so animated with rhythm, the grace of their hands folding, unfolding, dipping, swerving, and gliding, and the vivid facial grimaces coming and going as if a series of masks had been donned and then discarded. I was overwhelmed at this freedom to express one's self and to be understood. I excused myself, leaving Murray to sit in the circle of signs. On the tables, remains of dessert, bitten strawberries abandoned against scraps of cheesecake, glistening under the chandeliers, half-filled coffee cups standing neglected while hands floated, dipped, and folded nearby. A daughter had moved away, a teacher had retired, a Deaf man was redoing the shingles on the roof, and a grandson had been born. Over the sea of bodies gyrating and gesturing, my eyes swam with tears. I thought: *If I don't leave soon, I'll want to stay in the room for the rest of my life.* And: *I have to pull myself away from the blessed sight.*

Then I saw Murray. His face was gaunt and tired. I had to drive him back to our hotel. I motioned for him to come along.

Many of the Deaf paused their conversations to wave goodbye to me. Some rushed forward to hug me again. Murray and I walked past three men signing in earnest, whose cigarettes were forked between their fingers, the smoke trailing their swooping hands. Outside the hotel, Murray and I returned to the night. Snow flurries grazed the street lamps. Cold night air seeped up the hem of my coat. I felt a strange sort of relief: *I'm no longer alone in this province, now that Roger and Shelly have come back.*

Perhaps it's the beginning of the reversal of the exodus of Deaf professionals begun by the Task Force, nearly fifteen years ago.

Far away from the golden crowd high up in the hotel, I took Murray's hand as we walked back to our car.

৵

During the Christmas season, I was warm with optimism and contentment, relieved to have gotten past dredging up childhood memories. A deep magic was in the air: the sparkling snow outside, the ice-crusted roads, the high snowbanks, and the crunch of tires as Murray brought our crimson Olds 98 into the driveway. I was in a liminal space dissolving distinctions between Gina and me, between all living things. I thought: *After all, the Book of Kells has beasts entwined throughout its illuminated pages, and around the faces and limbs of saints. Snakes meeting face-to-face with fangs bared. The four evangelists are even depicted as animals: John is an eagle; Mark, a lion; Luke, an ox. Only Matthew is portrayed as a man. There are mythical animals: griffins, dragons, and unicorns. An otter with a fish. A peacock. Two mice nibbling a Eucharistic host. Two cats with other mice on their backs, solemnly watching the spectacle. Saints are accompanied by a dragon. Francis of Assisi was able to talk with a wolf, convincing it not to kill or terrorize the people of Gubbio.* I thought: *The dragon in my dreams, in my waking consciousness is a beast that lives within me, now in peace. Maybe. I hope.*

৵

In late January, Sophie came back from an errand she had run at Safeway during noon hour. She shuddered as she took her gloves off to sign to me: "I saw Gina. She was out there in her winter coat, pushing all those shopping carts together. Gina said, 'This is hard, but this is okay for now'."

I was not sure what this short report meant. I asked, hesitatingly: "So, she's not really happy with her job?"

Sophie shook her head: "No. She says she wants to get her Grade 12 and that she'll leave this job as soon as she can."

I threw up my hands and hissed: "She's so damn stubborn."

Later, I swivelled in my chair and spoke out into the nearly empty room: "I once read somewhere that humility is about accepting the truth of your limitations."

Sophie lifted her head and smiled: "And your potential."

I am my own wild bird, with nowhere to go, no matter how much I've achieved, no matter how many accolades I've gathered or praise I've accumulated. I'm now in a classroom. I can't impart to my students much about Deaf culture, sign language, or the great freedom in letting oneself be Deaf. I am trussed up in this province and in this small prairie city. Within me, there's only a pitiful child, more feral than human, trying to cover her body aid with her red coat. Her old, accusing voice counters me with: *You still don't pay enough attention to me.*

I pulled the dark curtains over the brilliant sunlight, and prepared to leave my classroom for the day, and with a hand raised to push down the light switches, I paused in the light from the hallway, realizing: *At Gally, I always signed off my exchanges with this irritating and demanding child in me, a quick image of myself curled under a roof of a house, with: I am sleeping in the house that love is building.* I thought more on it: *I've forgotten to do that for years.*

I turned away from my classroom. The door clicked behind me. That click had a sense of finality. I sensed that I was expelled from the classroom, propelled to a Deaf house within myself, a house whose walls were made of my skin, my bones, and my blood. I must stop looking for ways to escape my Deaf body and accept that this house truly shelters me, a most bitter and ferocious child. I whispered in my mind: *I accept myself*, and at that moment I remembered the end to the legend of Margaret of Antioch, how she realized that things that appeared menacing was not necessarily evil, and how it was at that moment that the dragon spat her out of his mouth.

Twenty-Eight

JOHANNA

This weary walk in the desert is not without travellers crossing my path who are even more parched than I am. How are they able to remain sane? How are they able to fend off the demons of self doubt, despair, and mockery? How do they manage to defeat *accedie*, that constant whine in the ears, urging them to lay down, to die of loneliness, to not hope anymore for any meaningful human contact. At least I have my books.

I sat beside Nay in the school conference room. He wore a grey jacket and a toque of the same colour jammed over his head, long swaths of hair framing his heart-shaped, coffee- skinned face. His large brown eyes swallow me, Sophie, the Karen interpreter, and the principal. His mother, a diminutive woman, sits across from us, wearing a traditional Karen dress woven in rows of emerald green, ruby red, lilac, and golden yellow. *Nay is so grey*, I shake my head. I touch him on the arm. He recoils.

Slowly, I sign: "SCHOOL TOMORROW, TEACH YOU," knowing that he has understood nothing of my signs. He is languageless, having lived in the jungle with his family until he was seven years old, and then moved to a Thai refugee camp along with his mother, his two brothers, and grandmother.

Except that he doesn't know who these people are. At first, he wants to sleep in my classroom. I pull the chair with him sitting in it, away from the table so that he can't use his arms as a pillow. I draw pictures. He finally picks up a pencil.

Then I show him a birthing video. His eyes open wide in fear. "MOTHER YOURS, BABY, YOU SAME," I sign. He nods slowly. He now has a mother.

Three weeks go by and he still lifts his hands to copy everything we sign. No matter how often we point at objects in our room, and provide the signs, he points and copies the signs. "WHAT?" I sign. "WHAT," he signs back. Nothing more.

This goes on for another month. Finally I say to Sophie: "He doesn't see the need to sign. Why should he sign? When he's gotten everything he's wanted by pointing. He's not connecting our signs to anything that is important to him."

In desperation, I lay bamboo reeds from a craft store on the table. I give him a knife and a glue gun. "HOUSE," I sign. "HOUSE MAKE." He copies me, "HOUSE." I sigh. He has no idea what I've just signed.

But he seizes the knife. We quickly insert a block of wood under the dry tough reeds and he saws away. In two hours, he has cut, glued, and shaped his bamboo house.

"SLEEP WHERE?" I ask him, adding a classifier, the shape of a person laying on a floor. He points to the far right side of the house. I show him the sign that means "bed" and "sleep" and wonder how he is going to understand the difference between the two words if he is only given one sign that means both.

"BROTHER WHERE?" I sign. He raises his eyes, puzzled. I pretend to be in pain of childbirth, popping out three babies between my legs. Tamla, Nay and Gler. He nods in recognition. "BROTHER," I say again. He points to his teeth. Then I realize. Gler has three top teeth missing. It's Nay's home name sign for his brother.

The lesson is finished and he is exhausted. I nod at Sophie. "Not yet," I sign. "He hasn't had his Helen Keller moment."

Sophie and I watch Nay point to everything in rapid succession. Sophie resolutely sits down every morning to review the book of a thousand pictures with him, patiently going through the signs. I manage to impress upon Nay that he has a father who is dead. I mimic man and woman having sex, making a baby. MOTHER FATHER. Then I feign death. I make signs for heart beating, and then stopped. Then I show a gun with my fingers. He now understands. His father was shot in the civil conflict between the Burmese and the Karen jungle fighters. He brings me a portrait of his family upon arrival in the Thai camp. His mother's arms are touching Nay's shoulders protectively while she looks dead in her eyes. The man beside her, Nay points. FATHER? His eyes seem to inquire. No, I tell him, it is the uncle who was hanged.

His mother, Thoe Paw, comes to me and says, "You are his mother now, he is your son as he will only listen to you." My eyes fill with tears.

From that day, Little Red Coat begins to speak to me. She tells me, *"You are finally paying attention to me. Let me tell you my real name. It is Johanna."*

A year later on Christmas Eve, the smell of sour cabbage, the holopsti welcomed us after the cold blasts of air rushing at our backs as we scurried to get inside my parents' house in Wilkie. The house was pulsing with people. David had brought his wife, Dawn, and their five children over from Unity. Ruth and Joe had already arrived an hour ago from the farm with their four children. Carol and Colin had packed up their five little ones in a van and driven on the icy roads from North Battleford. With Murray and our daughters, we were twenty-six people crammed into the house that my parents had occupied for the past thirty years. All day, children were playing everywhere, in the upstairs bedrooms, and on the main floor, winding their way among us women washing dishes and chopping vegetables, while the men sat in the cramped kitchen, their voices loud, faces red over the bottles of beer crowding the small kitchen table, and a turkey pan with neatly rolled holopsti rested on the range, ready to go into the dining room, and now we were around the table, and I couldn't make out a thing anyone was saying, and they were all talking at once.

"Ossy bull ow Loreen ay wit im, up or im even?" Carol's voice. Over the noise.

"Ill er o il, sez hees in ocen, av er from pain." Colin. He put his arm around Carol as she reached up to clasp his hand on her shoulder.

"Ow co e ay wit im?" My mother. She shrugged.

I rose from the table, upsetting my plate as I maneuvered out of the necklace of people surrounding the table.

David called: "Joanne, you want some dessert?"

Suddenly, the swirl of words was reduced to the occasional flutter of a vowel as everyone looked at me in expectant silence. Heads nodded sympathetically as I touched my ear and stood at the head of the table, beside my father.

I started slowly: "You know . . . uh . . . there's this space between us. It is as if we are on the opposite banks of the river and all of you are on the other side. Neither of us can swim across the river."

My mother. She said: "That's not true, Joanne. You're part of the family. We just have to behave ourselves." She glared at our family.

Gabriel howled as Dawn bent to give him another spoonful of mashed carrots.

I said, more firmly now: "No, Mom. It's not your way. It's not my way either. Things cut down to size. Served an abridged version without the spontaneity. Being treated like a child with a problem."

My mother, pleading: "If you could wear your FM system."

Still firmly: "It would help some, but I have to lipread. If I can't know who is speaking, all I'd have is a bunch of loud voices in my ear and I can't sort it out. No. There's really no solution."

My mother, the reconciler: "Murray could . . . "

More firm yet: "No, Murray cannot interpret for me. It's not fair to expect that of him."

My voice was loud. I touched my ear again, checking for volume control. The room remained silent, until I grasped the glass of wine by my plate and held it up, and said: "Look, let us just eat, and enjoy this food. You don't need to feel guilty about me not being able to hear. Not anymore. Here, let's drink to us." I toasted: "To our family!"

I sent off the first clink, which resulted in a slow waterfall of clinks. Everyone waited until the last swallow for me to say something again. Instead, my dad chuckled. He was about to tell a story, a story I'd heard so many times before but never tired of listening to, an oasis in this impossible conversation, something I could hear through anticipation of his words because they were so familiar.

He cleared his throat and began: "That reminds me. One day, while hanging around in the store at Revenue, I heard this man, his name was Joe and he was a bootlegger, kind of bragged that no one was ever able to locate his wine and steal any of it. I couldn't wait to tell my friends. We planned to watch him at the next dance in the Revenue hall and see if we could steal his wine. We noticed that night, that when a customer approached him, he'd leave the hall, jump on his bike, and with a whistle take off for his cache. By the time he'd rounded St. Charles' Church, heading west, we were following him. We heard a clink of a bottle and knew immediately that the store of wine was in a bit of buck brush about a quarter of a mile up the road. By the time Joe was back in the hall, two of us, the other two were lookouts, had found his goods. There were about five bottles in the box, but would you believe it, we took only one. One quart of wine for four kids. I don't remember much else about that night."

We all chuckled, even though we'd heard this story so many times while sitting among plates strewn with bits of shredded cabbage. The holopsti were gone, a few shreds of rice, carrot, and potato still clung to our plates, and the air was now warm and moist with smells of wine and freshly brewed coffee. The silence around the story drew us in, and we all looked at each other with amusement.

I stood and gathered my dessert plate and coffee cup. I said: "I'm going to sit in the living room with my dessert now. It's too noisy here." I thought: *I'm going toward death.* I wondered: *I choose it truly.* I felt: *A strange release, sensing an invisible crowd of Deaf and Hearing saints, living and dead, vilified, shot, tortured for their defense of the voiceless, their hands on my shoulder, signing, singing, signing me to my rest.* For now. I looked to Murray. And tonight, in his arms . . .

His eyes were compassionate, kind but daring: *Go on. Don't give up.* I went toward it, thinking it a new country.

Carol said: "Wait. I'll come with you." She stood up and handed over Sammy in his bib, his mouth full of potato, to Colin.

Carol and I conversed quietly in the other room, away from the noise and shrill cries of the children. She spoke of the books she read while struggling to care for five children under the age of twelve. I listened, marvelling at how she managed to remain so intellectually engaged with books while attacking daily mountains of laundry and dishes, and thought: *Stories nurture her too, especially when she's overrun by children and their incessant demands.* And: *Like me, she needs this quiet lull during this meal.*

As I drained the last of my coffee, I saw: *My Deafhood at the table has become a gift to her at this very moment. I've finally become generous without having to try.*

A few days later, we were back in Regina, carting jars of Mom's homemade soup, packages of lentil burgers, and a casserole dish of holopsti into the house. Dad's stolen wine story still played itself over and over again. My father, as a little boy, took some wine, but not all of it, not to get drunk but to outwit an adult who cherished an illusion. I realized: *His stories are full of subversion. His wildness as a little boy growing up in a German-Russian settlement in Revenue, how he smoked at the age of six, skipped school, fought other boys, stole candies from any store, even his father's and, as he often reminded us, how he became a teacher because he'd done everything that his wildest students could have done and even more. Most of his stories had encouraged me to be wild and ferocious in outwitting life's vicissitudes, to make friends with the part of me that can't be tamed. Every story had led me through labyrinths, to where the darkness shall be light, to a room of love in the centre.*

I've come to love this anonymity, this shunned Deaf body. It is my cell that taught me everything. It is a newfound freedom. I write of the failures that are now imprinted in my body. I speak of the darkness of my failures despite my successes. I'm not one of the great Deaf leaders who will change the face of Deaf education in this province or this country. I'll never be a famous researcher, activist, politician, or sign language literary giant who travels the world, sharing knowledge of Deafhood, Deaf culture, and linguistics. I'll never inspire great assemblies of the Deaf or the Hearing. I'll likely not become a Deaf university professor, like David Mason at York University, and teach Hearing teachers how to teach deaf children, and I won't likely train interpreters to work in a school setting, nor have any impact on diehard oralists who present auditory training and cochlear implants as the only options to parents newly-stricken with grief at discovering their child is deaf. I am, however, a well-educated Deaf woman in love with American Sign Language and books written in the English language.

My own failure to connect with those whom I love, the failure to empower other deaf children, the failure to speak out when I need to, the failure to be kind and patient with those who don't understand deafness are of more concern to me now. I must find a way to speak truth without the fire of the dragon escaping my lips. I am hidden away in a tiny classroom with Casey, Andy, Melissa, Nolan, and Gina, who remain unhealed and forgotten. I don't want their lives to be erased by ignorance, prejudice, or the egos of their family and friends. The world will be better for knowing about how to live with failure. In a culture obsessed with triumphs over adversity of every kind, I go on in the cell I live in. That small space in which I live is the house of my own Deaf body.

꙰

The warped floor creaked under my feet as I traversed the length of the family room and all its books. Winter howled outside. I drew the curtains more tightly over the windows. Upstairs, my husband lay sleeping. I opened my laptop, I didn't have my hearing aid on and I didn't hear the noises of the house or the computer as I began to type furiously. A few minutes later, I felt Murray's hand on my shoulder.

Murray signed to me: "Toby's barking."

I grinned at him, standing dishevelled in his bathrobe. It was two o'clock in the morning and our beagle, Toby, was awake and was now barking madly. I apologized and quickly closed down the laptop, slid into bed, warming my cold feet on Murray, warming myself with the beauty of my husband, and of our daughters. I heard voices in my Deaf body. They murmured: *Deaf and Hearing, attic and basement, man and woman, mother and child, city and desert, man and beast, God and man, dragon and angel,* as I fell asleep, dreaming of Caroline, the gorilla in the attic at Green Knowe, the *sweeooop* of those telephone wires, and the screech of the sundog winter day.

JOHANNA

After forty years of wandering in the desert, Mary of Egypt comes across an oasis. Standing on the edge of the desert, she can look down into the verdant green bank cradling a creek. Palm trees extend their long shadow fingers toward her, while the smell of grass nearly overpowers her. Yet she doesn't move toward the lush leaves of grass, the heavily burdened fig trees. Rather, she stands naked and shrivelled, her hair, white twisted wool-like strands. The sun warms her bare behind.

Then a cloak is suddenly flung about her shoulders. She backs away in alarm. The musty smell of the cloak is overpowering, and she can feel its collar, stiff with dirt and grease. A man steps back too, sensing her feral air. Then he introduces himself, weeping at the same time. He is Zossima, a monk from a nearby monastery in the oasis. Choking on tears of shame, he describes his own wanderings in the oasis, asking God if he could find a person holier than him, a person who could tell him more than what he already knows. He touches her skin, his fingers leaving a ring of moist fingerprints on her arm. He has seen every bird, beast, and flower. He has found birds of paradise. He has collected the dew in large broad leaves. He has been fascinated with the exotic lizards. Mary looks down at her feet, now crusted with soil moistened by his copious tears.

She doesn't want to leave the desert. But she could stand next to the oasis for Zossima's sake. She could talk to him, tell him of her travels. But her stories aren't going to help him much. He should listen to his own stories instead of running around trying to find someone who is holier than him. It isn't a competition.

Next year, she tells him. She points to a nearby grove of trees whose sheltering branches entwine together to make a roof. Already, the long grasses are bent as if to make a bed for her. *Meet me next year right here and maybe . . .*

Noises, both inside and outside of my head, are of little consequence. My body is here. This is what I sense when my mother tells me that the fridge has cut in, that the noise is not in my head, or when Murray tells me that the sudden crack I just heard was not Langley House emitting an arthritic yelp, but something inside my head.

This morning, Murray and I sat at the dining room table littered with newspapers and books. I was drinking his impossibly strong coffee.

He asked: "Do you remember the time when you wanted to hunt down every source of tinnitus, and find a way to solve it?"

I mumbled: "So?" I was becoming uncomfortable and started picking off the small white feathers that have buried themselves into my sweater. I'll never wear a goose down filled jacket again.

He said: "Ah, but I remember you listing off all the sources: the wine you really liked, the Chocolan (I bought you a case of it, so you still have to drink it all up), your medicine, the electric toothbrush, the car fan, vitamin supplements, the jazz concerts that Anna and Paula sang at, the sudden backfiring of our Olds 98."

I questioned: "What are you saying?"

Murray said: "I don't know. You figure it out." He gave his characteristic shrug, the shrug that aggravated his former Deaf students when they asked for answers to the questions they'd posed themselves.

I picked at the feathers on my sweater. The darn things refused to come off. I was hardly able to grasp their tiny filaments between my thumb and forefinger. I thought: *In between my ears there is a space, that is in command now, that decides what I am to see and hear, to know, to understand, and how to live, and I live in that space, it is my home. Technology and scientific knowledge will never conquer this space. Meanwhile, my house and its noises invade my body inhabiting its rooms, rooms constructed of mortar, brick, stone, and wood: Ladymint, Langley Hall, my classroom, the castles and cathedrals of England, they all emit noises which I cannot attend to. The noises are in the shadows, I've learned to leave them there. It requires a discipline of the mind, of the heart, to give them no more credence than what they deserve.*

There is no solution, no cure, no rehabilitation, there is my body that just is. Fired into the world, my Deaf body has become the house for me.

Note

This work is a fictionalized account of actual events in my life and in the lives of my students, and I have made some changes to the story's chronology. The names and descriptions of students, childhood friends, teaching staff, and educational interpreters bear no relationship to actual people, though the incidents are, in all essentials, true. Family members, Deaf community members, key people who inspired me and guided me are drawn from life and presented as themselves.

Acknowledgements

I wish to thank Thistledown Press for publishing this work. I particularly want to thank Seán Virgo for his brave editing, intuitively grasping the garguantan task at hand, and to hold my hand through it all. His astute directions, his wise commentaries, and "weasel" eyes have brought the manuscript to where it wanted to be; Harold Rhenisch for transforming what was once a bulky and unwieldy manuscript into a story with varied layers of "voices"; Saskatchewan Writers' Guild which promoted and administered the John V. Hicks Manuscript Award (for which this book was selected in 2011); City of Regina which provided a Writing Award toward the completion of this manuscript in 2008; my parents, Edward and Lois Weber. Without their love and support, I would have never become who I am; my two sisters and brother, Ruth Cey, Carol Keller, and David Weber who have cheered me on over the years; Regina Public Schools for their support of my writing and teaching adolescent students who are Deaf and hard of hearing. I especially want to thank my colleagues, Cathy

Arthur MacDonald, Morgan Reed, Cori Miller, Jewel Whyte, Jackie Frohlick, Lee Agarand, Sara Randall, and Cindi Orthner who supported me as a Deaf teacher; Gillian Sernich and Sherol Evans in their early readings of this manuscript and for their encouragement; members of my writing group: Joanne Gerber, Bruce Rice, Eric Greenway, Sharon Delint, Bonnie Dunlop; Paul Wilson for his support in promoting the manuscript; Karl and Ben Valiaho, Anna and Paula's brothers for their good cheer, music, and soul conversations along the way; Chrystene Ells, a noted playwright and film director, who demonstrated how to express complex ideas about the essentially Buddhist notion of "not two, not yet one", especially in her most recent work, *Kaleidocycle*; the Deaf community members who are committed to furthering the education of Deaf children and who have accompanied me throughout these difficult years of advocating for those who must learn through sign language, especially Roger Carver and Allard Thomas; Terry Swayn who vetted the manuscript from the family perspective; my daughters, Anna and Paula, who contributed their life material to this book; and finally, to Murray, who trusted me to write anything about him. Without him, this story would have never been told.

This work has been inspired by two books: Belden Lane's *The Solace of Fierce Landscapes: Exploring Desert and Mountain Spirituality*, the writings of Desert Fathers and Mothers and Paddy Ladd's *Understanding Deaf Culture: In Search of Deafhood*.

JOANNE WEBER obtained degrees in English, Library Science and Education and did graduate work at Gallaudet University in Washington, DC, where she became fluent in American Sign Language. She now teaches in the Deaf and Hard of Hearing Program at Thom Collegiate. Joanne and her husband live in Regina, Saskatchewan. *The Pear Orchard* was her first collection of poetry; *The Deaf House* is her first creative non-fiction.